# Predicting
# Politics

# Predicting Politics

BRUCE BUENO DE MESQUITA

The Ohio State University Press
Columbus

Library of Congress Cataloging-in-Publication Data

Bueno de Mesquita, Bruce, 1946–
    Predicting politics / Bruce Bueno de Mesquita.
        p.   cm.
    Includes bibliographical refverences and index.
        ISBN 0-8142-0898-3 (cloth : alk. paper) — ISBN 0-8142-5984-7 (paper:
    alk. paper)
        1. International relations—Forecasting.   2. World politics—1989–   I.
    Title.
        JZ1234 .B84 2002
        327.1'01—dc21
                                                        2001006329
                                                        Rev.

Jacket design by Diane Gleba Hall
Text design by Nighthawk Design.
Type set in Sabon by Bookcomp
Printed by Thomson-Shore

The paper used in this publication meets the minimum requirements of the
American National Standard for Information Science--Permanence of Paper
for Printed Library Materials. ANSIZ39.4-1992.

9 7 6 5 4 3 2 1

# CONTENTS

# PREFACE

*PREDICTING POLITICS* ATTEMPTS TO FULFILL TWO DISTINCT OBJEC-
tives. First, I offer a view of how changes in democratization around the
world are likely to influence the spread of peace and prosperity. A central
finding in this context concerns how national ranking on democratization
influences investment, growth, and the pursuit of peace as distinct from the
absolute level of democratization. Russia, for example, ranks lower now
than it did in 1980 relative to other countries on its degree of democracy
despite the fact that it is a much more democratic society today than was true
during the Cold War. Because the rest of the world, on average, has democratized more and faster than has Russia, Russia's attractiveness as a place for
investors has diminished and the danger that it will pursue war as a foreign
policy course has increased. These are, of course, extremely worrisome
developments for the future. Such developments are evaluated not only for
Russia, but also for China and many, many other countries.

The future is predicted with a game theoretic model that has a long pedi-
gree of use by governmental and business policy makers concerned with
high-stakes decisions. Demonstrating this model's potential to provide insights into the future constitutes my second objective. The main model presented here is applied to replicable data that is sufficiently old that we can
evaluate the model's performance over the recent past, and the data are sufficiently current that many of the dynamic model's projections include specific predictions about likely developments over the next three decades.
Thus, we can both see how well the model works and elaborate on a variety
of future prospects for the world.

It is my fervent hope that this model and other analytic tools will become
a routine part of decision making so that policy makers can simulate alternative domestic and foreign policy strategies and pick those most likely to
advance their vision for the future. In this way, through analysis as well as
wisdom, we can improve the prospects that the future will provide peace and
prosperity for all the people of the world.

I owe several deep debts of gratitude, which I am happy to acknowledge
now. Decision Insights, Incorporated (DII) is a New York-based consulting firm
that uses the model emphasized here. They have applied this model to governmental and business decisions as diverse as helping to limit the proliferation of

nuclear, biological, and chemical weapons, or keeping Taiwan in the Asian Development Bank, to evaluating the optimal strategies for businesses to complete successful mergers and acquisitions, resolve litigation negotiations, and succeed in contract negotiations. DII generously permitted me to use some data that it collected regarding Russia for the analyses performed in Chapter 6. I very much appreciate their assistance.

John Gaddis of Yale University and the Hoover Institution, Ned Lebow at The Ohio State University, and Kiron Skinner at Carnegie Mellon University provided the motivation for me to write this book as a consequence of stimulating conversations I have had with each of them over the years. They are not, of course, responsible for any errors I may have made. Malcolm Litchfield, Director of The Ohio State University Press, further stimulated my interest in working on this book, for which I am extremely grateful.

Much of the research and writing for *Predicting Politics* was done while I was a visiting professor in the Department of Politics at New York University. NYU and my colleagues there provided a stimulating and delightful environment—in fact, so stimulating that I have joined the department. I am particularly indebted to George Downs, Steve Brams, Adam Przeworski, my students, and indeed the rest of the department for their willingness to spend time discussing ideas with me about politics. Other parts of this book developed while I was at my other home base at the Hoover Institution, Stanford University, where I continue to be a Senior Fellow. As always, Hoover provides an exceptionally supportive environment for my research. I am most grateful both to NYU and to the Hoover Institution for their support and encouragement. My wife, Arlene, provides great support and encouragement, tolerating my travels here and there, with patience and good cheer. To all these good friends, thank you.

The future course of foreign policy is central to shaping the world as it will look decades from now. If this volume and the tools introduced here succeed in making some small contribution to a better future, I will be most gratified indeed.

Bruce Bueno de Mesquita
New York, February 25, 2002

ONE

# Predicting Politics

HISTORY MOVES IN FITS AND STARTS. RARE EVENTS CREATE TURN-ing points that wrench foreign policy from well-established patterns and shift international affairs down new, uncertain paths. Some new paths prove to be dead ends in a relatively short time, say a few generations. Soviet communism, disastrous for Stalin's tens of millions of victims, was longer-lived than Europe's equally disastrous fascist experiment between the world wars, but ultimately, like fascism, communism showed limited staying power. Other changes in policy establish more fundamental shifts that are sustained for centuries. This book presents analytic tools that help identify fundamental foreign policy shifts. It also marshals evidence about the character of such changes and uses that evidence to make predictions about the prospects of war and peace, and poverty or prosperity, over the next few decades.

Examples of long-lasting changes in international affairs are plentiful. Consider the seemingly narrow agreement known as the Concordat of Worms and the effects it had on politics for centuries to come. The Concordat of Worms, signed in 1122, brought the investiture controversy to an end. Under the terms of the Concordat, the pope alone was granted the right to nominate candidates to fill vacant bishoprics. Kings and the Holy Roman Emperor could reject nominees, but they could not propose candidates themselves. At one level, the Concordat of Worms was a narrow agreement resolving an important twelfth-century issue of little or no importance today. At another level, the Concordat can be seen as creating far-reaching consequences that reverberate through international affairs even today. This "deal" ensured the emergence of papal authority over Europe's monarchs and helped foster Catholic hegemony in Western Europe until it was superseded by the Westphalian system in the years following 1648. Indeed, a case can be made that the ultimate emergence of sovereign states as the dominant organization of international politics and the eventual decline of papal hegemony and even the broad outlines of the terms agreed to at Westphalia all followed from the forces put into motion by the Concordat of Worms (Bueno de Mesquita 2000a). In that sense, the Concordat ensured papal hegemony for centuries and also ensured eventual papal decline and the

1

ascent of secular authority. This, then, is an example of a short-term change in foreign policy that proved to have extensive, sustained impact.

Perhaps as a long-term aftermath of Worms, the Thirty Years' War set into motion changes in political incentives and political institutions that eventually contributed to the American and French Revolutions. These revolutions, in turn, put republican government firmly on the world stage. Liberal republican governance seems almost to have "never looked back," showing a gradual, nearly steady expansion to more and more countries. Thus it is that some policy movements endure while others prove ephemeral. Predicting why and how some shifts last and others dissipate is one path to a better understanding of the world in which we live and the world of the future.

This book is an effort to provide tools with which to identify and assess prospective turning events in foreign affairs. I offer such tools, grounded in the logic of game theory and social choice theory, along with analyses of seemingly crucial events, to evaluate the prospects we have to predict foreign and domestic policy futures and, perhaps, to help shape them. The undertaking here occurs at a time when many are focused on trying to sort out the likely shape of future foreign affairs. Many of us share the view that we live in a time of transition. When the Berlin Wall, and then the Soviet Empire and the Soviet Union itself, ceased to exist, the community of nations appeared to have undergone a change so dramatic as to lead to speculation that we were entering a period of an unknown new world order. That world order remains ill defined. Here I offer systematic means by which we can apply logic and evidence to alternative worlds in the hope of preparing better for the policy challenges that lie ahead. No one can speak with complete confidence about the future of domestic or foreign policy, but we can set out some useful aids to guide debate, discussion, prediction, and policy making. That is my central objective. Although I make specific predictions, the main emphasis is on tools of prediction.

Developing and applying game theory tools and social choice tools to an analysis of policy serves several purposes. The primary model utilized here has already found a place in published studies of foreign and domestic affairs (a sample includes Bueno de Mesquita 1984, 2000b; Bueno de Mesquita, McDermott, and Cope 2001; Bueno de Mesquita, Newman, and Rabushka 1985, 1996; Bueno de Mesquita and Stokman 1994; Feder 1995; Kugler and Feng 1997; Ray and Russett 1996). As such there is an established track record of reliable prediction, a track record I discuss at some length in chapter 3 when I explain the model. Having said that, it has only once been applied in academic research specifically to evaluating truly long-term foreign policy trends (Bueno de Mesquita 1998). The one instance, elaborated on in chapter 4, uses this policy forecasting model to evaluate the likely end of the Cold War based only on information about international politics known in 1948. In developing other such applications, I hope to provide a foundation from which future assessments will establish that this and related modeling tools are an important element in policy analysis, prediction, and formation. In trying to do so, I pursue two objectives.

The first objective is to provide a new outlet by which political scientists can provide assistance to decision makers. Currently, political scientists are called upon to advise governmental leaders and their agents on questions of fundamental domestic and foreign policy importance. Area specialists are frequently asked to evaluate developments within their region of expertise. I myself was asked to contemplate the implications of decisions in the late 1990s by the Indian and Pakistani governments to test nuclear weapons. It was my presumed expertise on South Asian affairs—the topic of my earliest research—rather than my knowledge of decision-making models that prompted others to seek my advice. Personal knowledge about specific parts of the world and experience in grappling with particular issue areas enhances the prospects that an advisor will have wisdom and insight to share. This is certainly an important and valuable asset in helping to improve decision making. But sharing personal wisdom and insight with decision makers is much like giving a few dollars to a poor person. It helps at the moment but rarely has a lasting impact. As the old saying goes, give a farmer food and he can feed his family for a day; give a farmer seeds and he can feed his family forever. So it is with wisdom as compared to analytic tools.

Wisdom is neither transferable nor imitable. Tools that assist in decision making, in contrast, can be mastered by many and can help give insight over and over again. They are like seeds to a farmer. A simpler version of the primary tool presented here has already become a routine part of foreign policy analysis within agencies of the U.S. government. For instance, after a demonstration of this model by officials from the U.S. government to officials and journalists in Russia, *Izvestia* reported on April 3, 1995: "The forecasts are given to the President, Congress, and the U.S. government and are substantial factors influencing the elaboration of the country's foreign policy course."

A second objective beyond the desire to build tools to assist in decision making is more narrowly academic in nature. I hope to lay to rest, or at least to help mute, objections that rational choice models and international relations theory in general are incapable of providing reliable assessments of outcomes that are unknown at the time studies are undertaken (Gaddis 1992; Walt 1999). That is, I hope to establish that we already have some reliable tools at our disposal for evaluating international and domestic politics in the short, medium, and long term. I also hope to lay to rest objections aired in the public media that rational choice models and modelers are not interested in addressing central policy questions (Cohn 1999). By demonstrating the predictive capacity of such models, I hope to establish some of the important benefits of a focus on the scientific method in developing cumulative knowledge about international affairs. Most of all, I hope to shed light on the merits of the tools offered here by showing their ability to predict important events and to isolate policy choices that can help improve the future.

## Organization of the Book

The book is organized as follows. In this chapter I discuss epistemological issues that seem to me to provide a sound basis for relying on rational choice models as an important element in the decision-making arsenal. I also examine some of the social forces that appear to be pushing international affairs toward greater democratization. In the next chapter I show how a simple game theoretic model can help elucidate very long-term trends in foreign affairs. I illustrate the possibility of anticipating the future by looking at how specific pressures shape strategic incentives, incentives that in time gradually can produce fundamental changes in international affairs.

The specific example in chapter 2 evaluates the impact of the Concordat of Worms on the rise and decline of papal hegemony and the eventual emergence of nation-states as the dominant organization of international politics. This chapter highlights how, even with a simple model, game theory can help illuminate subtle implications of decisions; implications that have been overlooked even in close historical studies. Chapter 3 introduces the main modeling tool used here. This model is more elaborate than the simple game described in chapter 2. Chapter 3 explains the logic behind this more elaborate model. The chapter also discusses the model's limitations and points to its externally audited track record based on previously published predictive studies. Chapter 4 applies the analytic model to data known in 1948 to see how accurately it predicts the end of the Cold War. For purposes of this and subsequent applications to long-term predictions, I introduce a modest but important modification that makes the model applicable to simulations of long-term expectations. The Cold War example is used to provide further foundation for the claim that, although inevitably imperfect, reasonably reliable long-term predictions can be made with this tool.

Chapter 5 uses readily reproducible data for the entire international system to predict changing international pressures to stimulate or retard democratization on a country-by-country basis. In this instance, the data used are based on information known as early as 1980, well before the end of the Cold War. The year 1980 is chosen because this is a time when the Cold War was not only in full swing, but fundamental international changes that occurred shortly thereafter had not yet occurred. Ronald Reagan had not yet become president of the United States, while Leonid Brezhnev remained in power in Russia. Mikhail Gorbachev was not yet even on the horizon. Likewise, the United States and China were just at the beginning of mutual diplomatic recognition, with Deng Xiao Ping having only relatively recently launched major economic reforms. The contest between the two superpowers seemed set to march on into the indefinite future. Some even contended that the U.S. was in decline. Yet a scant decade later the Soviet Union was on the threshold of complete collapse, with Soviet-style authoritarianism in retreat. Could these developments have been predicted in 1980 and can data from 1980 help elucidate the next three decades or so of changes in international democratization? Chapter 5 helps answer these questions.

Chapter 6 focuses on internal politics in Russia and China. Using data collected in November 1995, I simulate the unfolding of internal pressures among Russian elites and interest groups to see the country become more or less democratic. These data are used to project Russian democratization out to around 2010, long after the original data were collected. By using 1995 data, we also can check the model's predictions against what has happened over the past several years. Detailed predictions are made about the overall course of Russian democratization, but also about the evolution of preferences of specific individuals and interest groups in Russia. The results from this simulation of the internal thinking about democratization by key Russian actors is contrasted with predictions of Russian approaches to democratization based on external, international pressure.

Chapter 6 undertakes, as well, a detailed examination of the evolution of political views about democratization among Chinese leaders. For that analysis, I use data collected in the early 1990s and show how well the simulations do at correctly predicting the rise in political fortunes of some, like Zhou Rongji, and the decline of others, like Qiao Shi, who were once thought to be likely heirs to the mantle of political control in China. I go on to make predictions about the prospects for democratization in China through to about 2010. As with the Russian case, I compare predictions based on internal domestic considerations and those based on external, international pressures. In part the analysis evaluates the interaction of the two and leads to some perhaps surprising expectations.

Chapters 5 and 6 build on the assessment of social forces undertaken in the latter part of chapter 1. Chapters 5 and 6 provide falsifiable claims about important likely developments over the next decade or so. Both are based on earlier data so that they can be evaluated now against developments over the past five to twenty years, depending on the data set. At the same time, both are "played forward" far enough that, in addition to predictions about events that may already have happened, the chapters contain predictions about developments that lie squarely in the future. At the same time, the projections are not made so far into the future that none of us will be around to evaluate their accuracy. Thus, I am not offering predictions about the very distant future, but I am providing specific predictions about events that potentially can change the world order for decades or even centuries to come.

Chapter 7 expands on the earlier analyses to speculate about potential hot points for war in the future. Here I make use of well-established empirical regularities regarding territorial proximity, regime type, comparative prosperity, investment, and so forth to identify rivalries that are likely to subside and others that are likely to emerge or become exacerbated in the future. I highlight some surprising, novel results which suggest that the prospects for peace and prosperity are more dependent on the ranking specific countries have on indicators of relative democratization than on their absolute democracy "score."

## A Shift from Realism?

Although many journalists, scholars, and world observers early in the twentieth century wrote with alarm of impending war, equally many wrote confidently in the years leading to 1914 of the impossibility of a general war in Europe. Echoing the idealistic view among many of his time, Norman Angell, later a Nobel Peace Prize winner, concluded in *The Great Illusion* (1910), "The day for progress by force has passed; it will be progress by ideas or not at all." A decade earlier, the Polish businessman Ivan Stanislavovich Bloch wrote in *Is War Now Impossible?* ([1899], 1991):

> The war . . . in which great nations armed to the teeth . . . fling themselves with all their resources into a struggle for life and death . . . is the war that every day becomes more and more impossible. . . . A war between the Triplice [i.e., Germany, Austria-Hungary, and Italy] and the Franco-Russian Alliance [that is, two-thirds of the Triple Entente] . . . has become absolutely impossible. . . .The dimensions of modern armaments and the organization of society have rendered its prosecution an economic impossibility, and . . . if any attempt were made to demonstrate the inaccuracy of my assertions by putting the matter to a test on a large scale, we should find the inevitable result in a catastrophe which would destroy all existing political organizations. Thus the great war cannot be made, and any attempt to make it would result in suicide.

The First World War shattered confidence in such seemingly idealistic, utopian views of international politics. The Second World War completed the transition, turning attention to "realism" as the preponderant perspective on international affairs. To be sure, after the war there still were the World Federalists and other organizations that believed orderly international affairs could be achieved by bringing people together and educating them to their common interest. In counterpoint to the idealism that dominated prewar scholarship on international security, the postwar years witnessed a renaissance of efforts at positive rather than normative analysis. Principal among the early efforts to direct research in a more "realist" way were studies by Hans Morgenthau (1978), Kenneth Waltz (1959), Morton Kaplan (1957), and Kenneth Organski (1958). Each sought to identify the central factors that govern how nations interact with each other. In doing so, each subscribed to certain common principles that continue to dominate thinking about international relations.

The new realists saw the state, embedded in an international structure, rather than individual leaders facing domestic and international constraints, as the central actor on the world stage. The focus of attention was on the system, its central characteristics and the factors thought to give it stability. In this context, macro-level variables such as bipolarity or multipolarity, a balance of power or preponderance of power in a few hands, and liberal norms and rules or their authoritarian counterparts were the keys to the mechanical pressures emanating from what came to be known as the international system. States interacted somewhat like billiard balls or molecules colliding in a closed space. Emphasis was therefore placed on characteristics of the space, characteristics that presumably determined the range of possible interactions. International interactions were treated as almost devoid of political motivations, leaving little room for strategic considerations beyond state survival and stability. Echoing Marx's idea of a superstructure, the international system was viewed as the determinant of important changes or constancy in international affairs.

By drawing attention to characteristics of the international system, realist analysts and policy makers may have unwittingly embraced a new idealism. Whereas their predecessors saw hope in the constructive efforts of individuals to find negotiated paths through difficult issues, the realists denied the influence of individual decision makers. Structural factors provided the explanation of international politics. Perhaps, looking back on the dismal failures of their parents' generation, they sought a perspective that removed personal responsibility for the course of international affairs. While Thomas Carlyle, writing in the early nineteenth century, pondered the role of heroes in history, post–World War II realists wrote individual decision making out of the lexicon of international discourse. Hans Morgenthau distinguished between heroes—statesmen driven by international imperatives—and horse traders—democratic leaders responding to the will of the people (Morgenthau 1978). The latter clearly was a category of derision.

Debate turned to questions of mechanics rather than political incentives. Deterrence could mechanically prevent nuclear war because, presumptively, no issue could be important enough to risk national suicide, echoing Bloch's idealistic reasoning of a half-century earlier. Yet, only a few years before this viewpoint was enshrined as an axiom of Cold War foreign policy, Germany's leaders had taken just such a risk; they had pursued policies that risked national suicide and they lost. Only one generation earlier, Franz Joseph of Austria-Hungary had done the same in his contest with Serbia. He lost and the Austro-Hungarian Empire disappeared from the earth. Seventy years later, Mikhail Gorbachev made a similar gamble, though without resort to force, and the Soviet Empire and even the Soviet Union itself ceased to exist. Despite recurring national "suicides," international policy was constructed around the belief that, above all else, states seek to survive and are immortal. This apparently mistaken view may be central to the failure of realist international relations theories to predict fundamental events.

Few realists pondered even what it means to say that the state seeks survival above all else. After all, states are only metaphorically decision makers. States do not, in actuality, choose policies or have goals; leaders do. Consequently, it seems more likely that instead of states it is leaders who, as thinking beings, seek personal, political, and physical survival. But once we allow that perspective, realism unravels as the welfare of individual leaders need not—and often does not—match the "national interest" when construed as some measure of social welfare or national political persistence (Bueno de Mesquita and Siverson 1995; Bueno de Mesquita, Morrow, Siverson, and Smith 1999, 2000; Bueno de Mesquita, Smith, Siverson, and Morrow 2003).

Containment likewise was a mechanical, structural response to a foreign policy challenge. Soviet policy, in the American view, was a slave to a predetermined, implacable ideology. Marxist-Leninist ideology, rather than motives for personal advancement and aggrandizement, were assumed to be at the core of the struggle between American liberal democracy and Soviet communism. Where assessments of personal motives and incentives were sacrificed at the altar of ideological viewpoints, the range of responses was reduced to mechanical devices to contain the threat. Little thought was given to how best to alter or defeat rival incentives.

Mechanics go only as far as their tools will allow for managing foreign affairs. Here I take the perspective that individual decision makers attend to the domestic and international repercussions they can expect to follow from their actions. Therefore, my approach to understanding prospective policy futures is to identify tools that shed light on individual incentives and on strategic maneuvers designed to alter or operate within those incentives, taking institutional constraints into account as appropriate. Actors interact strategically, giving shape to the space they collectively occupy, the space that we call the international system. My approach, then, reverses the relative weight given to actors and the system from the positions these two elements occupy in structural theories. Rather than the system determining interactions among actors in the way a sealed pot under increasing pressure influences the prospects of collisions among molecules, I take the view that strategic maneuvers among and between competing actors give rise to changes in the characteristics of the international system; that is, they give rise to the shape of the pot and the pressure to which it is subjected. Decision makers decide when to turn on the heat and raise the pressure, or remove the lid or the heat to reduce the pressure.

While departing from a structural perspective, I must acknowledge that individuals are embedded in a social reality and that their reality is the product of the cumulative choices of a myriad of people beyond their control. My analysis, therefore, proceeds in two ways. I examine important social forces that may alter the choices or constraints leaders face, and I analyze and simulate illustrative key decisions against the backdrop of projected changes in such forces over time. Thus, I argue that decision makers inherit certain domestic and international constraints, but they are fairly free to maneuver in order to change the future characteristics of the international system inherited by tomorrow's decision makers.

In my investigation, I eschew the idea that random occurrences uniquely determine the path of history. Rather, I assume that paths chosen are the product of strategic calculations framed against the backdrop of the structural or institutional constraints decision makers inherit. To be sure, over the longer term those paths and constraints may lead to unanticipated consequences. Actions are chosen to maximize individual choosers' well-being on a human time scale. Looking over longer stretches of history we may see what appear to be major developments growing out of minor events. Many may infer that such consequences were random and wholly dependent on chance. From my perspective, these consequences may have been unforeseen by those who gave shape to them, but this is more likely to be due to their lack of interest in the longer run and the inadequate information at their disposal at the time choices were made than it is to be the product of random, exogenous forces.

In the next chapter I illustrate what I mean by discussing the origins of the modern sovereign state as a product of locally welfare-enhancing decisions in the twelfth century. Certainly none of the decision makers involved are likely to have foreseen the consequences their actions would have a century, two centuries, and even a millennium later. What is more, they probably did not care what the consequences would be even as little as thirty or forty years later. Even that brief a time placed the consequences beyond their remaining expected life-spans.

## Why Game Theory Analysis?

Of necessity, an assessment of foreign and domestic policy futures requires a certain amount of counterfactual reasoning. Throughout, I investigate alternative states of the world. In doing so, I do not rely simply on randomly chosen alternative states. Nor do I engage in frivolous hypothetical situations. You will find no counterfactual worlds grounded in assumptions like "What if Napoleon had a stealth bomber at Waterloo?" or "What if Hitler had not been born?" Rather, the counterfactual views of foreign policy examined here reflect alternative rational strategic paths that decision makers could have taken in the past or could take in the future. To be sure, I allow the possibility of unforeseen exogenous random shocks that may deflect events from time to time, but primarily I focus on unfolding histories as they might look if decision makers choose consistently with their own interests within their limited, rationally bounded local, historical, and temporal settings. The random shocks serve to identify the magnitude of a change in initial conditions required to fundamentally alter the projected course of events. Random shocks are used as a tool to calibrate the size of a social "earthquake" needed to change the expected course of events.

Every facet of policy making examined here is looked at through the lenses of rational actor models with a self-conscious effort to embed the analysis within the constraints imposed by the scientific method. That method, of course, requires a logically coherent explanation for presumed causal links among explicitly specified variables and assumptions. It also requires independent evidence as the means to evaluate the reliability of the explanatory or causal claims that are made.

In focusing on the scientific method I do not mean to suggest that other methods are not equally appropriate or more appropriate for some research strategies. I only mean to help the reader gain a greater appreciation for the application of scientific methods to the study of international affairs. Most essential features of the scientific method, of course, are no different in the social sciences than in other fields, although controlled experiments are clearly problematic in social inquiry, especially when concerned with relatively long periods of time. There is nothing about international relations research that makes it unusually well suited or poorly suited for scientific inquiry. The ability to predict classes of events or phenomena is often held up as a critical standard in scientific tests of hypotheses. I share the view that prediction is critical and so give it a prominent role throughout. After all, a motivation for this study is to evaluate methods for looking at *future*, as yet unobserved, states of foreign policy.

As I emphasize rational choice models, let me say a word about this approach. Science addresses issues of how to evaluate arguments and evidence. The scientific method is agnostic with regard to particular substantive or theoretical foci. Rational choice theories, therefore, are not inherently more or less scientific than other theories. Still, I focus on rational choice approaches to the study of international relations that rely primarily upon game theory. I do so for several reasons.

First, game theory is a body of reasoning designed explicitly to attend to the logic of strategic interaction. Strategic interaction, in which decision makers select a course of action taking into account expectations about how others will respond, is central to all of international affairs. It is difficult to imagine constructing any falsifiable, explanatory theory of international relations without thinking explicitly about the interdependencies between events and individual choices. Nongame theoretic points of view often assume away or greatly simplify the most interesting features of strategic interaction in international affairs. This is sometimes done by assuming that all foreign policy decision makers wish to maximize the same thing (e.g., national security; national survival) and wish to gain as much of that thing as possible before considering other types of benefits. As noted earlier, such theories often treat states as interacting in a mechanical, nonstrategic way. Game theory models, by contrast, embrace the idea of strategic maneuvering. In that sense, game theory seems like a particularly well-suited approach to the subject of concern.

Second, game theory provides tools for dealing with many of the concerns and assumptions of structural, behavioral, and psychological theories and so can help to integrate the important knowledge derived from these other approaches. Structure is a central element in games of sequential decision making in which choices are constrained by the situation decision makers find themselves in. Through a strategic analysis of the prior history of play, preferences, and beliefs, game theory provides a means to examine attitudes, perceptions, uncertainties, and learning on the part of decision makers. At the same time, game theory provides a systematic means of analyzing and predicting behavior across large classes of events whether they involve sincere behavior, bluffing, or other forms of strategic decision making. These are all crucial elements in the study of international affairs. Other approaches may take these features into account, but game theory is the only method with which I am familiar that explicitly *requires* attentiveness to all of these concerns. Having said that, we should keep in mind that there is not a single game theory of international relations. Rather, game theory is a mathematical foundation from which to construct different, even competing theories of international relations. As such, game theory is an axiomatically based theory of decision making. In international relations, game theory provides a method for explaining and analyzing strategic behavior. The quality of any given theory, of course, depends on the insights of the researcher. As a method, game theory only insures that certain crucial factors, including the ones I have enumerated, are taken into account.[1]

A third reason for focusing on game theoretic approaches to international relations is that they have enjoyed particular success in the area of prediction. As John Gaddis (1992) noted, structural, behavioral, and psychological perspectives failed to yield clear, specific, and detailed predictions of important events. Regrettably, he did not review the accomplishments or predictions based on rational choice theories, including game theory models (Ray and Russett 1996). I will try to fill that lacuna in his otherwise generally compelling assessment. In doing so, I enumerate examples of detailed predictions about important international events that were made using game theory methods, and I document the predictive character of these assessments and their rate of accuracy. I hope in this way to give the reader a better understanding of the potential this particular body of social science literature has for explaining and predicting international affairs.

The emphasis on game theory should not be taken as a criticism of other approaches. It simply reflects personal preference and a personal conviction about the strong advantages imparted by using a theory that explicitly requires attentiveness to strategic interaction. I investigate some large sweeps of history, as well as shorter-term perspectives on future international relations. In that sense, I hope to show how historical research and game theory models can be joined together to give a better understanding of the past and the future. With few exceptions, the methods of the historian and the methods of the social scientist are complementary. Each seems interested in resolving different and important aspects of our understanding of international relations.

Historians and social scientists share a common interest in the context, sequence, and meaning of events. However, they differ in the emphasis placed on, and the interpretation of, context, sequence, and meaning. And, of course, historians and social scientists differ in the methods used to evaluate evidence and to reach conclusions. At the risk of speaking for historians, which I certainly am not qualified to do, I express my view that many historians—certainly not all—are primarily interested in explanations that emphasize particular factors that distinguish one event, one sequence, one location from another. The meaning or explanation of events and actions is often assumed to be revealed through culturally and temporally bounded interpretations. Such a perspective naturally draws the scholar toward a close examination of particular events and actions. The historian's focus on particular, unique factors inspires the belief that little can be gained from explanations rooted in conjectures about motives for actions that are presumed to be quite general, if not universal. A common and perhaps correct claim is made, for instance, that medieval social, political, and economic relations cannot be understood through the application of modern notions of individual interests or welfare maximization.[2] Here the differences between social scientists and historians is rather explicit.

The belief in the existence of broadly applicable generalizations is at the core of scientifically oriented social inquiry and is at the core of this study. Social scientists, including game theorists, do not deny the relevance of cultural, temporal, or contextual considerations as means to understand past or future events (Bates et al. 1998; Rabushka and Shepsle 1972; Bueno de Mesquita 1981). Rather, such factors are embedded within theoretical constructs in which they serve as variables. Social scientists tend to be more concerned with how variables relate to each other than they are in explaining particular events or actions. Social science emphasizes the causation behind recurrent phenomena, while historical analysis seems more to emphasize the particular agents of causation for singular events. Put differently, the social scientist is more likely to emphasize general explanations of social phenomena, while the historian is more likely to emphasize unique features of individual episodes of social phenomena. The distinction should not be drawn too sharply, as there surely is a continuum of interests among researchers rather than a dichotomy. Still, the differences are real enough that history departments rarely hire people trained as social scientists and social science departments rarely hire people trained as historians.

For the social scientist, the events of history are a laboratory against which to test their claims about how variables are associated with each other, to test their theoretical propositions about causation. As such, the social scientist's task is not so much to explain particular events, but to identify relations among critical variables that explain classes of events or phenomena. For the historian, the search is for an evaluation of which variables were of relevance in a particular past case or sequence of events. The historian is more likely to be concerned with giving meaning to the events rather than defining the relations among variables. These are not logically equivalent exercises, though they are undoubtedly two important aspects of understanding human interactions.

The differences in the interests of these two groups of scholars have led to considerable confusion about "appropriate" methods. Historians emphasize discourse, meaning, context, and complexity—internal validity, if you will. Social scientists tend to emphasize regularities, replication, and parsimony—external validity, if you will. For many historians, path dependence, or the way in which one set of events influences another, is crucial to understanding historical events.[3] For many social scientists, sequence and path *inter*dependence are important because they help develop an understanding of the endogeneities behind the evolution of circumstances. That is, sequential analysis of specific choices investigates how the logic of a situation leads decision makers to choose strategically the values on key variables, making the unfolding of events interdependent in time and often in space as well. The circumstances, then, are not treated exclusively as exogenous elements, that is, elements whose value is dictated by factors outside the logic of the situation. For the historian, sequences of events set the stage for future developments, but often appear not to be shaped consciously by the expectations of decision makers about how those future developments may benefit or harm particular interests. Path dependence and its implications are very different for the historian and for the game–theoretically oriented social scientist. Chapter 2 illustrates these points by examining the consequences of the Concordat of Worms for the creation of new political institutions and the eventual demise of the papacy as the hegemonic power in Europe.

I put special emphasis on four aspects of the study of international affairs from a game theoretic perspective. These four aspects include (1) endogenous choices and their implications for path interdependence; (2) selection effects in theory and in data and how they can distort inferences from historical analysis; (3) the importance of independence between arguments and the evidence used to evaluate their merits if we are to distinguish between description, explanation, and prediction; and (4) prediction as a means of evaluating the potential of scientific inquiry to help improve future international affairs. These four items—endogeneity, selection effects, independence between argument and evidence, and prediction—represent areas where scientific inquiry into international affairs has proven to be helpful in clarifying problems that frequently arise in other modes of analysis. These four areas provide organizing principles behind the investigation set out here of prospective policy futures. A summary of my main claims is found in Table 1.1. As I have already written detailed discussions of my views on these issues, I refer the interested readers to earlier work (Bueno de Mesquita 1996, 2000b).

## Social Forces as Context

This volume emphasizes endogenous strategic choices, as well as explicit separation between theoretical arguments, evidence used to help inform theoretical development, and evidence used to evaluate the reliability of theoretical generalizations. It also recognizes that decisions about foreign policy are made within a political, economic, and social context. That context may well be the result of earlier strategic decisions not studied here.[4] Nevertheless, the context is an element that must be taken into account by decision makers in looking to the future. Therefore, I explore a few important examples of the context within which contemporary foreign policy choices must be made. These examples will be used in the final chapter on war to examine plausi-

**Table 1.1**
Summary of Differences between Social Science Inquiry and History

|  | Inductive or Historical Approach | Social Scientific (especially Game Theoretic) Approach |
|---|---|---|
| Flow of Events | Taken as given or as the product of "exogenous" developments. | Endogeneity is analyzed. Events are linked to strategic interaction. |
| Selection of Cases | Sampling on the dependent variables. Cases are chosen in which similar outcomes seem to be caused by similar factors. Cases with the same factors but without similar outcomes may be overlooked. | Sampling on the independent variables. Cases are chosen to evaluate whether similar factors occur with similar outcomes when variation in factors and outcomes are both represented in the cases analyzed. |
| Evidence | Often drawn from the same events as provided the basis for the hypotheses. | Evidence should be independent of the information used to derive hypotheses. |
| Objective of Study | To describe and explain specific events and actions in terms of contextual factors. | To make and test claims through prediction about causation as indicated by the proposed relations among variables. |

ble alternative contextual developments that may sway future foreign policies in different directions. How much of an effect they might have will be assessed by simulating alternative changes in or statistical implications of these contextual factors.

## Democratization

From the deepest recesses of recorded human history until the eighteenth century, the world's people were overwhelmingly dominated by monarchs. In much of Africa, tribal chiefs ruled their subjects with approximately the authority of European monarchs or Chinese emperors. Here and there, republics prevailed, as in the Italian city-states, in the Netherlands and elsewhere, but these rarely lasted. Military rule also has a long lineage, whether in Rome or Japan through the Tokagawa Shogunate, but by the eighteenth century, these, too, were mostly replaced by monarchies. Two hundred years later, in our own time, monarchy is a rare form of government. It, in its turn, was displaced by autocracy, democracy, and military dictatorship. Clearly, forms of rule are not immutable. Systems of governance come and go, always presenting the puzzle of why some thrive in one period, only to mostly die out in another.

Figure 1.1 shows the average (median) democracy score each year since 1800.[5] A few vertical lines are added to highlight major events. These include the ends of World War I (1918), World War II (1945), and the Cold War (1989). These benchmarks help isolate important trends.

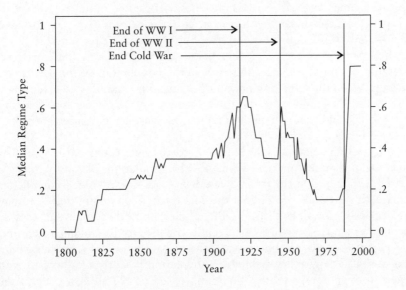

**Figure 1.1** Growing Prevalence of Democracy

From the French Revolution onward, governments experienced a long, sustained period of increasing democratization. The general increase in average governmental republicanism continued, with occasional fits and starts, almost unabated until the rise of fascism and communism in the 1920s. The end of World War I marked a downturn in global affinity for relatively more democratic regimes. By the start of World War II, the average government had retreated to the level of narrow, autocratic inclusiveness of the world nearly seventy years earlier, in 1870.

The end of the Second World War reflects a brief global struggle to resume the positive trend toward democratization. That trend was severely interrupted, however, by two important postwar developments. The Soviet Union defeated democratic movements in those states of Eastern Europe that fell within its sphere of influence. Additionally, the war's aftermath culminated in many newly minted countries that wrested freedom from colonial empires. Many of the newly liberated states shifted quickly from an initial semblance of democratic governance to more autocratic or even quasi-monarchic rule. The resulting diminution in "democraticness" returned the global governmental picture around 1975 to its vastly less democratic image of the 1830s and 1840s. The retreat of democracy appears to have been reversed around 1980, after which there is a sharp upturn in the average democracy score around the world. The substantial increase in average democraticness, it should be noted, predates the breakup of the Soviet Union.

Looking at the sweep of two centuries, Figure 1.1 highlights one fact above all others. With a few marked setbacks, national governments have shown a general, long-term trend away from monarchy and autocracy and toward democracy. Not every country has participated in this trend and not every year or decade has reinforced it. Still, the periods of retreat in movement toward more democratic forms of government are few and brief.

The graphic image of movement toward more representative regimes does not, of course, reflect differences in the populations of the constituent societies. With the large population of many authoritarian states, especially China, and their poor record on democraticness, we can be confident that the world is not becoming quite so representative when measured at the level of the experiences of individuals around the world.

Figure 1.2 re-examines the long-term trend toward democratization. This time, the median regime type is weighted by population. The graph is calculated by ranking countries from lowest democracy score to highest democracy score each year and then finding the country in this ranking that, summing the population of all countries in the ranking up to that point, includes the median person (i.e., the fiftieth percentile) relative to the global population.[6]

Figure 1.2 calls into question the thesis that the world is becoming more democratic. The graph weighted by population is vastly more erratic with regard to regime type than is the graph based on the median country displayed in Figure 1.1. The early years of the population-based graph show

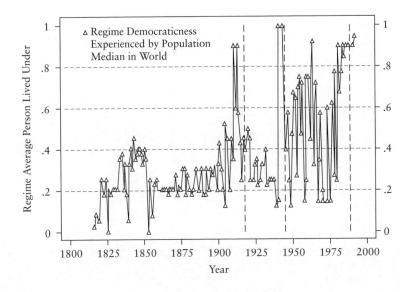

**Figure 1.2**  Is Democracy Growing More Prevalent?

much less of a positive trend toward democratization than is true for the plot based on the median country. Furthermore, although the very end of the time series does show high values on democracy, the surrounding years show wild fluctuations up and down. The average regime type, which reflects the democraticness of the average *government,* clearly increased throughout the nineteenth century, retreated during the second through third quarter of the twentieth century, and then resumed its upward journey. The same cannot be said with any real confidence for the experience of the average individual. Perhaps as an artifact of greater inclusiveness in the data set, and perhaps as a true reflection of changing conditions, the average individual has, on balance, become more likely to live with a highly volatile political arrangement. This suggests that much of the world's population lives with a state of turmoil regarding the nature of its government.

A pro-democracy optimist can find some reasons to be hopeful based on Figure 1.2. Beyond the volatility, the last quarter of the twentieth century shows a marked increase in the average individual's government's reliance on democracy. The volatility may reflect the unusually large number of institutional transitions taking place in the latter part of the twentieth century, transitions that, according to the figure, predate the collapse of the Soviet Union and the end of the Cold War. The easiest way to see the hopeful signs in Figures 1.1 and 1.2 is to strip away the volatility and just plot trend lines that show the propensity over time to increase the average democraticness score, whether as measured for the average country or the average citizen of the world. Figure 1.3 does just that.[7]

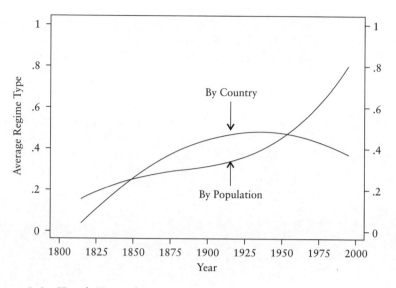

**Figure 1.3** Trends Toward Democracy

Figure 1.3 can, indeed, offer an optimistic view. Stripping away the volatility and fits and starts, we see some reasons for encouragement. But even here there are also reasons for caution. The trend as evaluated on a country-by-country basis was essentially flat for the past 100 years. The great acceleration in democracy took place in the nineteenth century and then apparently leveled off, perhaps even declining a bit recently. Of course, on the plus side it leveled off at a fairly high degree of democracy for the typical government, high at least by historical comparison. The population trend is much more reassuring. This, too, shows a long level period, but the past quarter-century has seen dramatic acceleration in the prospects that a global citizen lives in a government ruled by democracy. India, no doubt, is an important contributor here. Imagine how optimistic the picture could be if China became democratic.

Having provided an optimistic view, I would be remiss if I did not also reiterate some of the sources of caution. Looking back to an earlier period of potential transitions in governmental forms, that is, the years surrounding the revolutions of 1830 and 1848, raises a note of caution. Instead of liberalizing the world, these earlier revolutionary periods based on liberal principles seem to have produced retrenchment, leaving even fewer people subject to relative democracy than was true before. The aftermath of World War I, like the earlier efforts to promote liberal governance, yielded a renewed and sustained period of retreat from democracy. The retreat carried beyond the period of European fascism, incorporated the years of decolonization—motivated by liberal sentiments and forceful ejection where those sentiments were insufficient to produce voluntary withdrawal by European colonialists—seeming only to end around 1975.

Figure 1.2 and even 1.3 force us to question whether it is safe to assume that recent trends toward greater democratic governance reflects a long-term, sustainable change in world affairs or, like fascism and communism before, a temporary aberration. Optimism and normative wishes aside, the evidence is not yet in that democratization is increasing in terms of a sustained improvement in individual experiences. Chapter 5 is intended to shed some light on expectations for the future, indicating the likelihood that the world will retreat from or press forward toward further democratization.

## Prosperity

With occasional global setbacks, the history of the millennium just past is one of growing prosperity. Though for thousands of years there was little change in the material well-being of humanity, the period roughly from 1000 to 2000 was a time of considerable improvement. To be sure, the millennium had periods of severe reversal. Growth was so rapid during the years between 1000 and the Black Death in Europe that began in 1349 that the very idea of economic growth was essentially a new discovery during those centuries. The high Middle Ages marked a first industrial revolution among Europeans. The vertical water wheel, windmill, spinning wheel, sophisticated banking institutions, improvements in textile production, and countless other inventions improved daily life, helping to reduce the real cost of food at the same time that supply expanded. China saw the introduction and development of wet rice cultivation while also pulling back from technological innovation at which it had been the leader up until the high Middle Ages. Still, subsequent improvement in rice cultivation greatly expanded food supplies and enhanced average daily caloric intake. The world's population exploded in size in response to these and other improvements in living conditions.

The plague reversed the trend toward prosperity in Europe. Improvement in material welfare for the average peasant did not again reach the pre-plague levels until about the seventeenth or eighteenth century. At that time a second industrial revolution was about to begin, one that persists into our own time. Its flourishing brought previously unimaginable wealth to those millions of ordinary people lucky enough to live in societies whose governing structure permitted them to capitalize on the new opportunity for prosperity. Millions of others, starving under oppressive conditions, fled their homelands and migrated to countries that could offer them a chance to share in the new-found prosperity.

The post–World War II world represents a continuation of the period of the "bull market" that was launched by the second industrial revolution. Yet, abject poverty, famine, and misery persist in much of the world. Figure 1.4 depicts the growth in prosperity just since 1950. The three trend lines in the

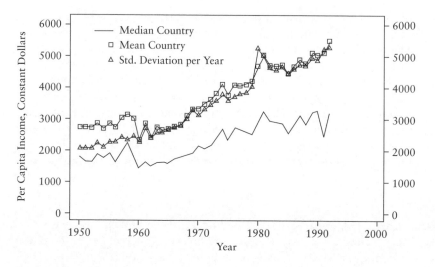

**Figure 1.4** Prosperity

figure reveal a story not unlike the tale of spreading democracy. While there is a general trend toward greater real per capita income around the world, that trend masks great differences across countries. Some few are growing fabulously rich while others fall farther and farther behind. To see this, let us dissect Figure 1.4 to better comprehend its details.

The lowest trend line shows the real per capita income of the median country in the world for each year between 1950 and 1992. There is a clear, slow trend upward in real median per capita income. That is, the average citizen in the median country is better off by several hundreds of dollars per year today than was true in 1950.

The highest trend line, made up of small squares, shows the mean country's real per capita income each year. The mean is much higher than the median and the gap between the two has grown. This suggests that the rich are getting richer faster than are the poor, as is confirmed by the third trend line. For the average citizen in the mean country, improvement in real per capita income is dramatic. Although both the median and the mean approximately doubled between 1950 and 1992, the gap in mean and median income widened from about $1,000 in 1950 ($1,766 for the median per capita income in 1950 versus $2,729 for the mean) to about $2,500 ($3,204 compared to $520).

The final trend line, made up of small triangles, is most disturbing and most informative. It plots the standard deviation of real per capita income each year. This line has a very strong positive trend and is always large relative to median per capita income. That is, the rich are pulling away dramatically from the poor, leaving them farther and farther behind. Thus, the global trend toward prosperity is extremely unevenly shared.

While the rich get richer, there could be a silver lining. Perhaps growth in per capita income is also trending upward. In that case, average material well-being at least is growing at an accelerating clip. Figure 1.5 examines the mean country's annual growth rate to evaluate whether this possibility is materializing. The mean alone is reported; the correlation between the mean and median is 0.9, making the two lines almost indistinguishable.

Alas, no such happy trend emerges. In fact, the trend across the years covered by the figure is significantly negative, though average annual growth is positive. Growth has slowed down for the average country over the period from 1950 to 1992. For a brief period in the early 1980s, the average country actually experienced economic contraction rather than growth. This is a disturbing story, especially if theories of relative deprivation and aggression prove correct (Gurr 1970). Those theories suggest that the gap between rich and poor, rather than absolute levels of prosperity, create the basis for friction between countries, with that friction at risk of being manifest, if not resolved, by violent means.

When I turn to a concrete examination of alternative policy futures and the risk of war, it will be useful to reflect back on the trend in declining growth rates. It will prove informative to examine alternative states of the world based on what we know about the relationship between prosperity, growth, democracy, and international violence. Then we can examine the prospective impact on foreign policy that is likely to arise if, for instance, economic expansion takes off around the world or if economic growth and democratization go hand in hand.

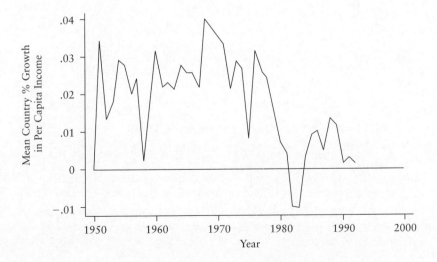

**Figure 1.5**   Annual Percentage Change in Per Capita Income

## Population Growth and Immigration

Before the relatively recent industrial revolution, few people wandered far from their place of birth. With the advent of the steamship and railroad, however, population movement became feasible for millions for the first time in history. Control over a substantial population is an important resource for those who want to exert influence over international affairs (Organski 1958; Organski et al. 1984). Populations grow or shrink in two primary ways: birth and death rates shift and people migrate into and out of countries. One first crude assessment of population change can be gleaned from Figure 1.6. Here I show the (often interpolated) annual change in the median country's population for the past two centuries.

Not surprisingly, the twentieth century was a period of population expansion. The very end of the period for which I have data offers a tantalizing hint of a great decline in the average country's population growth rate. Whether this is an anomaly or a newly established, persistent pattern cannot be said at this time. That such drops in growth rates are not new is certainly evident from an examination of the figure. Similarly large drops in demographic growth, relative to the immediately preceding years, were experienced around 1850, roughly the period of World War I, the start and end of World War II, and again about 1980.

Zooming in on the last half of the twentieth century, as is done in Figure 1.7, we can see a strong association between population growth and growth (or decline) in prosperity. As the average country's growth in per

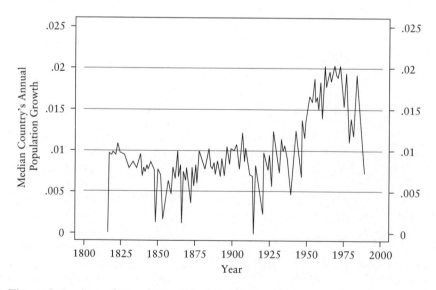

**Figure 1.6**   Annual Population Change: Median Country

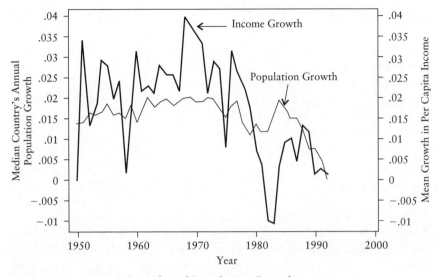

**Figure 1.7** Income Growth and Population Growth

capita income gradually arched downward in the latter part of the time series, so, too, did population growth. In fact, over the years for which we have relevant data, the correlation between growth in the average country's per capita income and growth in the median country's population is 0.5 (N=43). This suggests that either variable is a reasonable proxy for the other.

Population changes not only through birth and death, but also through immigration. If there is strength in numbers, then those governments and leaders who attract more immigrants may have a more influential future ahead of them than is true for those who prove unattractive to immigrants. Economic opportunity surely is related to immigration. Countries with higher per capita incomes are more attractive to immigrants than are poorer countries. But income effects are insufficient to eliminate another fundamental source of influence over prospective immigrants. Democratic regimes also hold out a substantial attraction for prospective immigrants, independent of income effects. This attraction is probably due to the fact that as governments become more democratic, they tend to emphasize public goods production over private goods allocations (Lake 1992; Persson and Tabellini 2000; Bueno de Mesquita et al. 2000; Bueno de Mesquita, Smith, Siverson, and Morrow 2003). Public goods, being accessible to everyone in a society, provide immediate benefits for immigrants (Bueno de Mesquita et al. 2003). Table 1.2 shows these separate influences on immigration. At the highest levels of democracy, immigration levels off, while rising steadily from the most autocratic to the nearly most democratic regimes.

**Table 1.2**

Immigration, Income, and Regime Type

| Variable | Coefficient | Standard Error | Probability |
|---|---|---|---|
| Real Per Capita Income | 0.019 | 0.001 | 0.000 |
| Democracy-Autocracy | 41 | 90.93 | 0.000 |
| (Democracy-Autocracy)$^2$ | −461 | 79.71 | 0.000 |
| Constant | −3.5 | 4.01 | 0.000 |
| N=91   F=65.40   P<0.000 | | | |
| R$^2$ = 0.1 | | | |

Figures 1.8 and 1.9 provide another way to look at the relationship between immigration and regime characteristics. Figure 1.8 shows the number of people, in millions, immigrating all over the world each year, as well as the number moving to the most democratic (Democracy-Autocracy = 1.00) and most autocratic (Democracy-Autocracy not larger than 0.10) regimes. Figure 1.9 examines the same phenomenon, but this time as a percentage of the total population of the relevant regime type (all regimes, most democratic, most autocratic). Both figures tell a dramatic story that shows a strong migratory preference to move to more democratic societies.

A careful examination of Figures 1.8 and 1.9 uncovers several important factors that will need to be attended to in subsequent analyses. Population migration does not show any particular temporal trend. Rather, it appears to rise and fall with major international events, especially (and not surprisingly) war. One important feature of war's aftermath is substantial

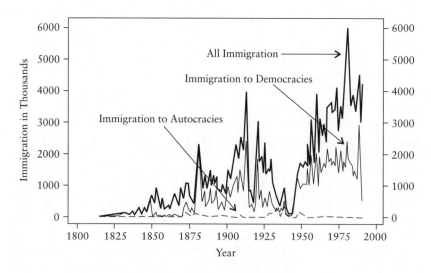

**Figure 1.8**   Population Migration and Regime type

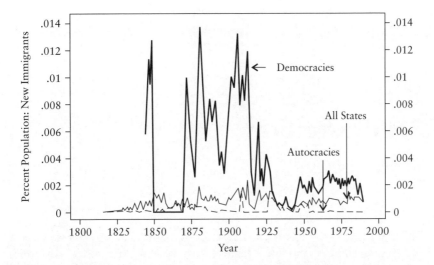

**Figure 1.9**  Percentage of Population Who are New Immigrants, By Regime Type

population movement. Even more notable, especially when viewed from the more normalized perspective of Figure 1.9, population migration is a miniscule proportion of global population, but a distinctly discernible and sizable factor in democracies. If the view of Organski and others is right that there is strength in numbers, then future foreign policy can be expected to favor democratic regimes in part because of their disproportionate demographic attractiveness.

## Conclusion

I suggest that the future of foreign policy depends on the interaction of social forces outside the immediate control of decision makers, combined with strategic maneuvering and decision making by political leaders. Contextual social forces are presumed themselves to be the product of choices by earlier generations of decision makers. By evaluating the interdependence between such social forces as changes in regime types, population migration, and changes in prosperity, with individual leadership incentives on human time scales, it may prove possible to predict important shifts in foreign policy in the future. Through the use of rational actor models attuned to relatively short-term leadership interests, I hope to demonstrate that rigorous methods can be brought to bear on international politics and can help predict longer-term developments.

# TWO

# Path Interdependence: An Illustration

THIS CHAPTER PRESENTS A SIMPLE MODEL INTENDED TO CONVEY how seemingly modest events can have dramatic long-term consequences. The focus is on the long-term endogenous consequences of the Concordat of Worms. In developing this example, I remain agnostic regarding whether the decision makers involved—the pope, a few key kings, and the Holy Roman Emperor—were conscious of the long-run implications of their agreement. It does not matter whether they consciously or unconsciously set into motion the consequences I infer from their decision at Worms. It is likely that they did not much trouble themselves with what would happen to the Holy Roman Empire or to the papacy several centuries down the road. More likely, they were concerned with what would happen in their lifetime and, perhaps, the lifetime of their children. Nevertheless, the actions taken in 1122 had predictable implications not only for the immediate future, but for the very long-term future as well. By examining the long-run consequences of short-term choices leaders make, I illustrate how strategic decisions can set into motion a long-term course of historical events. I also elucidate how game theory helps us discern that long-term course.

The theory offered here suggests that the development of important institutions of the modern sovereign state are partially an endogenous product of strategic maneuvering between the Catholic Church and European kings over relatively short-term political control within their domains. The theory further implies that the Concordat of Worms created incentives for the pope to stifle economic growth. This view stands in contrast to the general accounts of economic growth or of institution building found in the sociological literature beginning with Weber or in the historical and much of the political economy literature (Weber 1958, 1968; Rosenberg and Birdzell, Jr. 1986; Wesson 1978; Greif 1998; Kantorowicz 1957; Baldwin 1986; Tuchman 1984). If my case is persuasive, then it highlights important differences between theories of endogenous choice and more standard, path-dependent historical accounts.

I begin by providing the text of the Concordat of Worms and analyzing its central implications. Then I offer a brief historical review, suggest a game theoretic model of the agreement, and explore the implications that follow from it. I show how Worms sets into motion the creation of institutions that proved fundamental to the creation of sovereign states. I investigate how these elements are tied to Church-king competition over the appointment of bishops. I show that the resolution of the Investiture Struggle established a property right that adhered to sovereign territory, placed the king in a new fiduciary role regarding that territory, and that this property right fostered competition which influenced economic growth in Europe for centuries and was an important element moving kings and popes to erect new political institutions. The property right established at Worms in 1122—the right of kings to certain income from the territory defined by the domain of each bishop— was essential to the rise of the modern, territorially based, state system.

## Text of the Concordat of Worms

### *Privilege of Pope Calixtus II*

I, bishop Calixtus, servant of the servants of God, do grant to thee beloved son, Henry—by the grace of God august emperor of the Romans—that the elections of the bishops and abbots of the German kingdom, who belong to the kingdom, shall take place in thy presence, without simony and without any violence; so that if any discord shall arise between the parties concerned, thou, by the counsel or judgment of the metropolitan and the co-provincials, may'st give consent and aid to the party which has the more right. The one elected, moreover, without any exaction may receive the regalia from thee through the lance, and shall do unto thee for these what he rightfully should. But, he who is consecrated in the other parts of the empire (i.e., Burgundy and Italy) shall, within six months, and without any exaction, receive the regalia from thee through the lance, and shall do unto thee for these what he rightfully should. Excepting all things which are known to belong to the Roman church. Concerning matters, however, in which thou dost make complaint to me, and dost demand aid—I, according to the duty of my office, will furnish aid to thee. I give unto thee true peace, and to all who are or have been on thy side in the time of this discord.

### *Edict of the Emperor Henry V*

In the name of the holy and indivisible Trinity, I, Henry, by the grace of God august emperor of the Romans, for the love of God and of the holy Roman church and of our master pope Calixtus, and for the healing of my soul, do remit to God, and to the holy apostles of God, Peter and Paul, and to the holy catholic church, all investiture through ring and staff; and do grant that in all the churches that are in my kingdom or empire there may be canonical election and free consecration. All the possessions and regalia of St. Peter which, from the beginning of this discord unto this day, whether in the time of my father or also in mine, have been abstracted, and which I hold: I restore to that same holy Roman church. As to those things, moreover, which I do not hold, I will faithfully aid in their restoration. As to the possessions also of all other churches and princes, and of all other lay and clerical persons which have been lost in that war, according to the counsel of the princes, or according to justice, I will restore the things that I hold; and of those things which I do not hold I will faithfully aid in the restoration. And I grant true peace to our master pope Calixtus, and to the holy Roman church, and to all those who are or have been on its side. And in matters where the holy Roman church shall demand aid I will grant it; and in matters concerning which it shall make complaint to me I will duly grant to it justice. (MG LL folio II, pp. 75 ff., translated in Ernest F. Henderson, *Select Historical Documents of the Middle Ages,* London: George Bell and Sons, 1910, pp. 407–409).

The agreement at Worms gave the pope sole authority to nominate candidates for bishop. These candidates would be freely elected so that the office of bishop could not be sold, thereby shifting the authority to select bishops from the Holy Roman Emperor to the pope, eliminating simony. In exchange, the Holy Roman Emperor (and, under comparable agreements, other kings) would receive the income from the bishopric so long as it lay vacant, but would return authority over its income (through the regalia) once a bishop was consecrated. The new bishop would, in return, owe allegiance to the king and would provide support through force of arms in times of necessity (through the lance). The remainder of this chapter is concerned with understanding the implications and consequences of this agreement.

## The Power of the Pope

The power and authority of the pope reached its high point roughly from the papacy of Innocent III (1198–1216) to that of Boniface VIII (1295–1303). During the preceding three centuries, the pope's influence was dramatically transformed. Where once he was no more than the bishop of Rome, by the period discussed here he had expanded the authority associated with his title as the Vicar of Christ, the presumptive living embodiment of Jesus Christ's will. Having once been subservient to secular rulers, serving largely at their pleasure, the pope had become essential to the coronation and legitimation of the Catholic kings of Europe (Schimmelpfennig 1992, pp. 170–97; Kantorowicz 1957). The pope was elevated to such a degree that the bishop of Rome now claimed the authority to excommunicate or depose kings.[8] Indeed, some, like the king of England, explicitly owed fealty to the pope. The infallibility doctrine which had originally constrained popes to follow precedence was, sometime between 1316 and 1334, converted into something closer to its modern interpretation in which the pope can overturn precedence by invoking infallibility. It was a time when the pope was arguably the most powerful leader in the world and when the Roman church was hegemonic in Europe. After the early 1300s, the pope's influence went into a slow decline as the authority of sovereign kings rose to replace the church as the dominant political factor in Europe. The Thirty Years' War marked the culmination of that process. After the war, Catholicism no longer could claim successfully to be the one true faith among European monarchs.

The institutional arrangements that elevated the pope and church to such an exalted position during the twelfth and thirteenth centuries also planted the seeds of the church's slow demise as a secular European or world power. In addition, they fostered creation of the nascent modern, territorial state, gradually shifting political control from the pope to heads of state. The Concordat signed in 1122 presented a dilemma. The terms agreed to at Worms provided incentives for the church to try to retard economic growth in the secular domain. Indeed, papal hegemony depended on this effort. Yet, Worms created incentives for kings to stimulate economic growth within their domain and, if possible, to stifle such growth within the Church. These claims are at odds with widely accepted historical accounts.

The standard view holds that:

1. The church promoted growth;
2. Institutions, both secular and ecclesiastic, developed without a strategic link to the relationship between the church and the monarchies of the day; and
3. The appointment of bishops reflected the decision by monarchs, like Philip Augustus in France, to cooperate with the pope, rather than a decision by the pope to cooperate with monarchs.

This standard perspective is clearly reflected in the following statements by distinguished historians examining these very questions. John Gilchrist (1969, p. 3), for instance, writes, "During the vital period of growth the church did not impede but fostered economic progress." Ernst Kantorowicz (1957, p. 197), observing the emergence of new institutions, claims: "When in the twelfth century the church, including the clerical bureaucracy, established itself as the 'mystical body of Christ,' the secular world sector proclaimed itself as the 'holy Empire.' This does not imply causation, either in the one way or the other. It merely indicates the activity of indeed interrelated impulses and ambitions . . . [that] happened to emerge simultaneously—around the middle of the twelfth century."

John Baldwin (1986, p. 68) maintains that "Louis VII's policy of un-coerced cooperation [with the pope] worked still more advantageously for his son."

In contrast, I argue that the church did try to impede growth in the secular sector as a strategic maneuver to sustain the pope's political power. Kings developed new administrative and judicial institutions as a strategic response designed to increase their power and to counteract the efforts by the church to enhance the pope's authority. One consequence of these strategic efforts was that, where monarchs were successful in the promotion of economic growth, they were able to compel the pope to appoint bishops that satisfied monarchic interests at odds with those of the Catholic Church. This then enhanced the political power of monarchs and the independent, sovereign authority they exercised over the territory defined by the bishoprics within their domain.

I set out a game theory model for the appointment of bishops. Through comparative static analysis, I examine the appointment process in the light of different levels of economic development. I show that the pope, as leader of the church, had incentives to retard those aspects of economic growth that gave disproportionately greater advantages to secular rulers relative to the advantages conferred on the church. I contend that the pope promoted new institutions designed to thwart growth and that kings, responding to the shifting strategic environment, invented new political institutions to promote their authority over the Catholic Church. Following the theory, I offer empirical evidence and indicate how it contradicts previous historical accounts. The evidence is presented in two forms. First, I offer a narrative discussion of some of the important institutions that emerged within the church and in France and England after the Concordat of Worms and show how they were associated with the concessions each side made at Worms. Then I offer statistical evidence drawn from data on the appointment of bishops in France between 1179 and 1223. The statistical evidence, in conjunction with the narrative account, points to a shift in influence between the pope and kings in a manner consistent with the notion that Worms undermined the feudal order and set the sovereign, territorial state into motion. Thus, a seemingly simple agreement designed to resolve a specific dispute turns out to have profoundly influenced the future of foreign and domestic policy for centuries beyond the direct concerns of those who struck the "deal." Before presenting the model, I provide a brief historical review to familiarize the reader with essential aspects of the period.

## A Brief Historical Review

From approximately the tenth century until the Black Death in the fourteenth century, the economies of Europe experienced remarkable expansion. Although agricultural pursuits remained dominant, an extraordinary commercial and technological revolution took place (De Roover 1948; Miller and Hatcher 1995; Gies and Gies 1994; Duby 1991; Ladurie 1971; Lopez 1976). During this period, a money economy flourished and the foundations were laid for modern banking practices. Contracts became more sophisticated and more standardized, setting the stage for the ascent of merchants and lawyers as influential community leaders. Indeed, even popes became increasingly likely to be trained in law, rising to the papacy through the church's law offices.

Technology was harnessed to improve productivity to a degree unprecedented in the preceding millennium. Mills powered by water and wind became commonplace, mining on a large scale occurred in much of Europe as this period's industrial awakening called for new sources of metal, fuel, and other industrial materials. The technology of textile production, Europe's most important industry, made great leaps forward, as did international trade in textiles. Fuels for industrial production were diversified as coal and coke assumed an increasing role alongside wood.

The growth in wealth did not bypass the Catholic Church. As the owner of about one-third of Europe's land, and as a source of voracious demand for new construction, the church was an intimate beneficiary of and agent for economic expansion during the high Middle Ages. Indeed, many technological innovations were first applied on church lands, especially the lands of the newer monastic orders, most notably the Cistercians and the Crusading Orders like the Hospitalers and the Knights Templar. These new orders, unlike their predecessors who eschewed money-making labor (e.g., the Benedictine order), became wealthy through leadership in industry and banking. It is worth noting that these entrepreneurial orders, which refused to engage in such churchly activities as performing burials or hearing confession, came into existence beginning around 1100, and grew to great influence, wealth, and prominence over the next two centuries. I will return to them later, as they are an example of the new institutions promoted by the papacy to prevent the erosion of church influence by kings.

The growing wealth of the church contributed to the pope's rising stature and influence. By the twelfth century, the pope had diligently pursued elevation to the status of first among equals. He had risen above all other bishops, especially after the break with the Eastern Orthodox Church, and now strove also to rise above the kings of Europe and even above the Holy Roman Emperor. The adoption of the purple robe for the pope as of 1075 and by the secondary position accorded the Holy Roman Emperor at papal coronations after 1122 exemplify the pope's increasing prominence (Robinson 1990). The pope succeeded over a span of a few generations to rise to such a level that the kings of Catholic Europe were subservient to him. English kings, from the Conqueror on, pledged fealty to the pope.

In France, King Philip Augustus is said to have "promised royal bishoprics and abbeys freedom to elect their leaders as long as the canons and monks chose men who were both 'pleasing to God' and 'useful to the kingdom.' Cooperation, with both parties respecting mutual interests, was Philip's guiding principle" (Baldwin 1986, pp. 176–77). That is, Philip Augustus ostensibly would not interfere in the pope's prerogative under the Concordat of Worms and the specific agreements with France when it came to selecting nominees as bishops. The sentiment that called for supporting the interests of the church, even when they opposed those of the king, are cogently stated by Louis IX (Saint Louis) in his letter of advice to his son, who became King Philip III (Philip the Bold, 1270–1285) of France:

> I wish here to tell you what is related concerning King Philip [Augustus], my ancestor, as one of his council, who said he heard it, told it to me. The king, one day, was with his privy council, and he was there who told me these words. And one of the king's councillors said to him how much wrong and loss he suffered from those of Holy Church, in that they took away his rights and lessened the jurisdiction of his court; and they marveled greatly how he endured it. And the good king answered: "I am quite certain that they do me much wrong, but when I consider the goodness and kindness which God has done me, I had rather that my rights should go, than have a contention or awaken a quarrel with Holy Church." (Medieval Sourcebook at http://www.fordham.edu/halsall/source/stlouis1.html)

These observations naturally encourage the conclusion that the pope was hegemonic in Europe and that, therefore, the economic expansion probably occurred with the church's participation and blessings. Indeed, as the earlier quotation from Gilchrist indicates, historians of this period argue that the church favored growth. How, then, can we reconcile such observations with the claim I make that the Concordat of Worms stimulated competition between the church and secular authorities, competition that eventually and almost inevitably was won by the monarchs of Europe?

## The Model

The Concordat of Worms lays out a clear strategic game between the papacy and the Holy Roman Emperor. To model that game I begin by elucidating a few assumptions that are embedded in the agreement signed in 1122.

I assume that Catholic kings found papal opposition to their policies costly and, likewise, the king's opposition to church views was costly for the pope. That is why it was customary for nominees for high church office to be individuals both pleasing to God and useful to the kingdom (*qui Deo placeat et utilis sit regno*). One important arena in which the pope and kings hoped to coordinate their behavior was in the appointment of bishops. Naturally, the pope and each king had his own preferences among prospective candidates.

Why should the pope and monarchs have cared to coordinate over the appointment of bishops? Bishops were important emissaries between the pope and secular rulers in part because bishops possessed specialized information. They were in touch both with what went on within their own territory and within the counsels of the church and the monarchy. As in general principal-agent problems, bishops, depending on personal loyalties, might use their expertise to more faithfully reflect the interests of the king or the pope. They also were major tax collectors who could be used to help advance royal or papal financial interests. Under the terms of the Concordat of Worms, bishops owed allegiance to both pope and king. Bishops were obligated to guarantee the king's right to call upon them for military service. For both the king and the church, loyal bishops were potential sources of armed knights, major sources of tax collection, and large-scale property owners and ecclesiastical landlords with the power to turn the population in the bishopric in favor of or against a monarch or pope. They were a central source of information, capable of swaying policy debate to favor the interests of the king or the church within the territory of their See. Indeed, bishops routinely used these advantages to advance their welfare, sometimes limiting the impact of the pope in Rome and sometimes limiting the options of the king.

Under the Concordat of Worms, the pope gained the right to nominate bishops and the king the right to approve the nominees. To protect the interests of the king, the Concordat required that each bishop swear fealty to the king upon installation. In other words, in exchange for the return of the bishop's regalia by the king to the new bishop, the bishop promised military assistance and loyalty to the king as sovereign of the territory occupied by the bishopric.[9] In this way, the king transferred back to the church and the bishop as its agent the right to the tax revenues from the See. During the vacancy between the death of the old bishop and the consecration of the new bishop, the revenue from the bishopric went to the king under the terms of the Concordat of Worms and associated treaties. This revenue was substantial. It represented a property right that adhered to the king as sovereign over the territory of the See and not to the king as an individual. The king could not sell the future right to control the regalia, nor could it be inherited except by ascent to the throne. The right belonged to the king's successor, who might be his child or might be from an entirely new line. The king held the right to this income, then, as a fiduciary for the kingdom and not as his personal, private property. This is a significant departure from typical feudal practice. It establishes the sovereign claims of the king on behalf of his citizen-subjects within the territory of each bishopric in his domain. It is the beginnings of the state.

There was competition between each Catholic king and the pope to ensure that a newly appointed bishop was likely to view the pope or the king respectively as his primary master. The king could use delay in accepting the pope's nominee as a lever to encourage the pope to select a candidate to the king's liking. The pope could use the threat of excommunication or interdiction (and both were used) to encourage the king to accept the church's candidate.

Excommunication was accepted by believers as an action that placed their souls at eternal risk of damnation. Interdiction, which prevented residents in the interdicted area from receiving the sacraments, placed their souls at risk because of actions taken by the pope against the king. Excommunication and interdiction called for people to shun the excommunicated or interdicted king. This had the effect, even among nonbelievers, of making normal activities difficult and costly. Furthermore, interdiction raised the specter of civil unrest against the king by subjects deprived of the sacraments. These were powerful weapons in the hands of the pope.

Because of the privileged access to revenue and information enjoyed by bishops, they could sway important policy choices and negotiations in favor of the pope or a king. Consequently, their loyalty was a valuable resource.[10] Indeed, if this were not so there would have been no basis for the Investiture Struggle or for the Concordat of Worms and associated agreements. Under the terms of these agreements, the pope nominated bishops whose election required the king's consent. There was a general understanding, though certainly not a binding commitment, that the king would approve the pope's nominee. Indeed, with a few exceptions kings routinely accepted the pope's nominee for bishop. In the early years of his reign, Louis VII in France contested three elections, but did not again intervene directly in the election of bishops from 1149 until his death in 1179. Philip Augustus appears to have followed his father's lead by intervening only rarely, though he, too, contested some elections. Similar patterns are found elsewhere in Europe; however, I focus on France for empirical evidence as relatively reliable data are available from France during the reign of Philip Augustus.

It is evident that the king stood to benefit financially from vacancies in bishoprics just as the pope stood to benefit from minimizing the length of interregna. The significance of vacant Sees can be inferred from their duration, which the king could manipulate, and by the income they generated. From at least 1139 onward, the pope had called for vacancies to last no more than three months. Of the eighteen vacancies during Philip's reign that can be measured in months, thirteen lasted more than three months with only five falling within the time sought by the pope. Of Philip's total income in 1202–1203, one of the few periods for which the data exist, 5 percent came from regalia. This was about 17 percent of his discretionary income (Baldwin 1986, p. 156).

The period of vacancy, and, therefore, the monarch's control over income, could be extended by a failure of the king to accept the church's nominee. The acceptance of nominees, then, is a puzzle that requires explanation since it was costly. Of course, we must keep in mind that repeated rejection of the pope's nominees would also have been costly. It would have been tantamount to rejection of agreements like the Concordat of Worms, leaving the struggle over investiture to loom over church-king relations and to jeopardize the eternal soul of the king, not to mention his ability to conduct business as usual within his realm and between his realm and the church. As noted earlier, the pope, after all, had powerful means to retaliate against recalcitrant kings. Interdiction and excommunication were not mere idle threats, but were measures invoked by the pope to have his way not only on theological questions, but also on decidedly secular matters, as in the cases of interdiction of France's Philip Augustus and England's Henry II (Robinson 1990).

The competition between the church and the French king over the appointment of bishops was indicative of a broader issue of sovereignty. Control over bishoprics was a central theme of the reform movement in the church since before the revolutionary papacy of Gregory VII. The practice of simony not only harmed the religious mission of the church, but also represented a potential threat to church revenues and the church's political discretion. By putting bishoprics up for bids, secular authorities deprived the church of important control over the flow of tax revenues and alms given to the church through bishops and their underlings. The church also lost control over a key source of information and a key agent for policy implementation. As John Gilchrist has aptly noted, "although some of the opposition to church reform may have been genuinely religious, a large part derived from concern over the implied threat to lay, and individual clerical, control of church property and income" (1969, p. 22). It is evident that a delicate balance existed in which kings and the church had mutual incentives to reach agreement on the selection of bishops, but each also had private incentives to shift the selection toward a candidate of his own choosing. It is also evident that the Concordat of Worms and the associated agreements established a property right that adhered to the king as head of state rather than adhering to the monarch as an individual. Thus, this revenue source represented an early element in the establishment of modern state sovereignty, including the right to tax within a well-defined territory, one of the central sources of sovereignty pointed to later in the Treaty of Westphalia. From the resolution of the investiture struggle, then, there emerged a bargain between church and state.

The decision over nominations and election of bishops can be characterized as a simple game. The game in Figure 2.1 is a close approximation of the nomination and election procedure, and the payoffs fairly reflect the terms established at Worms.

Assume a two-player game consisting of the pope and a king. Each is charged with joint responsibility for selecting bishops in accordance with the agreement at Worms. The pope, moving first, nominates a candidate. He prefers candidates who are expected to be loyal to him, while the king prefers

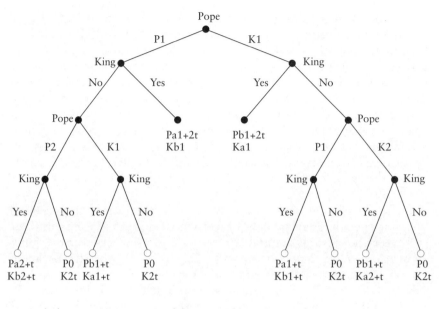

ai > bi for Pope, King          Candidates: P1, P2, K1, K2
                                Pope prefers Pi candidates and King prefers Ki candidates

**Figure 2.1**   Selection of Bishops: The Game of Competition Created at Worms

candidates, such as relatives or members of his court, expected to be loyal to the royal family. The pope's first nominee is designated as P1 or K1, with the pope preferring candidates who are identified in the game as P1 or P2 to any candidates designated with the letter K. The king prefers candidates designated as K1 or K2 to any candidate identified with the letter P. After the pope nominates a candidate, the king decides whether to accept the candidate. If the king accepts the candidate, the pope receives the payoff associated with that candidate (a1 if P1 is chosen and b1 if K1 was nominated and approved) plus 2t, where t represents the one-period income from the bishopric. The add-on to the payoff is 2t to denote that in this two-stage game, the pope gets this income from the bishopric during both periods. The king's payoff is b1 if P1 was approved and is a1 if K1 was approved. For both the king and the pope, a1 > b1. All of the king's utilities are prefaced with the letter K in Figure 2.1 and all of the pope's are prefaced with the letter P.

If the king rejects the pope's nominee, then the pope offers a new candidate. If P1 was offered first, the pope nominates either P2 or K1. If the pope nominated K1 originally, then the pope nominates P1 or K2. If the king approves the new nominee, the pope receives a2 (if the approved nominee is P2), b1 (if the nominee is K1), a1 if the nominee is P1 and b2 if the nominee is K2. With approval, the pope also receives the income from the See for the one remaining period and so gets an additional payoff of t. The king is rewarded comparably and also receives t because, by rejecting the first nominee, he received the income for one period. Finally, if the king again rejects the pope's nominee, the pope receives a payoff of 0 and the king receives 2t. Of course, in reality the king could reject the pope's nominee an indefinite number of times. Two stages, however, are sufficient to elaborate the central themes.

Let us examine the cases that point to alternative equilibrium outcomes of the game in Figure 2.1. The first case of interest arises when t, the regalian revenue, is sufficiently small that the king in the final round strictly prefers to approve the pope's nominee rather than take the income. In this case the pope will never give the king either of the two prospective candidates (K1 or K2) most desired by the king. On the left side of the tree, the king's choice reduces to approving P1 immediately or collecting some of the regalian income and approving P2 later. The pope presumably can find a candidate P1 whom the king likes sufficiently more than P2 that the king will forego the regalian income by making the interregnum as short as possible. This outcome mirrors the general account offered by historians.

If the pope likes P2 better than P1 as bishop sufficiently that he is willing to forego some regalian income to get P2, and the pope anticipates that the king will reject P2 if he is not compensated with some regalian revenue, then the pope can nominate as P1 someone sufficiently unattractive to the king that the king will prolong the interregnum a bit and let the pope have his more preferred bishop in the end. On the right side of the tree, assuming t is small enough, the king would choose to accept K1 in the first instance because he is better for the king than P1, who is the choice by the pope if the king rejects K1. Naturally, facing a choice between K1 or either P1 or P2, the pope nominates P1 and not K1 at the outset, ensuring that a candidate more desirable for the pope is elected. If t, the regalian income, is small enough, the pope gets his preferred choice as bishop.

Suppose now that t is not so small that the king will always prefer to approve a papal nominee rather than take the regalian income at the end of the game. If t, the regalian income, is large enough that the king prefers to take the income rather than cooperate with the pope by approving either P1 or P2, but is not large enough for the king to prefer the income to K1 or K2, then the pope's hands are tied. The pope can avoid losing any of the regalian income by nominating as K1 someone the king prefers by enough to K2 that the king will approve K1 right away, foregoing any regalian income. If the pope prefers K2 over K1 enough to give up some income and if the king prefers K2 (a2 + t) to K1 (a1) without an interregnum, then the pope can ensure his third most preferred candidate is selected over his least preferred candidate. But, in any event, the pope must give the king one of his two preferred candidates. This scenario contradicts the standard historical accounts.

Should the value of the regalian income rise still further, it becomes easier for the pope to avoid his least preferred candidate and it becomes harder for the pope to keep the interregnum short. Indeed, if the income becomes sufficiently valuable, the pope loses all ability to obtain the king's approval, the agreement at Worms breaks down, and the king monopolizes the taxes raised from the bishop's territory. This, in essence, marks the end of the pope's prospects of being a European hegemonic power and is essentially what happened by the end of the Thirty Years' War and the rise of Protestantism as a rival to Catholicism. This result, like the previous equilibrium, contradicts standard historical accounts of relations between kings and popes resulting from Worms.

Summarized a bit more formally, the game leads to six different equilibria. These are:

Equilibrium 1: P1 is bishop and regalian income is small

If $b2 > t$ (implies $a1 > t$), then pope chooses P2 if king rejects P1 ($t > b1 - b2$) on left side. However, if $b1 - b2 > t$, then king chooses P1 over P2. On right side, $b1 > t$ (implied by $b1 > b2 + t$ implying $a2 > t$) and P1 chosen by pope if king rejects K1. If, however, $a1 - b1 > t$, then king chooses K1 over P1 and pope chooses P1 as his initial nominee and gets P1.

Equilibrium 2: K1 nominated immediately and becomes bishop, regalian income is moderate

If on the left side, $t > b2$, but $a1 > t$, then pope chooses K1 on left side if king rejects P1. In this case, the king will always reject P1 on the left side, so that K1 is chosen and approved on the left side. On the right side, suppose $b1 > t$ (implies $b1 > b2$, i.e., for the king P1 > P2 and also $a2 > t$), then the pope chooses P1 over K2 if the king rejects K1. If a $1 - b1 > t$, then the king approves K1 on the right side. In this case, the pope nominates K1 immediately ($b1 + 2t > b1 + t$) and the king approves K1.

Equilibrium 3: K1 nominated immediately and becomes bishop, regalian income is moderate

If on the left, $t > b2$, but $a1 > t$, then pope chooses K1 on left side if king rejects P1. In this case, the king will always reject P1 on the left side, so that K1 is chosen and approved on the left side. On the right side, suppose $b1 < t$, but $a2 > t$, then the pope chooses K2 over P1 if the king rejects K1. If $a1 - a2 > t$, then the king approves K1 on the right side. In this case, the pope nominates K1 immediately ($b1 + 2t > b1 + t$) and the king approves K1.

Equilibrium 4: K1 or K2 eventually becomes bishop, regalian income is moderate

If on the left side, $t > b2$, but $a1 > t$, then pope chooses K1 on left side if king rejects P1. In this case, the king will always reject P1 on the left side, so that K1 is chosen and approved on the left side. On the right side, suppose $b1 < t$, but $a2 > t$, then the pope chooses K2 over P1 if the king rejects K1. If $a1 - a2 < t$, then the king approves K2 on the right side. In this case, the pope is indifferent between nominating P1 initially and ending up with K1 or nominating K1 initially and ending up with K2.

Equilibrium 5: Pope nominates K1 and gets K2 as bishop: regalian income is moderate

If on the left side $t > a1$ (implies $t > b2$, $t > b1$), then the pope is indifferent between nominating P2 and K1 because either will be rejected by the king and P1 will also be rejected by the king. If, on the right side, however, $a2 > t$ (implies $a2 > a1$), then the pope will nominate K2 if the king rejects K1, which the king will do. The pope therefore will initially nominate K1 and get K2.

Equilibrium 6: The king disapproves of all nominees: Regalian income is large

If on the left side $t > a1$ (implies $t > b2$, $t > b1$), then the pope is indifferent between nominating P2 and K1 because either will be rejected by the king and P1 will also be rejected by the king. If, on the right side, $t > a2$, then no matter who the pope nominates, the king rejects the nominee.

## Implications for Pope and King

The game leads to several hypotheses about relations between popes and kings as well as about the incentives popes and monarchs had regarding the creation of wealth in the secular domain. So long as bishoprics remained poor enough, the pope could ensure that the elected bishops would be loyal to the church, ensuring the pope's political control (equilibrium 1). In fairly wealthy Sees, political control shifts from the pope to the king (equilibria 2–5). In sufficiently wealthy bishoprics, the king values the income from a vacant See more than the value he derives from cooperating with the pope. In such a circumstance, the pope had no choice but to nominate as bishop a man expected to be more loyal to the king than to the pope, thereby yielding significant political influence to the king. If the wealth became really large, the king would prefer, in essence, a perpetual vacancy so that he gained the tax benefits in perpetuity (equilibrium 6). Under such a circumstance, the church could no longer vie with the monarch for political control and so would be reduced to the role of the modern church as a major religious body, but not as a major political-military entity.

Because in wealthy Sees the pope would choose candidates especially pleasing to the king, it is evident that we cannot properly infer whether the king was obedient and deferential to the pope or whether the pope was deferential to the king without examining the wealth of the bishopric and the anticipated loyalties of the bishop- nominee. In other words, the observation by historians that Philip Augustus accepted all papal nominations for bishop after the beginning of his reign cannot, by itself, be taken as evidence of his cooperation with or subservience to the pope.

Because the pope's prospects of getting a loyal bishop elected depend on the value of the income from the diocese, we can see that the Concordat created an endogenous incentive for the pope to retard economic growth in the secular domain. How could the pope or the king influence their competition over the selection of bishops? In answering this question I elaborate on the endogenous, strategic incentives created at Worms.

The value of t can be taken as endogenous. The value of the income from a See depended on the wealth of the area. Since the revenues extracted from the Sees were generally proportionate to the wealth in the diocese, the pope had incentives to keep any wealth accessible to secular authorities at a low enough level that the king would accept as bishop a candidate preferred by the pope. The pope could facilitate the prospects of getting bishops who were loyal to him by retarding economic growth in the secular portion of the economy. Naturally, the king had incentives to promote growth for many reasons, one of which was that it gave him a general advantage vis-à-vis the powerful Catholic Church. In a period already experiencing marked economic expansion, the pope's recently acquired hegemony was certainly at risk. In fact, the conflict between the pope and the French king erupted in virtually open warfare by the time of Philip IV (the Fair, 1285–1314) and Boniface VIII (1294–1303).

## Narrative Account of Evidence

The church's hegemony benefited from policies that hindered economic expansion, prolonging the time before the game shifted to yield bishops loyal to the king or, in the extreme case, made bishops largely irrelevant from the perspective of the king (as occurred by the time of the Treaty of Westphalia). By holding down the value of t, the pope could ensure that more bishops would be of type P (equilibrium 1) and fewer of type K (equilibria 2–5). Unfettered economic expansion in the secular realm meant that the expected value of t would rise, making it increasingly likely that the revenues earned by the king during interregna exceeded the value the king attached to agreement with the pope. Such a shift would have marked the decline of papal influence, at least in bishoprics with sufficient wealth.

The popes of this period introduced policies whose consequences included retarding secular economic growth relative to what one would have expected in their absence. In the first Lateran Council (1123), at which hundreds of bishops confirmed the agreement at Worms, celibacy was elevated and reinforced by prohibiting the clergy from marriage or having concubines. This insured that the property of the clergy would devolve to the church rather than to heirs. At the second Lateran Council (1139), more serious changes were instituted that must have limited secular economic growth. The council dealt with questions of inheritance and usury. On the inheritance of the private property of deceased bishops, now more fully elaborating on the consequences of the celibacy arguments at Lateran I, the church raised the stakes and insured that they, and not any secular venue, would be the beneficiary:

> [T]he goods of deceased bishops are not to be seized by anyone at all, but are to remain freely at the disposal of the treasurer and the clergy for the needs of the church and the succeeding incumbent. . . . Furthermore, if anyone dares to attempt this behaviour henceforth, he is to be excommunicated. And those who despoil the goods of dying priests or clerics are to be subject to the same sentence. (Lateran II text is found at http://www.netins.net/showcase/dewa/catholic/ecum10.html)

By imposing excommunication on violators, the church raised the risks families or monarchs ran in trying to seize the "personal" property of deceased clerics.

The Council ruled regarding usury that:

> we condemn that practice accounted despicable and blameworthy by divine and human laws, denounced by Scripture in the old and new Testaments, namely the ferocious greed of usurers; and we sever them from every comfort of the church, forbidding any archbishop or bishop, or an abbot of any order whatever or anyone in clerical orders, to dare to receive usurers, unless they do so with extreme caution; but let them be held infamous throughout their whole lives and, unless they repent, be deprived of a Christian burial.

In Lateran II the church also erected other barriers to lay or secular authority that might jeopardize church interests. For instance, the church forbade lay people to receive tithes from churches, even if given by the bishop or the king, and subjected any who took such financial benefits to excommunication. It further decreed that "lay people, no matter how devout they may be, have no power of disposal over ecclesiastical property," thereby attempting to deprive nobles of the right to dispose even of their private, proprietary churches and chapels.

Prior to 1139, usury was forbidden the clergy, but was not elevated to a mortal sin for lay people, nor was a ban on usury by lay people long discussed and debated at the highest levels in the church. The effect of banning usury was to raise the price of money and to create a potential shortage of would-be lenders. Just as modern-day central banks increase interests rates to slow growth (and inflation), so the twelfth-century church raised interest rates by denying heaven to those who loaned money for profit. Though the church used scripture to justify its action, there was a widely held view among church canonists that there was no doctrinal ban on usury in early Catholic teachings or scripture. And, of course, the church had not used scripture to ban such usury in its preceding thousand years.[11]

Enforcement was a problem. The church recognized the difficulty inherent in determining whether a lender *intended* to commit usury; that is, to derive any profit from allowing the use of one's money. To deal with intent, the church wisely shifted enforcement from the canonists to the theologians. They reasoned that while human law might fail to recognize a usurious loan, God knew whether a lender intended to make a profit no matter what subterfuge was used to mask the return. Therefore, anyone having made such a profit and failing to make restitution or to show sufficient contrition before death was condemned eternally. This was the consequence of being denied a Christian burial.

To facilitate restitution for usury and to heighten the threat of damnation associated with lending, the church established new institutions. The fourth Lateran Council (1215), for instance, made annual oral confession mandatory. This period also saw the distribution of confessors' manuals with specific instructions for dealing with merchants and others likely to have engaged in usury (Le Goff 1980). Through the confessional the church provided a means by which those otherwise damned for usury could save their souls. The path to forgiveness, however, generally was strewn with a combination of making financial restitution to the church and cessation of the sinful behavior. While the threat of eternal damnation was powerful indeed in the twelfth century, still, money lending continued. Merchants and others devised clever schemes of their own (including misleading contracts, exchange-rate manipulation, and false stock companies) to hide their true financial arrangements, but the risks (including eternal damnation) had been raised and so, naturally, the expected rate of return had to rise commensurately (De Roover 1974). The upshot was to make loans costlier and, thereby, to diminish growth relative to what it otherwise would have been.

During the twelfth century, the church's rhetoric also shifted in ways that may have dampened economic growth. At the same time that the Cistercians built and operated mills and other labor-saving devices to improve efficiency, the church began to promote the view that idle hands are the work of the devil. The church discouraged the spread of machines and other technology in the secular realm, ostensibly fearing that labor-saving devices would lead to idleness and that idleness in turn would lead to sin. Certainly, by discouraging the spread of labor-saving technology, the church was reducing productivity and, therefore, economic growth in the lay sector. By the thirteenth century, with the rising wealth and influence of merchants, the church gradually abandoned its arguments against improvements in technology, but then this shift coincides with the diminution in church authority hypothesized to be associated with growth in secular wealth.

The church erected or strengthened other institutions as well in this period to bolster the pope's political position. The election of the pope had previously been the responsibility of the electors of the Holy Roman Empire. The College of Cardinals, introduced in the eleventh century, grew steadily in importance after Worms. Before the twelfth century, the College did not have authority to elect the pope. Beginning in that century, a two-thirds vote in the College became a necessary condition for papal election, though approval by secular authority, especially the Holy Roman Emperor, also remained necessary. By the beginning of the thirteenth century, the College of Cardinals became the dominant body for selecting the pope, wresting control over that fundamental process from the secular realm.

It is also noteworthy that entrepreneurial monastic orders, like the Cistercians, Templars, and Hospitalers, came into existence at the end of the eleventh century. This is the exact time when the pope was driven out of Rome and when the Holy Roman Emperor had created a schism by selecting an anti-pope, itself a clever secular institutional maneuver to strengthen the emperor in competition with the pope. By being driven out of the papal states, the "real" pope was cut off from financial support. That the new, entrepreneurial orders were organized and recognized by the exiled pope in this period seems hardly coincidental. Quite the contrary: Pope Paschal II (1099–1118) and Innocent II (1130–1143), for instance, exempted monks from tithes. The Cistercians, founded in 1098, took advantage of this exemption to obtain a virtual monopoly on the highly valuable wool trade. Not until the late thirteenth century, as kings rose in prominence relative to the pope, were the Cistercians subjugated to the interests of the king. By the end of the thirteenth century they were driven into bankruptcy by the heavy taxes of the French crown (Gilchrist 1969).

In the late eleventh and early twelfth centuries, these new monastic orders looked to the pope for protection from taxation by kings and their local bishops. The new orders were freed from all secular authority, including secular taxation, and put directly under the supervision of the pope. In exchange for his protection, the pope derived a significant portion of his income from the new entrepreneurial orders during the long periods he was driven out of the papal states by the anti-pope and the Holy Roman Emperor.

So, the new orders served to finance the pope against the secular authorities and, in exchange, were given a free hand to generate great wealth for themselves (and the papacy), an activity that had been anathema for earlier monastic orders.

Kings were no less innovative than the pope in erecting institutions to wrest political control and to increase their wealth and enhance their competition with the pope. The decades immediately after the Concordat of Worms saw a dramatic burgeoning of political institutions in England and France. Whether intentionally or not, many of these had the effect of weakening the pope's influence and securing a higher growth rate for the king's subjects and, therefore, higher tax revenues for the king. Consider, for instance, the series of legal reforms introduced by Henry II in England during the mid-twelfth century. These reforms became the foundation of English common law. Most noteworthy for the issues raised here are the writs of *novel disseisin, mort d'ancestor, utrum,* and *darrein presentment.*

The first protects property rights and the second, rights of inheritance. These two writs provided an important improvement in a person's ability to predict whether he or she would maintain access to and the benefits from the land being worked. These writs greatly shortened the judicial process for determining rights of access to the land and enhanced a smoother operating agricultural system. They proved highly popular and effective in securing the property rights that are essential to economic growth; they also enhanced the king's credibility as the person who would insure order and justice in matters of property (Van Caenegem 1988; Barzel 1989; North and Weingast 1989; Eggertsson 1990; Przeworski 1991). These rights were especially powerful in protecting the interests of tenant widows and their children against land-grabs by unscrupulous landlords.

The third and fourth writs deal with restrictions on ecclesiastical rights. *Utrum* established the king's primacy in determining whether a dispute belonged in his secular courts or in the church's ecclesiastical courts. Prior to Henry there was a presumption in favor of the jurisdiction of the ecclesiastical courts. *Utrum* reversed this presumption among litigants in England, and the period of which I write was a litigious age. *Darrein presentment* addressed Henry's interest in protecting the tradition of patronage that gave landowners the benefit of presenting or selecting clerics for appointment in their proprietary churches. This ran directly counter to the efforts of the church to take all such influence away from the secular domain, as is evident from the rulings in Lateran II (1139) and III (1179), some of which are quoted above. In *darrein presentment,* as in *utrum,* Henry challenged church authority and, as in the first two writs, he sought to protect a property right that, in this case, the church was trying to usurp for itself (Van Caenegem 1988).

The four major writs of Henry II were also accompanied by the introduction and spread of the jury system to replace trial by ordeal.[12] Henry sought to insure "victory of a reasoned, rational mode of proof over the old irrational appeals to God or the obscure forces of nature" (Van Caenegem 1988, p. 63). This effort is also found at the same time in France and elsewhere on the continent. Probably not coincidentally, the shift to a jury system from trial by ordeal also weakened church institutions and income. Trials by ordeal were supervised by the clergy, who were well compensated for their participation. For instance, two priests are known to have been paid 10 shillings for blessing the ordeal pits near St. Edmund's Bury in 1166. At the time, a worker's daily wage was about one penny and a villein and his entire family could be purchased for 22 shillings (Van Caenegem 1988, p. 64).

The administrative structure of the modern state likewise began to emerge in the twelfth and thirteenth centuries. The king's right to levy taxes for reasons other than necessity gradually developed in exchange for political concessions to his subjects, most notably in 1297 when Edward I accepted *Confirmatio Cartarum*. These tax revenues gave the king the ability to muster an army without having to rely on the intricate rights and restrictions implied by the feudal order. Consequently, the bishop's military guarantee to the king "through the lance," granted at Worms, diminished in importance. The pope, in contrast, continued to rely on feudal commitments to raise an army.

King's courts at a fixed location in England and in France replaced the itinerant justice of an earlier time, thereby centralizing judicial control in the hands of the king, further diminishing the role of the church as an adjudicator of disputes, and further emphasizing the king's territorial sovereignty. Additionally, kings began to claim that they ruled by divine right, thereby challenging the pope's special position as allegedly chosen by God. In the jockeying back and forth for control, both kings and church evolved new institutions and methods to foster or stymie economic growth and wrest political control.

## The Selection of Bishops: An Empirical Assessment

The narrative account suggests a period rife with institutional innovation, much of which influenced the relative autonomy of the pope and monarchs. Whether these institutional changes and the level of political influence shifted with growth, as suggested by the game, can now be examined with available statistical evidence.

The reign of Philip Augustus was a period of economic expansion in France. This implies that later in Philip's reign more bishoprics would have had large enough revenues to tie the pope's hands in nominating bishops than was true earlier in his reign. In fact, we can make a pretty good estimate of when economic growth would have pushed many dioceses over the threshold to insure that the king would get the bishops he wanted. Philip renounced his regalian rights in 1203; that is, he ostensibly gave up his right to the income from bishoprics during interregna. While some interpret this gesture by Philip as an act of contrition toward the church (Baldwin, 1986), it is possible that Philip knew he now had a winning strategy in most dioceses that would lead to the selection of his preferred candidates for bishop. In that case, Philip could afford to appear magnanimous by renouncing the rights hard earned in the resolution of the investiture controversy. After all, Philip's declaration itself was not binding. In fact, Philip later reneged in some Sees. If the theory presented here is correct, the pope should have recognized the increased need to select bishop candidates who were acceptable to the king. The game had changed from one of domination by the pope (equilibrium 1) to one of domination by Philip (equilibria 2–5).

If the game structure proposed here is correct, we should observe an increase in the proportion of new bishops who were Philip's candidates after 1203 relative to what we observe before. If the standard historical account is right—that Philip learned to cooperate with the church—then we should observe a decrease in the nomination (and selection) of candidates believed to be preferred by the king.

Table 2.1 shows the distribution of bishops appointed during Philip's reign based on whether they were more likely to be loyal to the king or to the pope.[13] The historical record is clear. After 1203 Philip increasingly got bishops who were loyal to him. This is consistent with the explanation associated with my argument.

Less than one-fourth of all new appointees in Philip's first twenty-four years in office were expected to be favorable to the king rather than the pope. In his last twenty years, after 1203, despite renouncing his regalian rights, 50 percent of those appointed were relatives and close associates expected to be his supporters. If, as the standard historical accounts suggest, Philip had learned to comply with the wishes of the church, then we must wonder why the pope switched to appointing the king's relatives late in his term rather than earlier, when Philip was seemingly less contrite toward the church?

Other measures of the relationship between economic growth and the appointment of bishops are available for Philip Augustus's France. Since the general thesis is that where there was sufficient wealth, the pope would nominate—and Philip would approve—bishops loyal to the king rather than the pope, we can test the proposition spatially as well as temporally. Maps of

**Table 2.1**
Selection of the King's Man for Bishop:
Before and After Renouncing Regalian Income

| Bishop | Before 1203 | After 1203 |
|---|---|---|
| Pro-King | 11 | 17 |
| Pro-Pope | 36 | 18 |

$\chi^2 = 5.65$   P < .01 One-tailed

twelfth- and thirteenth-century France identify towns with significant textile industries, in touch with the Champagne fairs, or located on major water or land-based trade routes (Lopez 1967). The Sees in these areas presumably generated more wealth than the Sees not on any of these trade routes or involved in the merchant and export markets. These wealthier communities can be matched against the locations of the Sees to ascertain whether a pattern exists between the expected loyalties of newly appointed bishops and the wealth of the bishopric.

Table 2.2 shows the relationship between papal nominees and whether the bishopric is located on a major trade route. Table 2.3 shows the same relationship, but this time the independent variable is an index categorized as 1 if any of the three wealth criteria (trade route, cloth manufacturing, or being in touch with the Champagne fairs) is satisfied. Neither cloth manufacturing nor being in touch with the Champagne fairs, by themselves, are statistically significantly associated with the bishop-nominee's type, though each is in the predicted direction. Unfortunately, the wealth data other than with regard to location on a major trade route are spotty, with missing information for many regalian Sees. Finally, Table 2.4 shows the interaction effect of both wealth and being post-1203 on the likelihood that the nominee was expected to be loyal to Philip or to the pope.

Tables 2.2, 2.3, and 2.4 point to a substantial proclivity for the pope to nominate bishop candidates who were relatives or close associates of Philip's in those bishoprics that were wealthy and to nominate papal loyalists more often in poorer Sees. This is consistent with the expectations from the game.

The tables tell a story that reinforces the view that the struggle over growth was also a struggle over political control and that, gradually, the king

**Table 2.2**
Selection of the King's Man for Bishop:
See Is On or Not On a Major Trade Route

| Bishop | Trade Route | Not a Trade Route |
|--------|-------------|-------------------|
| Pro-King | 20 | 8 |
| Pro-Pope | 27 | 27 |

$\chi^2 = 3.46$   P < .03 One-tailed

**Table 2.3**
Selection of the King's Man for Bishop: See Is Wealthy or Not Wealthy

| Bishop | Wealthy | Not Wealthy |
|--------|---------|-------------|
| Pro-King | 22 | 6 |
| Pro-Pope | 30 | 24 |

$\chi^2 = 4.21$   P < .02 One-tailed

**Table 2.4**
Selection of the King's Man for Bishop:
Interaction of Wealth and Year > 1203

| Bishop | Wealthy and Year > 1203 | Not Wealthy |
|---|---|---|
| Pro-King | 14 | 14 |
| Pro-Pope | 9 | 45 |

$\chi^2 = 10.15$   $P < .01$ One-tailed

was winning against the efforts of the church. The French king was 2.5 times more likely to have a relative or close associate nominated as bishop by the pope in Sees on important trade routes than he was elsewhere. In wealthy dioceses, as measured by satisfying any one of the three economic indicators, the king was more than three times more likely to get a loyal bishop than in less wealthy dioceses. After 1203—when according to standard historical accounts Philip conceded control to the pope—61 percent of new appointments in wealthy Sees went to Philip's loyalists, whereas elsewhere and before, only 24 percent of appointees were expected to be loyal to Philip.

The standard historical account is difficult to sustain in light of the evidence. Papal appointments varied systematically with the wealth of each bishopric. Where wealth was minimal, the pope and church, rather than the king, controlled the appointment of bishops. As the loyalty of bishops was a major factor in the exertion of political control, the church had a strong incentive to minimize growth in wealth and, therefore, the influence of the king over the appointment of key political figures. Church policies aimed at reducing growth helped prolong papal hegemony, but the new secular institutions invented in the twelfth and thirteenth centuries gradually insured the demise of papal influence. In the process, these new institutions, many being outgrowths of the competition over economic expansion fostered by the property right granted by the Concordat of Worms, gave rise to the modern sovereign state system. By the end of the Thirty Years' War, the wealth and influence garnered by kings became so great that the game against the pope entered its final stage. With the Protestant Reformation and the defeat of the church, the Treaty of Westphalia made the appointment of bishops irrelevant to kings and so ended the pope's role as a central political figure in Europe. From that time forward, the state, rather than the church, was the primary seat of political authority.

## Summary

The Concordat of Worms created a property right over territory (specifically, bishoprics) that adhered to the sovereign as a fiduciary rather than to the sovereign as an individual. This fiduciary role was new. The property right created competition between kings and the pope over political control. The contest for control manifested itself, in part, through the erection of new political institutions. Some of these institutions on the side of the church appear to have been designed to slow economic growth, thereby prolonging the political ascendancy of the papacy. The institutions erected by monarchs appear to have stimulated growth and hastened the day when they would be politically ascendant over the church. The struggle for political control gave advantage to the church in the first century or two after the investiture struggle, and a gradual decline in papal authority after that, culminating in the rise of Protestantism and the modern state at the end of the Thirty Years' War.

The competition that was institutionalized at Worms fomented the construction of new executive, judicial, taxing, and legislative apparatus that eventually emerged as the state as we know it. Worms set in motion the evolution of many of those institutions, insuring that the territorial property right it created would form the foundation for a new political structure. Over the span of about 500 years, the agreement at Worms served to preserve and protect papal authority. It also served to insure the development of new means to produce growth, including much of the administrative apparatus of sovereign states, so that kings could escape the powerful grip of the pope. Those new means ultimately resulted in the demise of the Catholic Church as Europe's hegemonic power and the emergence of the terms at Westphalia that codified the sovereign authority of the territorial state.

Foreign policy was firmly and markedly redirected as a consequence of the agreement at Worms. The effect, felt for centuries, has been shown to follow directly from the terms of the agreement once we accept the notion that decisions about promoting or retarding economic growth were made endogenous by the way Worms tied the fate of popes and kings to the value of the revenue generated by vacant bishoprics. That is, the rise of the sovereign state was not the product of path dependence and happenstance, but rather the product of path interdependence set into motion in 1122.

We saw that a simple game can improve our understanding of how institutional choices reshape foreign affairs. The examination of the Concordat of Worms in game theoretic, strategic terms allowed us to "predict" the course of events, including the promotion or retardation of the spread of prosperity. It also allowed us to see how conflict could have developed between the papacy and Europe's monarchies, culminating in the Thirty Years' War and the demise of papal hegemony. Thus, we saw indirectly how a game theoretic approach could help us understand the prospects of peace and prosperity across the Middle Ages. Of course, thus far we have only looked retrospectively at hoary decisions. The rest of this study is focused on applying some lessons learned in this chapter to an effort to predict the prospects of peace and prosperity in the future. We move, then, from postdiction to real prediction.

THREE

# Tools for Predicting Politics

CHAPTER 2 USED A SIMPLE MODEL TO ILLUSTRATE HOW SMALL
events can create emergent properties that carry weight in shaping international affairs for decades and even centuries. Now I offer a more general model that can be used to analyze a broad array of policy decisions. This model, sometimes referred to as the expected utility model (hereafter EUM), might better be described as a dynamic median voter model with coercion. Here I explain how the model works, how it explains political decision making, and how well it has done in actual real-time use. I also suggest limitations of the model and areas for further improvement.

The EUM is an example of *applied* modeling. It is a tool designed for practical application. As such, some sacrifices in theoretical or analytic purity are made to gain empirical leverage. At the same time, the model remains faithful to the rational choice perspective which suggests that decision makers do what they believe is in their best interest. The decision makers in this model, however, are not fully rational. Rather, they are modeled as individuals with bounded rationality, unable to look ahead over an unlimited time horizon. They are sufficiently myopic that they see only one move ahead of their current choice. Furthermore, while they update information, they do so crudely. Some rules governing choices in this coercive median voter model are ad hoc approximations of what one would expect in a model of full rationality. These concessions to tractability are unfortunate from an analytic point of view, but they are essential to make this a useful tool for real decision makers concerned with applying it in real time. I mention these points in the hope that the reader will bear in mind that the objective behind this modeling exercise is to emphasize application over analytic purity. This is not to say that the model is not rigorous, for it surely is. Rather, I wish to convey the understanding that most means for making it more rigorous theoretically would also limit its use to deriving general propositions—an important feature of any field of inquiry—at the expense of abandoning its applications to strategic planning and prediction. This model is meant to be used actively to explain and to shape politics. It is designed to allow its falsification or improvement by taking it beyond the realm of mathematical formalism and placing it squarely in the realm of empirical prediction.

## Logical Foundation of the Model

The model is concerned with explaining how policy positions of competing players evolve over time and shape policy outcomes. Therefore, it leads to predictions about policy outcomes and identifies strategic opportunities for altering them. As such, it can be used to explain and predict political decisions at any level of analysis, including, of course, foreign policy and international relations. It can also be used by policy makers to anticipate outcomes and to reshape them to be more in line with their own interests. Indeed, this model has been used in just such a context for two decades.

The model focuses on the application of Black's (1958) median voter theorem and Banks's (1990) theorem about the monotonicity between certain expectations in asymmetric information games and the escalation of political disputes. These theorems, along with ideas from bargaining theory, foster the development of a quasi-dynamic political model that includes detailed expectations about the agreements or compromises that decision makers are willing to make over time. It also includes an assessment of the anticipated ultimate resolution of the issues in question.

Two constraints are assumed to facilitate prediction and explanation: (1) that issues are unidimensional, so that preferences can be represented on a line segment; and (2) that preferences (and associated utilities) for potential outcomes diminish steadily the farther in Euclidean distance a possible settlement is from one's preferred outcome.[14] These two constraints are requirements of the median voter theorem. Black's theorem proves that the outcome the median voter desires is the winning position under the constraints just assumed provided a simple majority is required for victory. Since many interesting political problems do not involve voting, I assume that the exercise of power by mobilizing political influence or power is the nonvoting analog of votes in most political interactions. The decision rule need not require a majority of power in support of a position, and can be adapted, as with other spatial models, to require a super-majority or to empower one or more stakeholders with a veto.

The model deviates from the conditions assumed by the median voter theorem in one other important way. Black assumed that all voters vote and that they do so strictly according to their preferences over the alternatives. This is a natural way to look at decision making in democratic systems. However, as already noted, Black's theorem has much to tell us in nonvoting situations as well. In applying the median voter theorem to these other settings, we must recognize that not everyone is free to "vote" or act according to his or her own preferences over outcomes. Indeed, Black's theorem does not allow for the possibility that votes are coerced, but coercion is a distinct possibility in many political settings. The model discussed here recognizes this. It allows for the possibility that some decision makers are compelled to throw their support behind an alternative that they seem to prefer less than some other feasible choice. Through coercion, it is possible for players to cross over the median voter position, having been compelled—or attracted—to back an outcome farther away from their "apparently" true policy wishes than is the median voter. This creates the possibility that the median voter outcome can shift over time, though new voters neither enter nor leave the system. Even without being compelled by the imposition of costs or the threat by someone to impose costs, a rational actor can move across the median-voter divide. I explain this movement related to interests in being a "deal maker," shortly, but first I develop the model's ties to Banks's monotonicity theorem.

The monotonicity theorem provides a basis for predicting when policy debates are expected to produce negotiated settlements or are expected to lead to an escalation of friction between competing interests. Banks's monotonicity theorem highlights an important feature of all politics. It tells us that in any asymmetric information game, the more one expects to gain from challenging a rival perspective, the more likely one is to undertake the challenge. This simple statement turns out to have interesting and sometimes surprising implications for political intercourse. In particular, Banks's monotonicity result provides part of the theoretical basis for the introduction of coercion into spatial analysis. It offers insights into how to expand the analysis of decision making into arenas in which rational actors can be compelled to back policies that in a less constrained environment they would prefer to oppose.

By using the monotonicity result and the median voter theorem I suggest a way to estimate and simulate decision-maker perceptions and expectations. The resulting model helps us comprehend bargaining and shapes an understanding of the conditions that can lead a negotiation to become excessively conflicted or to break down. I capitalize on the perceptual features of the proposed model by using comparative static techniques to describe the process by which negotiations unfold, moving from one set of circumstances (and outcomes) to another and another.

The model itself depicts a game in which actors simultaneously make proposals and exert influence on one another. They then evaluate options and build coalitions by shifting positions on the issue in question. The above steps are repeated sequentially until the issue is resolved or the players break off discussions, having concluded that agreement is not possible. Resolution or breakdown occurs when the costs of continued negotiation are estimated to exceed the expected benefits from such continued discussions. The model assumes that each player has the same time discount rate. When the shift in the median voter position (or position based on some other pertinent decision rule) predicted from one round to the next is small enough, given the time discount rate, then the model assumes bargaining ends. The outcome predicted at this point depends upon the decision rule in force. If majority rule (or some super-majority rule) is in force, then the policy outcome that corresponds with the rule (e.g., the median voter's policy position at the end of bargaining if majority rule is in force) is the predicted outcome. If there is a veto player and that veto player does not agree with the identified outcome, then agreement is not reached and the result is that the issue remains unresolved.[15] If there is more than one veto player, then, of course, for there to be a predicted agreement, the veto players must have converged to about the same position.

In the game, each player knows three factors: the *potential power* and *stated or inferred policy position* of each actor on each issue examined, and the *salience* each actor associates with those issues. The decision makers, stakeholders, or players do not know how much others value alternative outcomes or what perceptions others have about their risks and opportunities. Each decision maker chooses based on his or her perceptions and expectations, with these perceptions and expectations about the play of others and the general situation sometimes being in error.[16]

Strategies in the game consist of sequences of policy proposals (including no proposal) from each player to each other player. Naturally we must ask what each player is trying to achieve through her or his strategic decisions. In answering this question, I emphasize important differences between the theory here and the median voter theorem. I have already noted one important difference, namely, that players can be coerced. I have also hinted at another, namely, that player positions in the model are not policy ideal points. Now I elaborate on that and suggest insights that might be gleaned from a spatial model that does not rely on policy ideal points.

In the median voter theorem, actors locate themselves at their ideal point on a policy continuum. Their ideal point, of course, represents the policy choice on the continuum that they most prefer. No actor with single peaked preferences would ever move voluntarily or agree freely to a policy that is on the other side of the median voter position relative to their ideal point. There would be no reason to do so. In the model discussed here, however, players are interested in maximizing their welfare on two dimensions rather than one. One dimension is explicit—policy—and the other—personal welfare—is imputed.

Decision makers care about the policy choice on the issue continuum and so, from that perspective, are reluctant to move from the position with which they have associated themselves to a position on the opposite side of the median voter. However, they also are interested in enhancing their personal welfare by being seen as instrumental in helping to form a winning coalition. Naturally, the location of the winning coalition may not be constrained to fall on the same side of the issue continuum (relative to the median voter's position) as their own stated negotiating stance. If a player values credit for helping to forge a winning coalition sufficiently, then the player will be prepared to shift positions, even moving to the opposite side of the policy space provided doing so supplies sufficient utility regarding credit for helping to "make a deal." Such a player can be attracted to a new position without being coerced. Such a player may strike a policy compromise with others in order to gain credit as the broker of an agreement. Just such a motivation, for instance, might help explain why Palestinian leader Yasir Arafat in the early 1990s forsook the Palestine Liberation Organization's historic stance to drive Israel into the sea and accepted modest territorial concessions from the Israeli government (Bueno de Mesquita 1990).

Decision makers vary in their willingness to sacrifice personal political advantage in exchange for steadfastness behind policy principles. Some are prepared to sacrifice their policy position to reach agreement and resolve differences with adversaries (e.g., Anwar Sadat of Egypt and Menachem Begin of Israel, Bill Clinton of the United States and Kim Il Jung of North Korea) and others are not. Margaret Thatcher, for instance, opposed British participation in ongoing efforts by the European Union to further integrate the states of Europe under a semi-federal structure. Her opposition cost her leadership of Britain's Conservative Party, resulting in John Major replacing her as prime minister. Thatcher's stance was in the tradition of John C. Calhoun in the United States and many other leaders around the world. Calhoun, you will recall, declared that he would rather be right than be president. Whether he was right or not, he assuredly did not become president.

One way to describe bargaining styles might be to examine how ready a negotiator is to trade policy goals to forge an agreement. In hundreds, perhaps thousands, of applications of the EUM to political issues, one recurring pattern is that most individuals who rise to the highest leadership position in a democracy (prime minister or president) show remarkable flexibility on issues. That is, they are willing to trade away their policy stance to gain an agreement. This is less clearly true of autocrats. They tend to hold more steadfastly to their initial policy stance, suggesting that the incentives in such regimes, as well as leadership recruitment, are very different from those experienced by leaders in more democratic polities.

## Selecting from Among Policy Proposals

Of the infinitely many possible proposals to resolve some issue—let us call it issue $a$—how are we to predict which will be chosen? To answer this question, let us first learn a little more about each actor $i$. In this analysis, each decision maker is endowed with three characteristics. Each player attaches some *utility* to each possible outcome on issue $a$, as already noted. Each participant in the bargaining process is also endowed with the *power* to exert some influence over decisions. Let $c_{ia}$ be the capabilities (or power) actor $i$ could bring to bear on issue $a$, such that the sum of the capabilities of the participants in a multilateral decision-making setting is 1.[17] $c_i$ is, then, actor *i*'s share of the total *potential* influence that could be brought to bear in the negotiations over some issue *a*. Each participant has its own agenda of priorities or *salience* that it attaches to the issues that must be confronted. Thus, *i* may attach considerable importance to one issue and considerably less importance to another.[18] Any aggregation of individuals with identical values on all three of these variables can constitute a stakeholder for the purposes of this model. Differences in the available pool of resources or on preferred outcomes or on salience mean that the aggregation of individuals makes up more than one group and must be so treated.

Note that actors are defined only by the three characteristics of capabilities, policy preference, and salience. This means that an actor can be an individual, a group, an entire nation, a bloc of alliances, an international organization, or anything in between. In that sense, this is a quite generic model that is equally applicable to interpersonal decision making, group decision making, and interstate interactions. Its application recognizes no level of analysis restrictions. Chapters 4 and 5, for instance, apply it to actors that are nation-states, while chapter 6 applies the model to data that is a mixture of individuals, groups, organizations, and nations.

When alternative courses of action are pitted against each other, the array of forces on either side often determines victory. Of course, this array depends on more than the relative potential power or clout of the competing interests. It depends also on the willingness to spend influence on the issue in question [$s_i$] by focusing attention on it—a budget constraint—and the intensity with which each actor prefers one proposed settlement.[19] Thus, each group has a total number of *potential* "votes" equal to its capabilities, a factor that may be influenced by external considerations and/or by the institutional arrangements that provide structural constraints on the decision-making process. Where structural constraints are relevant, as in qualified majority voting in the European Union, congressional voting following a presidential veto, Security Council choices, and the like, the model can be readily adapted by changing its key decision rule—the median voter rule—to reflect the operative rule in the situation (Volgy and Imwalle 2000).

The "votes" cast by actor *i* in a comparison of alternatives $x_j$ and $x_k$ are said to equal $v_{ia}^{jk}$ where:

$$\left( v_{ia}^{jk} \mid x_j, x_k \right) = (c_i)\,(s_i)(u^i x_j - u^i x_k) \tag{1}$$

Thus, the "vote" or power mobilized by actor *i* in a comparison of two alternatives ($x_j$ and $x_k$) is equal to the potential capabilities of *i* discounted by how important the issue is to *i* (i.e., $s_i$) and by how much *i* prefers one proposal over the other ($u^i x_j - u^i x_k$).

The "voting" scheme reflects, if you like, what takes place "inside the smoke-filled room" before the formal, visible decision-making process occurs. It assumes that any formal process echoes the agreements reached beforehand. Put differently, it assumes that stakeholders anticipate future action in the immediately next stage of decision making, using backward induction. They anticipate how the formal decision-making setting will influence all actions and pick proposals in the "smoke-filled room" that they believe will survive the formal process. Stakeholders are bounded in their rationality, however, in that they are unable to look farther ahead than the next stage of decision making. So, their choices are locally rational, but may turn out to be inefficient two or more steps down the road.

The prospect that a proposal will succeed is assumed to depend on how much support can be mustered in its favor as compared to the feasible alternatives. This is calculated as the sum of "votes" across all actors in a comparison between $x_j$ and $x_k$. This sum equals $v^{jk}$ with

$$v^{jk} = \sum_{i=1}^{n} v_i^{jk} \tag{2}$$

If $v^{jk}$ is greater than zero, that implies that $x_j$ defeats $x_k$ because the tacit coalition in favor of $j$'s proposal is more motivated and powerful than the coalition supporting $k$'s proposal. If $v^{jk}$ is less than zero, $x_j$ is expected to be defeated by $x_k$, and if $v^{jk}$ equals zero, the competing interests are collectively indifferent between the two alternatives.

In any negotiation, there are likely to be many more than two proposed settlements. By pitting all alternatives against one another two at a time, the outcome the median voter prefers (weighted by power, salience, and intensity of preference) is found. Barring perceptions or beliefs that lead decision makers to switch their position, the median voter position is the predicted outcome (Black 1958). In the original version of this model, the median voter position was always the predicted outcome. However, the version explained here allows decision makers to switch positions in response to proposals, pressures from one another, and calculations of the trade-off between policy gain and personal credit for being a deal maker. By doing so, the model now provides a quasi-dynamic element.

In practice, perceptions or beliefs often lead decision makers to grant concessions or to give in to a rival's point of view, sometimes needlessly. Such concessions or capitulations can change the location of the median voter. For now we only note that the initial median voter outcome can be the predicted outcome provided key actors do not switch positions in a way that alters the location of the median voter. Of course, providing an accounting of when such switches in position are expected to take place is crucial and is included in the EUM.

The basic, median voter prediction is not the final prediction of the model. The beliefs and perceptions of the relevant actors frequently suggest compromises and concessions that one or another actor is willing to pursue and that other actors are willing or compelled to accept. These beliefs and perceptions may influence the array of interests sufficiently to require re-estimating the median voter, perhaps several times, until perceptions and positions stabilize around the outcome predicted at the moment when the model's time discount rule is hit. That rule stipulates that the change in the predicted outcome in the next round must be large enough, given the cost of continued negotiation (i.e., the time discount rule) to warrant continued discussions. The rule is currently an ad hoc decay function that demands larger and larger predicted shifts in outcome the higher the number of rounds of bargaining (i.e., sequences of proposal exchanges). Future improvement in the time discount function certainly could help to enhance the model's reliability.

## Perceptual Analysis

The forecasting element of the model reveals what decision makers should expect if everyone acts sincerely according to her or his underlying preferences. What, however, can a decision maker do if the predicted outcome is not to his or her liking? Are there strategic maneuvers that can improve the expected outcome?

It is possible and indeed likely that actors will engage in private, sophisticated deals to rearrange the prospective resolution of a controversial issue. These deals may be the result of cooperation and coordination among a subset of stakeholders or they may be the product of conflict and coercion. When deals are produced by coordination among actors, the "deal making" reflects the essence of negotiations. The perceptual model guides inquiries to facilitate understanding which "deals" are feasible and which are not. It points out how to construct the outcome with strategically sophisticated approaches to resolve a policy issue. If an interest group is dissatisfied with the expected outcome, there are essentially four courses of action by which this group—the focal group—might improve its prospects:

1. Alter its own level of effort (i.e., change $s_i$);
2. Shift its revealed position;[20]
3. Influence groups who are willing or can be compelled to make concessions to the focal group to alter their level of effort (i.e., $s_k$); or
4. Influence groups who are willing or can be compelled to make concessions to the focal group so that those other groups alter their revealed position.[21]

Here I focus only on point 4, maneuvers that involve persuading or coercing other groups to switch positions, with the direction and size of any changes in position being dictated by the logic behind the model. Changes in salience are treated analogously. Decision makers interested in learning what leverage they can exert could benefit from estimating the beliefs held by each other actor.[22] These are used to estimate each player's expected utility from challenging or not challenging the policy proposal backed by each potential rival. They also help approximate the utility each actor $i$ believes its rival expects to derive from challenging or not challenging the policy goals of actor $i$. This latter value can be thought of as proportionate to the costs a decision maker expects a rival will inflict on her. The higher a rival's expected utility from challenging a given policy stance, the costlier it will be to resist the challenge. This directly reflects the central implication of the monotonicity theorem. In any asymmetric information game, the likelihood that an actor will escalate pressure on another player increases with that player's expected gain from the use of pressure.

Decision makers are assumed to calculate the expected consequences of challenging and of not challenging alternative proposals. The expected utility for $i$ from not challenging rival $j$'s position is denoted as $E^i u^i \Delta x_j | \bar{d}$, with $\bar{d}$ denoting the failure to challenge or make a proposal. This expected utility is estimated by projecting what the relevant decision maker believes is likely to happen without the exertion of pressure on a rival to persuade the opponent to alter its behavior. One of three contingencies may arise: actor $i$ may anticipate that with some probability $(Q^i)$ rival $j$ is the type that will not alter its current policies over the period of concern to $i$, giving group $i$ whatever utility it receives from the preservation of the status quo between itself and $j$ [with ($u^i \Delta x_j^* | \bar{d}$) being the associated utility]; $i$ may anticipate that $j$'s position on the issues will change $(1-Q^i)$, in which case there is some chance $(T^i)$ that, from $i$'s perspective, the policies of $j$ are anticipated to get better [with $u^i \Delta x_j^+ | \bar{d}$ being the associated utility] or to get worse, with probability $1-T^i$ [with ($u^i \Delta x_j^- | \bar{d}$), so that $u^i \Delta x_j^+ | \bar{d} > u^i \Delta x_j^* | \bar{d} > u^i \Delta x_j^- | \bar{d}$) being the associated utility]. $i$'s expected utility if it leaves $j$'s proposal unchallenged is described as:

$$E^i u^i \Delta x_j \mid \bar{d} = Q^i u^i \Delta x_j^* \mid \bar{d} + (1 - Q^i) \left[ T^i u^i \Delta x_j^+ \mid \bar{d} \right. $$
$$\left. + (1 - T^i) u^i \Delta x_j^- \mid \bar{d} \right. \tag{3}$$

$i$ can challenge $j$'s position on an issue by proposing a change in $j$'s position. In doing so, actor $i$ presumably takes into account the probability that $j$ does not care enough about the issue to resist the proposed settlement by $i$ $(1-s_j)$. $i$ also considers the possibility that $j$ will resist $i$'s proposal $(s_j)$. If there is resistance, then there is some likelihood that $i$ will succeed in enforcing its wishes on $j$ $(P^i)$ and some probability that it will fail $(1-P^i)$. Should $i$ succeed, then $i$ will derive the utility associated with compelling or convincing $j$ to switch from its current policy stance to that supported by i. This is denoted by $u^i \Delta x_j^+ | d$, which equals $u^i(x_i - x_j)$. Should $i$ fail, then it confronts the prospect of having to abandon its objectives in favor of those pursued by $j$, denoted by $u^i \Delta x_j^- | d = u^i(x_j - x_i)$. The expected utility for challenging $j$'s proposed resolution of the multilateral dispute $(E^i u^i \Delta x_j | d)$ is:

$$E^i u^i \Delta x_j \mid d = s_j \left\{ P^i \left[ u^i \Delta x_j^+ \mid d \right] + (1 - P^i) \left[ u^i \Delta x_j^- \mid d \right] \right\} +$$
$$\left[ 1 - s_j \right] \left[ u^i \Delta x_j^+ \mid d \right] \tag{4}$$

so that the overall expected utility of $i$ with respect to $j$'s outlook on issue a is:

$$E^i u_{ij} = E^i u^i \Delta x_j \mid d - E^i u^i \Delta x_j \mid \overline{d} \tag{5}$$

Equations (3) and (4) reflect each actor's effort to look ahead and estimate the consequences of alternative actions. The difference between the two initial actions—challenge or not challenge—is represented in equation (5). If equation (5) is greater than zero, then $i$ believes that challenging $j$'s position is superior to not challenging it. In that case, $i$ is assumed to make a proposal of its own. If equation (5) is less than zero, then not challenging is preferred and $i$ is said to be deterred. If equation (5) equals zero, then $i$ is indifferent between challenging and not challenging $j$'s proposed settlement. Each actor evaluates equation (5) vis-à-vis each other actor. In doing so, actors consider the expected actions of third parties. The estimates of $P^i$, the subjective probability that $i$ will be successful, include calculations of how $i$ expects all other parties to respond to a dispute over policy settlements between $i$ and $j$. In particular, $P^i$ places each other actor in $i$'s coalition, $j$'s coalition, or in a neutral position as indicated by each third party's preference for $i$'s policy proposal or $j$'s. $j$ makes a comparable calculation (as does each $k \in N$). Because equation (5) includes such subjective elements as utilities and subjective probabilities, it is possible to estimate a complete matrix of expected utilities that capture all possible confrontations, compromises, and capitulations among all the participants in the relevant political arena.

Once the expected utility values are estimated, we can denote each relationship between pairs of stakeholders. If equation (5) is positive for $i$ and negative for $j$, then the relationship implies either compromise or coercion. If the value of (5) for $i$, is greater than the absolute value of (5) as calculated for $j$, then both players agree that $i$ has the upper hand. In this instance, $j$ is expected to be willing to offer concessions to $i$, although the concessions are not likely to be as large as what $i$ would like. The likely resolution of their exchange is a compromise reflecting the weighted average of $i$'s expectations and $j$'s. This weighted average approximates, in the limit, both Nash's cooperative bargaining solution and Rubenstein's non-cooperative game bargaining solution (Nash 1950; Rubenstein 1982). If equation (5) is positive for $i$ and negative for $j$ and the absolute value of (5) from $j$'s point of view is larger than the value of (5) from $i$'s perspective, then $j$ is compelled to accept $i$'s wishes unless someone else offers $j$ an enforceable compromise that spares it from having to capitulate to $i$. That is, $j$ cannot inflict sufficient costs on her challenger to get the challenger to settle for less than a complete capitulation by $j$. If both $i$ and $j$ believe that they have the upper hand in the relationship, then conflict is likely and that conflict has an uncertain outcome, reflecting the high costs each can impose on the other coupled with a strong motivation to pursue the contest. In international disputes, this situation is highly correlated with the probability of a war (Bueno de Mesquita 1985). Should both $i$ and $j$ believe that equation (5) is negative for them, then there may be blustering and bluffing. Nevertheless, the expectation is that the relationship is a stalemate because the costs of pursuing a challenge are believed to exceed the expected benefits. The most likely outcome is that the status quo will continue to prevail between $i$ and $j$.

## Estimating the Model

The various components of equation (5) must each be measured for the model to have practical value. The measurement procedures are explained in considerable detail elsewhere (Bueno de Mesquita 1985; Bueno de Mesquita, Newman, and Rabushka 1996; Bueno de Mesquita and Lalman 1992), so here I provide only brief, summary descriptions of the methods used for estimating each of the key variables.

The estimation of the subjective probability of success for $i$ in a competition with $j$ is accomplished as follows:

$$P^i = \frac{\sum\limits_{k|u^k x_i > u^k x_j} v_k^{ij}}{\sum\limits_{k=1}^{n} v_k^{ij}} \quad \text{for all} \quad k \in N.$$

The probability measure has its origins in earlier theoretical work on third party choices during disputes. Altfeld and Bueno de Mesquita (1979) report a high rate of accuracy in predicting third-party decisions to join ongoing wars based on a model that yields an expression that is virtually identical to the numerator for $P^i$. The denominator simply normalizes the value in the numerator so that the overall term falls in the interval (0,1). The numerator and denominator have straightforward political interpretations. The numerator calculates the support $i$ can expect to receive in a confrontation with $j$. This support depends upon the capabilities of each actor who prefers $i$'s policy objective to $j$'s. However, capabilities alone are not sufficient information to estimate the value of each third party's support. The capabilities are diminished by the degree to which the issue in question is not salient to the actor whose support level is being estimated. The lower an actor's salience score, the less likely the stakeholder is to spend resources on the issue as it is not an issue of much concern to the decision maker. Finally, the capabilities must also be discounted by the intensity of preference of the actor in question for the outcomes under contention. If a third party is just about indifferent between supporting what *i* wants and supporting what *j* wants, then putting much effort behind helping *i* win is not likely. If, however, a stakeholder intensely favors *i*'s objective over *j*'s, then it uses more of its capabilities to help *i*. Thus, the numerator captures the expected level of support for *i*. The denominator reflects the sum of the support for *i* and for *j* so that the overall expression shows the gambling odds for *i*.

The probability calculation is subjective in that *i*'s estimate of its chances for success may be quite different from *j*'s estimate of the same value. The subjective component is introduced by using estimates of the individual risk-taking profiles of each decision maker. In particular, the utilities for the specific proposals (e.g., $x_i$, $x_j \in R_a$) that enter into the calculation of $v_k$ are evaluated so that:

$$u^i x_j = 1 - |x_i - x_j|^n \tag{6}$$

with ri—the indicator of risk-taking propensities—estimated as described below and giving curvature to the utility function.

The risk-taking component is complex. The risk indicator estimates the size of the trade-off, discussed earlier, made by each decision maker between pursuing political satisfaction (i.e., forging agreement) and policy satisfaction (Lamborn 1991). By political satisfaction I mean the desire to be seen as an essential deal maker, as a key member of the winning coalition. Political satisfaction enhances personal political security and welfare. By policy satisfaction I mean supporting a substantive policy outcome close to the actor's preferred policy choice even if that means losing to an inferior choice. I assume that all decision makers trade off at some rate between the pursuit of policy goals and political goals.

Decision makers differ, however, in the rate at which they are willing to give up one form of satisfaction for the other. This difference across actors means that purchasing policy support from or granting political credit to some players is easier than from others, as reflected in Figures 3.1 and 3.2. Figure 3.1 shows that the current levels of satisfaction on the two dimensions influences the ease with which deals can be made, given a constant shape to the indifference curve. That is, the marginal rate of substitution between policy satisfaction and political satisfaction depends on the current endowment. Those who have a lot of security are willing to give up more of their political welfare to gain a small amount on the policy dimension. Those who are well endowed with policy satisfaction are willing to trade relatively large amounts on that dimension for small increments in their political well-being.

Figure 3.2 reminds us that different decision makers are willing to trade policy and political satisfaction at different rates. That is, holding the political and policy endowments for two actors constant, they may still trade to another mix of satisfactions at different rates. Actor A in Figure 3.2 requires

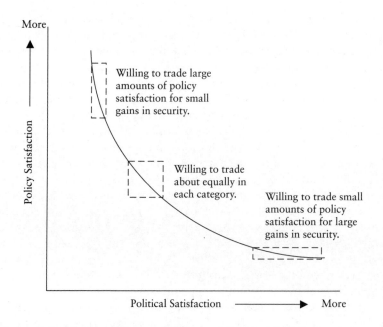

**Figure 3.1** Trade-off Between Policy and Political Satisfaction

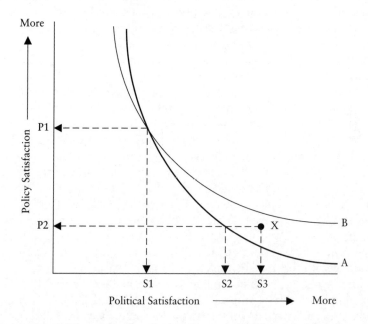

**Figure 3.2** Different Trade-off Rates between Policy and Political Satisfaction

less additional political security than actor B to give up the same amount of policy satisfaction. Holding P1-P2 constant, we can see that S2-S1 is smaller than S3-S1. S2-S1 is sufficient for A to make the policy/political security trade. S3-S1 would really please A, moving that actor to a higher indifference curve. But player B would not give up P1-P2 policy satisfaction even for a gain in personal welfare equal to S3-S1. Doing so places B on a lower indifference curve, a trade that is flatly unacceptable to B.

Political security is, of course, a central idea in much of politics, but what does it mean in this context? The answer to this question is at the heart of the difference between the model discussed here and standard median voter spatial models.

Players choose their bargaining position—the position measured here—strategically. It represents an ideal mix of political and policy satisfaction for the actor. By observing the location of the actor's stated bargaining position, we can infer aspects of his or her willingness to trade between policy and personal credit for helping to make the deal. The closer to the median voter position in expected utility terms an actor's public or stated position is on a policy issue, the more secure and the more committed the actor is to gaining personal credit. The median voter position is the most politically advantageous location on a unidimensional continuum with majority rule, whether that majority is votes or power. After all, the key characteristic of the median voter position is that in head-to-head competition it beats all alternatives. Therefore, the decision to locate close to the median voter in expected utility terms is assumed to reflect a fear of vulnerability or a tendency to be risk averse with regard to being excluded from the winning coalition. This presumption of risk aversion follows from the notion that the actor has chosen a position that minimizes threats to its security at the expense of pursuing the policy outcome she prefers. The farther the decision maker's expected utility score is from being at its possible maximum, while remaining within the feasible set of alternative proposals, the more risk acceptant the decision maker is presumed to be and the more committed the actor is to staunch support of his chosen policy stance. Algebraically, this "risk" calculation is:

$$
R_i = \frac{2 \sum_{i=1}^{n} E^i U_{ij} - \sum_{i=1}^{n} E^i U_{ij_{\max}} - \sum_{i=1}^{n} E^i U_{ij_{\min}}}{\sum_{i=1}^{n} E^i U_{ij_{\max}} - \sum_{i=1}^{n} E^i U_{ij_{\min}}}
$$

with $r_i = 1 - \dfrac{R_i - \frac{1}{3}}{R_i + \frac{1}{3}}$

The measure of risk taking provides one perspective on how much each decision maker appears to have exchanged personal political security for policy goals or vice versa. In doing so, this measure also provides a basis for estimating the value attached to the status quo. The first term in the numerator of the main expression for estimating risks is equal to the security and policy value of actor $i$'s actual or "stated" position, its value for the status quo. The next two terms place the "status quo" value within the boundaries of what could have been attained in terms of political security or policy satisfaction, two reference points that serve to frame the chosen policy stance in the context of the range of options on the policy and political dimension.

In the sense of evaluating choices against reference points, the EUM has a commonality with prospect theory, though the EUM is set in a game theoretic mode rather than a purely decision theoretic perspective as is true of prospect theory (Kahneman and Tversky 1984; McDermott 1998; Bueno de Mesquita, McDermott, and Cope 2001).[23] In prospect theory, decision makers are risk averse in the domain of gains and risk seeking in the domain of losses. Here decision makers can be risk averse or risk seeking in either domain, where the domains pertain to gain in personal credit or gain in steadfastness behind a policy point of view. To the degree that they are not risk neutral in one domain, their risk propensity is opposite in the other domain. For example, those who enjoy high levels of personal political satisfaction will, in the model's logic, end up being risk averse on that dimension and, therefore, be risk seeking when it comes to policy satisfaction. In this way, the model here approximates an important insight from prospect theory, while embedding this insight in a strategic, game theoretic framework. I justify the use of prospect theory insights in an expected utility framework by noting that the S-shaped utility function characteristic of prospect theory does not violate assumptions of rationality and by observing that the experimental results from prospect theory can be accounted for in an expected utility framework provided the experiments' subjects are seen to be in a strategic, signaling environment. As I have explained this elsewhere, I do not repeat the details here (Bueno de Mesquita 2000b).

The three framing values—the actual expected utility, the maximum feasible expected utility, and the minimum feasible expected utility—can be estimated. They evaluate three levels of political satisfaction: the one realized by the decision maker, the most political welfare the actor could have realized within a given bargaining setting, and the least the actor could have realized. Because we already have estimated utilities or satisfaction on the policy dimension, those utilities plus these three scores provide sufficient information to plot estimated indifference curves of the sort found in Figures 3.1 and 3.2.

Bargaining style and elements of culture are captured within the model by comparing the three values: status quo expected utility, political satisfaction, and policy satisfaction. Although culture and personality are far more complicated concepts, still these three elements seem to reflect a good deal of how people bargain and what lies at the core of their value system. Some cultures socialize people to be deal makers, while others discourage horse trading. As the model's track record, discussed later, suggests, the model does equally well in its application to problems all around the world and also in problems involving interactions between negotiators from different societies and cultures. This suggests that essential values are captured by the model.

Utilities for the marginal gains $[(u^i\Delta x^+_j|d$ and $u^i\Delta x^+_j\bar{d}]$ or losses $[(u^i\Delta x^-_j|d$ and $u^i\Delta x^-_j\bar{d}]$ from shifts to alternative proposals are evaluated, using the basic "risk" building block just described, in the manner delineated in Bueno de Mesquita and Lalman (1986) and following equation (6). $u^i\Delta x^+_j|\bar{d}$ and $u^i\Delta x^-_j|\bar{d}$ are approximated by comparing the value actor $i$ attaches to the current median voter prediction to the value $i$ attaches to the median anticipated if $i$ accepts $j$'s preferred outcome.

Equation (5) is estimated from four perspectives, with relevant superscripts on equation (5) showing from whose perspective the calculation is being viewed:

1. $i$'s expected utility vis-à-vis each rival $j$'s proposal;
2. $i$'s perception of each $j$'s expected utility vis-à-vis $i$'s proposal;
3. $j$'s expected utility vis-à-vis each $i$'s proposal;
4. $j$'s perception of each $i$'s expected utility vis-à-vis $j$'s proposal.

The expected utility values summarized in (1) and (2) and in (3) and (4) respectively describe each actor's perception of its relationship vis-à-vis each other actor. With Banks's monotonicity of escalation result in mind, these relationships can be described in continuous form. According to Banks's theorem, the probability with which an actor anticipates confronting a given rival increases with its expected utility for challenging the rival's proposal. This means that the higher $i$'s expected utility from persuading $j$ to accept $i$'s position, the higher the likelihood that $i$ will confront $j$.

What information does the perceptual model uncover? Recall that every decision maker is assumed to know the array of potential power, positions, and salience of each other decision maker. That information is common knowledge. The private information possessed by each decision maker involves the shape of its own utility function and the belief it holds about the expected utilities of each other actor. Thus, everyone is assumed to know the basic information that goes into the expected utility model. Everyone knows the shape of their own utility function, but can only form a belief about the shape of the utility functions of other decision makers.

The beliefs of each actor imply actions. Those actions, as the extraction or granting of concessions over support for this or that specific position, lead to a re-evaluation of the situation by each decision maker. As stakeholders respond to revised proposals, with their responses supported by their beliefs and expectations, the prospects for a favorable or unfavorable settlement change for many participants. Beliefs and expectations provide the foundation for a quasi-dynamic assessment of the evolution of issue positions and for recalculations of the location of the median voter.

When actors are persuaded or coerced into accepting a proposal different from their initial (or current) position on an issue, the decision process enters a new phase. Coalitions change and the support or risks associated with alternative proposals vary. New proposals are brought forward as revised beliefs and expectations open new possibilities or foreclose old ones. Each such sequence of revised stances on an issue is called an *iteration* or *bargaining round*. These two terms are used interchangeably. The model computes as many iterations as it takes for the policy issue to resolve itself or for the discount rule to be reached before there is agreement among the necessary players (i.e., if a super-majority is required or if there are veto players). Issues are resolved by reaching a stable outcome, an outcome from which there does not seem to be a meaningful possibility of change given the estimated expectations of the actors.

The model portrays a process of decision making during each iteration or negotiating round. To gain an intuitive sense of what happens within the logic of the model during each iteration, think of the decision makers as engaged in a game of cards. At the outset, each player is dealt a hand. The quality of the hand dealt to each player depends on the commonly known characteristics of each player. Stronger players (or those with strong backing from others) generally draw better cards than weaker players do. Because of variations in salience, some players pay closer attention to their cards than do others and so form different perceptions of the situation. Based on the cards they hold and the known characteristics of other players, each decision maker forms perceptions about how good the hand is of each rival relative to the hand dealt the particular decision maker. With that information, each player decides on proposals or bids to make to the other decision makers.

If a player believes his or her hand is very weak compared to a specific rival, then no proposal is made to that actor. If $i$ expects to lose to $j$, for instance, then $i$ does not make a proposal to $j$. If, however, $i$ thinks it holds a good hand relative to $j$, then $i$ makes a proposal in the form of a suggested change in position by $j$ on the issue at hand. If $i$ thinks $j$ stands to lose quite a lot, then $i$ will propose that $j$ accept $i$'s current position. If $i$ thinks it has a good enough hand to shift $j$'s position, but not so good that $j$ will give in to what $i$ wants, then $i$ proposes a compromise somewhere between $i$'s position and $j$'s.

After all the players have submitted their secret proposals to one another, each player now reviews the new cards—the proposals—that it holds. Of course, some proposals are better for the recipient than others. Indeed, some proposals turn out to be frivolous in that the proposer cannot enforce the proposal, something that the proposer might learn only at the end of the round of proposal making. Other proposals received by a decision maker are potentially enforceable, but fall by the wayside because a superior, enforceable proposal was made by a different player. Each player would like to choose the best offer made to it and each proposer enforces its bids to the extent that it can. Those better able to enforce their wishes than others can make their proposals stick. Given equally enforceable proposals, players move the least that they can. Each actor selects from among the bids it made and the bids it received. The bid chosen is the proposal that is the optimal choice for the player given the constraints under which it operates. These constraints include its own perceptions and the reality of which proposals turn out to be enforceable and which turn out to be beaten back by rivals or rejected outright as unenforceable by the recipient.

At the end of a round of proposal making, players learn new information about their opponents. If, for instance, a player finds that some proposals it thought of as enforceable are successfully rejected, then it learns the proposal was unenforceable (i.e., the player has less support than it thought). By monitoring responses to its proposals a player learns how much leverage it has with other decision makers. If a proposal is accepted, then a player learns that it made the best offer among all the proposals made to the recipient of its accepted bid.

When the players finish sorting out their choices among proposals, each shifts to the position contained in the proposal it accepted. Of course, when a decision maker agrees to a compromise with another actor, it hopes that the other player will also live up to its end of the compromise bargain. But this is a game in which promises are not binding. Proposals are enforceable if a decision maker has the means to make sure that another actor does what it says it will do. Each player is free to renege on a proposed deal so long as it can enforce another agreement or so long as someone else can enforce an agreement on it.

What consequences follow from the actions implied by the first iteration through the model? How do those actions influence the location of the median voter? How do we decide when the median voter outcome at a particular iteration is to be taken as the actual resolution of the issue at hand? If no stakeholder believes it has a remaining credible proposal, then the game ends. Similarly, if the value of remaining proposals is sufficiently small that the cost of continuing to bargain outweighs the value for each player of the expected improvement in the outcome, then the game ends. The median voter at that stage of the game is the predicted policy outcome, assuming majority rule is the relevant decision criterion. If, however, credible proposals are believed to remain, then the game continues. (For a fuller description of the sequential process, see Bueno de Mesquita and Stokman 1994.)

## Developing the Data

Political outcomes, whether they involve intra- or intergovernmental relations or negotiations between public and private organizations or even within a single organization, can be and have been explained and predicted using the EUM. To do so, however, requires converting theoretical concepts into practical application. Although this can be a difficult task, there is, fortunately, a body of knowledge that can be called upon to estimate the critical variables. By combining the perspective of this rational actor model with the knowledge and expertise of area or issue experts, it is possible to estimate the variables of interest and to solve the perceptual and "voting" components of the model discussed here. Chapter 6 contains an example of analyses based on expert data. Chapters 4 and 5, however, rely on data that are extracted from readily replicated sources, namely Correlates of War data for chapter 4 and Polity data for chapter 5. Thus, data can come from experts or from standard sources, depending on the issue under examination.

The forecasting and perceptual models require the identification of the groups or actors interested in trying to influence a policy outcome on the issues in question. For each actor, data must then be estimated on three variables: capabilities, strategically preferred outcome, and salience. Sometimes, in institutionally structured settings, it is also important to take into account structural constraints that operate to help shape outcomes. The model (and its software) is readily adapted to reflect requirements other than a majority, as in institutional settings where a super-majority is required, or can take into account players with veto power.[24] With just this minimal information in hand, it is possible to predict what the likely actions and outcome will be. This is done without any other information regarding, for instance, the history of the situation, the history of relations between particular actors within the situation, other sunk costs, or without even interviewing the actors involved to assess their own judgment about their beliefs and expectations.

For most problems to which this model has been applied, data have come from individuals with area or issue expertise who have great insight into who the players are likely to be on an issue. What is more, although area experts often doubt that they possess the essential information to quantify capabilities or salience, eliciting such information is generally possible through careful interactive techniques. Most of the data used in this volume, however, are derived from easily replicated objective sources. The data and their derivation are explained in the appropriate chapters related to the applications developed here. Those interested in developing data should consult the later chapters as well as the instructional manual at http://bdm.cqpress.com. The latter explains how to frame issues and interview experts to obtain the necessary information when that information cannot readily be derived from less subjective sources.

One question frequently asked about this methodology when the data come from issue or area experts is: How sensitive is the model to the biases or perspective of the particular experts who provide the data? It is surprising to most people initially to learn that the outcomes predicted by the model are robust across different experts. Upon reflection, however, this should not be too surprising. Since experts are not asked their opinion, but rather for very basic information—who are the stakeholders, what do they say they want, how influential could they be, and how much do they care about the issues with which we are concerned—it turns out that the vast majority of specialists basically view this information in the same way. Naturally, different specialists will give different labels to some stakeholders (especially when the stakeholder is a group and not an individual), but the underlying structure of the data turns out analytically to be remarkably similar from specialist to specialist. Indeed, in some sense, knowing the information asked for to apply this model is a minimal condition for being a specialist.

That the predicted results are not terribly sensitive to which specialists provided the input information is easily seen to be so by examining the track record the model has achieved. Later I review some of that track record. For now, let me just mention that independent audits of the accuracy of this model in making real-time predictions indicate that it has achieved an accuracy rate of around 90 percent based on thousands of applications. The *Far Eastern Economic Review* (June 13, 1996, cover story, p. 6) evaluated the accuracy of the predictions made by Bueno de Mesquita, Newman, and Rabushka in their book *Forecasting Political Events* (1985) as a means to test the reliability of predictions made in their newer book (1996). William McGurn, the author of the article, reports, "They applied the same model in March 1984 to project the impact of what would become the Joint Declaration. Based on their findings, they predicted twelve developments, of which only one proved inaccurate (a technicality about how land would be valued). The others proved pretty much on the mark: increased welfare spending, the growing importance of demonstrated 'loyalty' to China in the award of key contracts, and an 'ongoing reinterpretation' of the Joint Declaration's provisions long after they were signed." More recently, the *Financial Times* (1998) reports that the EUM played an instrumental role in forecasting correctly the possibilities and limitations in prospective mergers to consolidate Europe's defense industry.

It is very unlikely that in these and so many other cases users of this model were fortunate enough to pick just the right experts to get the right information that led to the right prediction. Indeed, the experts often disagree with the very predictions produced through the modeling process. It is more likely that the results are not as sensitive as one might think to variations in the personal perspectives of the experts.

## Model Output

The above discussion provides an abstract sense of the modeling process incorporated into the expected utility model. To flesh out the process a bit more, I discuss here the elements of the model's printout and what they tell us about politics. Table 3.1 contains an example of the data required by the model. The issue examined in Table 3.1 asks, "What is the stated position of

**Table 3.1**
Model Inputs on Political Reform in China: A Domestic Assessment
Assuming the Death of Deng Xiao Ping

| Stakeholder | Resources | Position | Salience |
|---|---|---|---|
| Zeming | 80 | 25 | 50 |
| Lipeng | 90 | 15 | 80 |
| Qiaoshi | 85 | 15 | 80 |
| Shanghai | 30 | 35 | 50 |
| Ruihuan | 60 | 30 | 75 |
| Tianjiyun | 50 | 20 | 40 |
| Zhurongji | 60 | 35 | 80 |
| Zoujiahua | 80 | 15 | 75 |
| Shangkun | 100 | 20 | 85 |
| Baibing | 85 | 15 | 85 |
| Wangzhen | 85 | 15 | 80 |
| Wanli | 60 | 25 | 60 |
| Xiannian | 60 | 20 | 60 |
| Chenyun | 100 | 10 | 85 |
| Boyibo | 75 | 20 | 70 |
| Pengzhen | 90 | 15 | 80 |
| Challdem | 20 | 100 | 90 |
| Chspring | 20 | 100 | 90 |
| STU/INTEL | 40 | 100 | 90 |
| USA | 70 | 100 | 40 |
| Japan | 50 | 60 | 50 |
| Europe | 55 | 90 | 30 |
| Hong Kong | 25 | 100 | 85 |
| Guandung | 30 | 50 | 70 |

each stakeholder with regard to supporting greater centralization (position 0 on the scale) or greater democratization (full democracy at position 100 on the issue scale) in China?" The data were collected in October 1991.[25]

Table 3.2 illustrates the round-by-round simulation of policy positions based on the initial input data shown in Table 3.1. I display just five bargaining rounds here, but discuss twenty-five such rounds for these data in chapter 6. The first five rounds appear to paint an optimistic picture of Chinese liberalization, a picture that is diminished when we look farther out in time in chapter 6.

Table 3.2 shows a broad view of position shifts for each player and also displays the predicted outcome; that is, the median "power" position in each round. The model provides considerably more detail, however. For each player and also overall for each round, the model calculates the proportion of interactions expected to involve positional stalemate, conflict, compromise, and acquiescence. Also, for each player vis-à-vis each other player, the model identifies whether that specific interaction is expected to involve stalemate, conflict, compromise, or acquiescence. In those cases for which the

**Table 3.2**
Predicted Policy Positions across 5 Rounds

| Stakeholder | Round 1 | Round 2 | Round 3 | Round 4 | Round 5 |
|---|---|---|---|---|---|
| Baibing | 15 | 53 | 53 | 53 | 53 |
| Boyibo | 20 | 15 | 23 | 23 | 23 |
| Challdem | 100 | 100 | 100 | 100 | 100 |
| Chenyun | 10 | 34 | 34 | 34 | 34 |
| Chspring | 100 | 100 | 100 | 100 | 100 |
| Europe | 90 | 90 | 79 | 70 | 67 |
| Guandung | 50 | 46 | 43 | 43 | 43 |
| Hong Kong | 100 | 100 | 100 | 100 | 100 |
| Japan | 60 | 56 | 54 | 53 | 53 |
| Lipeng | 15 | 52 | 52 | 52 | 53 |
| Pengzhen | 15 | 52 | 52 | 52 | 53 |
| Qiaoshi | 15 | 52 | 52 | 53 | 53 |
| Ruihuan | 30 | 42 | 42 | 42 | 42 |
| Shanghai | 35 | 32 | 32 | 32 | 32 |
| Shangkun | 20 | 15 | 15 | 15 | 15 |
| STU/INTEL | 100 | 100 | 100 | 100 | 100 |
| Tianjiyun | 20 | 21 | 25 | 52 | 52 |
| USA | 100 | 100 | 100 | 100 | 100 |
| Wangzhen | 15 | 52 | 52 | 53 | 53 |
| Wanli | 25 | 20 | 20 | 20 | 20 |
| Xiannian | 20 | 21 | 21 | 21 | 21 |
| Zeming | 25 | 28 | 28 | 28 | 28 |
| Zhurongji | 35 | 35 | 35 | 35 | 35 |
| Zoujiahua | 15 | 51 | 52 | 53 | 53 |
| Median "Power" | 20 | 51 | 52 | 52 | 53 |

model predicts a potential compromise, it identifies the precise policy shift or shifts that are predicted, who is the source of the proposal leading to the shift, and whether a player had received other proposals that also were interpreted as credible. By credible I mean that in the absence of a more attractive option, the player in question believed, according to the model's logic, that there was a sufficient coalition in support of some other proposal that it could have been enforced. Further details about the output can be garnered from experimenting with the software at http://bdm.cqpress.com or from earlier publications, especially Bueno de Mesquita (2000b).

## Prediction and International Relations

Ultimately, the best way we have to evaluate the explanatory power of a model is to assess how well its detailed analysis fits with reality. This is true whether the reality is about a repeated event, like the price of a commodity or the evolution of regime types around the world, or about important one-time political decisions. This can be done with retrospective data or prospective data. In the latter case, when actual outcomes are unknown at the time of investigation, there is a pure opportunity to evaluate the model, independent of any possibility that the data have been made to fit observed outcomes. Indeed, perhaps the most difficult test for any theory is to apply it to circumstances in which the outcome events have not yet occurred and where they are not obvious. It is with this difficulty in mind that later chapters explicitly examine as yet unknown domestic and foreign policy futures.

Of course, predicting that the sun will rise in the East and set in the West is not terribly interesting. Neither is predicting that there will be an American presidential election on the second Tuesday in November every fourth year. The prediction of uncertain events is demanding exactly because the researcher cannot fit the argument to the known results. This is a fundamental difference between real-time prediction and post-diction.

The EUM has been tested in real time against problems with unknown and uncertain outcomes thousands of times. Many of the applications have been conducted within the framework of Decision Insights Incorporated, a New York-based consulting firm, where few applications have been widely available for scrutiny. However, one commercial user of the model, the Central Intelligence Agency, declassified its own detailed evaluation of the accuracy of this model. Additionally, and perhaps more importantly, I and others have published many predictions in the academic literature during the past two decades. These, of course, have always been accessible to the scholarly community. Some academic assessments by others of these predictions are also available in the published literature. After discussing the U.S. government's independent assessment, I will return to the academic published record for further evidence about the reliability of the technique described.

In 1989, Dr. Stanley Feder of the CIA gave a speech reported on by the *Salt Lake City Tribune* (March 1, 1989). He said that "the 'Spatial Theory of Politics' has been gaining increased acceptance at the agency and has resulted in accurate predictions in 90 percent of the situations in which it has been utilized." In response to that article, Professor James Ray, now at Vanderbilt University, contacted Dr. Feder to find out more about the claim of predictive accuracy. On October 22, 1991, Dr. Feder wrote to Professor Ray:

> The article correctly reports that I said that political forecasts made with a model based on the "spatial theory of voting" were accurate about 90 percent of the time. . . . The forecasting model about which I lectured at the University of Utah was developed by Professor Bruce Bueno de Mesquita, now at Stanford University. . . . Since 1982 a colleague and I have used Bruce's models to analyze and identify policy choice scenarios for over 1,000 issues in scores of countries around the world. . . . At

the end of 1985 we did a systematic analysis of the accuracy of forecasts made with the policy choice model. That assessment showed the policy decision model *with inputs provided by recognized country or issue experts* correctly identified the configurations of political forces that would lead to specific, well-defined policy decisions over 90 percent of the time. The model made it possible to identify easy-to-observe differences among alternative political situations and to forecast correctly the policy decision associated with each. . . . [The models] provide specific forecasts, something few other methods or pundits can do with more than a moderate degree of accuracy. (Emphasis in original)[26]

Charles Buffalano, Deputy Director of Research at the Defense Advanced Research Projects Agency, expressed a similar view in a letter dated June 12, 1984. He said:

[O]ne of the last (and most successful projects) in the political methodologies program was the expected utility theory work of Professor Bruce Bueno de Mesquita of the University of Rochester. The theory is both exploratory and predictive and has been rigorously evaluated through post-diction and in real time. Of all quantitative political forecasting methodologies of which I am aware, the expected utility work is the most useful to policy makers because it has the power to predict *specific* policies, their nuances, and ways in which they might be changed. (emphasis in original)

Feder referred to a systematic assessment in his letter, which was subsequently published in a volume edited by H. Bradford Westerfield of Yale University. As that article contains many specific, detailed examples, I take the liberty of examining it in depth (Feder 1995). What types of issues has the CIA analyzed using the models offered by Decision Insights? A sampler, taken from table 2 in the declassified article, includes:

What policy is Egypt likely to adopt toward Israel?
How fully will France participate in SDI?
What is the Philippines likely to do about U.S. bases?
What stand will Pakistan take on the Soviet occupation of Afghanistan?
How much is Mozambique likely to cooperate with the West?
What policy will Beijing adopt toward Taiwan's role in the Asian Development Bank?
How much support is South Yemen likely to give to the insurgency in North Yemen?
What is the South Korean government likely to do about large-scale demonstrations?
What will Japan's foreign trade policy look like?

What stand will the Mexican government take on official corruption?
When will presidential elections be held in Brazil?
Can the Italian government be brought down over the wage indexing issue?

As is evident from this sampler, the modeling method can address diverse questions. Analysts have examined economic, social, and political issues. They have dealt with routine policy decisions and with questions threatening the very survival of particular regimes. Issues have spanned a variety of cultural settings, economic systems, and political systems.

Feder's assessment compares the forecasts based on this expected utility model to more conventional approaches used by the intelligence community. He notes that the model makes specific, detailed predictions 60 percent of the time, a level well below the nearly 100 percent with today's version of the model. He goes on to report that such specificity is found only 33 percent of the time in "traditional" intelligence analyses (Feder 1995). He also observes that while traditional and expected utility analyses both scored well in terms of forecast accuracy, the latter offered greater detail and less vagueness.[27] He notes that the expected utility predictions hit what he calls the bull's eye twice as often as standard intelligence analyses. Perhaps more importantly, Feder notes that while the data for the model generally are obtained from area experts, the predictions frequently differ from those made by the very experts who provide the data. That is, the model is not a Delphi technique that asks experts what they believe will happen and then reports back that information. Feder reports that every time the model and the intelligence community made different predictions, the model proved correct, and he offers many detailed examples (Feder 1995).

Feder's assessment is not the only basis on which to evaluate predictions from this rational actor model. Additional evidence can be found in the published articles that contain predictions based on the EUM. Professors James Ray and Bruce Russett (1996) evaluated many of these publications to ascertain their accuracy. Motivated by John Gaddis's claim that international relations theory is a failure at prediction, they note that

> he does not mention a set of related streams of research and theory that justifies, we believe, a more optimistic evaluation of the field's ability to deliver accurate predictions. The streams of research to which we refer are, specifically: a rational choice approach to political forecasting. . . . The origins of the political forecasting model based on rational choice theory can be traced to *The War Trap* by Bruce Bueno de Mesquita. The theory introduced there was refined in 1985, and served in turn as the basis for a model designed to produce forecasts of policy decisions and political outcomes in a wide variety of political settings. . . . This "expected utility" forecasting model has now been tried and tested extensively. [T]he amount of publicly available information and evi-

dence regarding this model and the accuracy of its forecasts is sufficiently substantial, it seems to us, to make it deserving of serious consideration as a "scientific" enterprise. . . . . [W]e would argue in a Lakatosian fashion that in terms of the range of issues and political settings to which it has been applied, and the body of available evidence regarding its utility and validity, it may be superior to any alternative approaches designed to offer specific predictions and projections regarding political events. (Ray and Russett 1996, p. 469)

These authors go on to report that John Gaddis, in private correspondence, has agreed that the expected utility model "strikes me as an important advance over earlier approaches to predictive modeling because it takes into account the emergent properties of complex adaptive systems . . . [and] there has been a sort of Bueno de Mesquita–John Lewis Gaddis convergence" (Ray and Russett 1996, p. 469).

Ray and Russett report on specific studies as well as general principles. They note that in a 1984 article (Bueno de Mesquita 1984), the model was used to predict that Ayatollah Khomeini would be succeeded by Hasheimi Rafsanjani and Ayatollah Khameini as leaders of Iran following Khomeini's death. At the time of publication, Khomeini had designated Ayatollah Montazari as his successor so that the predictions were contrary to expectations among Iran specialists. Khomeini died five years later, in 1989. He was succeeded by Rafsanjani and Khameini. They also note that a 1988 article correctly predicted the defeat of the Sandinista government in elections; the elections were held in 1990.

Other predictions over the years can be found in articles dealing with the prospects of a peace agreement in the Middle East, prospects of political instability in Italy over the budget deficit, the dispute over the Spratly Islands, the likelihood that Taiwan will develop a nuclear weapons capability, outcome of the Maastricht referendum in Europe, progress on the Good Friday Agreement in Northern Ireland, and others (Bueno de Mesquita and Berkowitz 1979; Bueno de Mesquita 1990; Bueno de Mesquita and Beck 1985; Wu and Bueno de Mesquita 1994; Morrow, Bueno de Mesquita, and Wu 1993; Organski and Bueno de Mesquita 1993; Kugler and Feng 1997; Bueno de Mesquita, McDermott, and Cope 2001).

Ray and Russett focused attention on Gaddis's critique of international relations theory. With his appropriately influential concerns as a backdrop, I continue the review of the EUM's track record.

In Gaddis's 1992 article, he pointed to the failure to predict three events as evidence for the inadequacy of current international relations theory. He wrote, "The abrupt end of the Cold War, an unanticipated hot war in the Persian Gulf, and the sudden disintegration of the Soviet Union astonished almost everyone. . . . [T]he fact that they arose so unexpectedly suggests that deficiencies persist in the means by which contemporary princes and the soothsayers they employ seek to discern the future course of world affairs" (Gaddis 1992, p. 5). While I wholeheartedly agree that deficiencies persist, I wish to establish the *prima facie* basis for my claim that reliable prediction of specific international events is possible by quoting from an interview in *U.S. News and World Report* on May 3, 1982, in which I said, "Applying my theory on why nations go to war . . . I will go out on a limb and cite places where I think war is likely: . . . War between Iraq and Saudi Arabia or between Iraq and other states on the Arabian Peninsula once the Iran-Iraq war is settled." The Iran-Iraq War ended in mid-1988 and, of course, the hot war in the Persian Gulf that Gaddis referred to as unanticipated began in the summer of 1990 with the Iraqi invasion of Kuwait. So at least one of the three events to which he referred was publicly predicted well in advance, including the timing of the event, using the model applied here.

The prediction of the Gulf War was not a solitary, isolated prediction, as should be evident from the above examples. However, I wish to point specifically to another of the events Gaddis addressed. Representatives from the U.S. government who use an in-house version of the expected utility model (called Factions) bragged to the Russians in 1995 about its effectiveness, as reported in *Izvestia*. As that article notes, "Experts engaging in studies within the framework of this system state that on the basis of long experience of using it, it can be said with a great degree of confidence that the forecasts are highly accurate. In particular, according to them, the 'Factions' method was used in May 1991 to predict the August putsch." The 'putsch' or coup, of course, was the crisis that precipitated a second of John Gaddis's exemplars of unpredicted critical events that was anticipated with the EUM: the collapse of the Soviet Union. The next chapter applies the model to data knowable to anyone in 1948 to see if it could also predict the end of the Cold War.

To be sure, some predictions have been wrong or inadequate. The expected utility model successfully predicted the break of several East European states from the Soviet Union but failed to anticipate the fall of the Berlin Wall, although chapter 5 makes clear that, had the model been applied to this problem, it could have done very well using data publicly available in 1980 or even earlier. The model predicted that the August 1991 Soviet coup would fail quickly and that the Soviet Union would unravel during the coming year, but it did not predict the earlier, dramatic policy shifts introduced by Mikhail Gorbachev.

The expected utility model certainly was not applied to that situation so that such predictions could not have been made. That, of course, is an important difference between prediction and prophecy. The first step to a correct—or incorrect—prediction is to ask for a prediction about the relevant issue. Alas, no one asked me or my colleagues for any predictions about the demise of the Soviet Union before critical events had begun to unfold.

## Limitations

The model, of course, has many limitations as well as strengths. It is inappropriate for predicting market-driven events not governed by political considerations. It is imprecise with respect to the exact timing behind decisions and outcomes. The model can have timing elements incorporated into it by including timing factors as contingencies in the way issues are constructed, but the model itself is imprecise with regard to time. The dynamics of the model indicate whether a decision is likely to be reached after very little give and take or after protracted negotiations. Nevertheless, it cannot say how long in clock-time a round of negotiations will last. Most importantly, for many issues of interest "objective" data are not available, so that the model by itself is often of limited value without the inputs from area or issue experts. They, of course, are quite valuable without the model. Still, the combination of the two is substantially more reliable than the experts alone. The limitations remind us that scientific and predictive approaches to politics are in their infancy. Still we can draw some encouragement from the fact that in many domains it has already proven possible to make detailed, accurate predictions.

# FOUR

# The End of the Cold War: Predicting an Emergent Property

T HE END OF THE COLD WAR IS A TURNING POINT NOT ONLY FOR the world of international affairs, but also for the smaller world of international relations research. Decades of thought by area specialists, historians, philosophers, statisticians, journalists, and pundits failed to provide a clear, explicit prediction that the Cold War was about to end. In light of this apparent failure, and as noted in chapter 3, John Gaddis (1992) argued that international relations theory was a failure. Gaddis challenged the core of international relations theorizing, stimulating a lively, sometimes heated exchange over whether international relations theory was a failure or not. That debate challenged the very notion that the absence of explicit predictions about the end of the Cold War was germane to the questions he raised.

Others have raised equally strong concerns about the ability of rational choice models to address topical policy concerns (Cohn 1999; Walt 1999). These critics ignore or are unaware of the American government's use of the EUM. Here and in the subsequent chapters I hope to offer some food for thought for those who maintain that rational choice models and modelers do not or cannot address important policy questions. The questions addressed here are very broad, but the sampling of analyses discussed in the previous chapter makes clear that the EUM has also been used to examine problems of immediate foreign policy importance, as well as issues of short-, medium-, and long-term consequence.

The purpose of this chapter is to use the EUM retrospectively to see if the structure of relations among states after World War II contained an emergent property, the seeds for the unfolding development and end of the Cold War. By this I mean that the exercise I undertake here is attempting to see, in a probabilistic sense, what the likely evolution of international relations looked like, given the characteristics of the pre–Cold War, but post–World War II period. I will show that one can demonstrate, just from information about the world in 1948, that it was highly likely that the United States would emerge as the victor over the Soviet Union in a peaceful resolution of the Cold

War. Once that assessment is completed, I turn in the remaining chapters to addressing equally long-term evaluations of the future world order.

In the approach I take, national leaders are assumed to adapt strategically to changing circumstances by choosing the course of action they believe at any given time is best for them (or, by extension, their nation). Their behavior is adaptive and it is complex. It is adaptive in that behavior responds to shifting circumstances. It is complex in that each state (or leader) has a strategic interest in structuring the way in which the environment changes so as to encourage others to adapt in a manner favorable to the state in question. In particular, but not exclusively, the United States and the Soviet Union, as the main protagonists in the Cold War, each had an interest in shaping the adaptive behavior of all other states. Each, of course, hoped to promote a situation in which the international system evolved in its favor.

I show that, by simulating a wide array of plausible counterfactual histories, we can see that the initial starting point of the Cold War had embedded in it an emergent property. Specifically, the probability of an American Cold War victory was much higher than the probability of a Soviet victory, given the initial Cold War conditions and rationally complex, adaptive behavior. The results of my analysis support the contention that critical aspects of the Cold War's end were predictable and that many of its specific characteristics were highly likely, but not inevitable. It suggests a reorientation of discussion about path dependence, shifting instead to a case for path interdependence, while highlighting the importance of some policy choices over others.[28] It provides a means to view counterfactual histories in a rigorous way and suggests policies by which the Cold War could have ended sooner or even have been avoided altogether.

## Application of the Model to Predicting the Cold War's Evolution

To apply the EUM to the Cold War without taking advantage of ex post knowledge, I have undertaken numerous simulations, all based on the same initial data. The initial data, drawn from the Correlates of War Project, include a list of the thirty-six most powerful sovereign countries as of 1948.[29] For each country, there is an estimate of their 1948 national capabilities and their position on a security dimension scaled from -100 to +100.

The security dimension is measured in terms of the similarity in military alliance portfolios for each pair of countries as of 1948, using Correlates of War alliance data, as explained in Bueno de Mesquita (1981). That is, each state can have any possible mix of defense pacts, nonaggression pacts (or neutrality pacts), ententes, and no alliance relationship with each of the other states in the international system. A security portfolio or military alliance portfolio is defined as the array of military alliance agreements a state has with all other states. The degree of shared security interests of any pair of states is evaluated as the correlation (using Kendall's tau b) of their security portfolios with one another.[30] For instance, by the height of the Cold War, the United States and the other members of NATO shared very similar security portfolios with one another. They tended to form mutual defense pacts with the same sets of states and they also tended to avoid alliances altogether with the same set of states. Thus, if I were taking advantage of actual information about the similarity in alliance commitments in, say, 1965, the measurement procedure I use would show a high degree of similarity of interests or correlation on the security dimension between, for instance, the United States and the United Kingdom or the Netherlands, and between the Soviet Union and Bulgaria, but a low level of similarity or correlation between Bulgaria and the United Kingdom or the United States and the Soviet Union.

The measure of shared interests reflects the focus in 1948 on security concerns, while capturing the world before the clear emergence of a bipolar structure between the friends of the United States and the friends of the Soviet Union. This measure has been widely used in numerous studies in the literature on security and, while certainly imperfect, has been demonstrated to vary in theoretically predicted ways across a large array of security-related concerns. The initial security policy score for each simulation is calculated by examining the difference in the similarity of alliance portfolios for each country vis-à-vis the United States and the Soviet Union. A score of +100 indicates a security policy most like that of the United States. A score of -100 indicates a security policy most like that of the Soviet Union. A score of 0 indicates complete neutrality between the two sides, with negative values being increasingly pro-Soviet and positive values being increasingly pro-American. This normalized scale reflects openly declared policy positions and not political or military power per se.

As of 1948, sides had not yet been clearly drawn in the Cold War struggle so that, as the data reflect, the central tendency was toward neutrality in choosing between the United States and the Soviet Union. It is changes in these scores over time that I am interested in predicting, especially changes in the score that reflects the policy position at which power was balanced between the competing world views at any given time. Of course, I am equally interested in predicting changes in the policy positions of the United States and the Soviet Union. The balance-of-power policy position is defined here as the security policy position (between -100 and +100) for which it is true that as much aggregate power falls above that security position as falls below it. That is, the balance-of-power security position is the position of the state that is the median power whether we sum power from below or from above on the security policy dimension.

Capabilities are measured using the Correlates of War Composite Capabilities Index. This widely used indicator is the average of six components: share of the system's military expenditures and military personnel, urban population and total population, and steel production and commercial fuel consumption. The capabilities of the thirty-six most powerful states in the system as of 1948 are included in the analysis. Their capability scores are normalized so that they sum to 100.[31] It should be noted that because the starting date is 1948, neither Japan nor East and West Germany were sovereign states and so are not included in the analysis. If anything, this introduces a pro-Soviet bias into the analysis, as Japan and West Germany certainly emerged as more powerful states than did East Germany. The capabilities data are further biased against the finding here that the United States was especially likely to win the Cold War because the Correlates of War Capabilities Index is known to overweigh both the Soviet Union and China. This overweighing results from the fact that iron and steel production had diminished in importance as actual power factors in the post–World War II era and also because both had large but relatively poor populations.

Salience for national security policy is set equal to 100 for each country in 1948. This reflects the situation at that time when the early signs of the Cold War were upon us. The year 1948 is chosen because it is a key dividing year. The World War II alliance between the United States, Britain, and the Soviet Union was clearly shattered by the conflict over Iran in 1946, as well as by disagreements with the Soviet Union over the fate of Eastern Europe and over the governance of divided Germany, etc. However, neither NATO nor the Warsaw Pact had emerged to define the central parameters of the international order for the next forty or so years. Of course, by 1948 there were bilateral alliances between the USSR and what became the membership of the Warsaw Pact, but no multilateral agreements were yet in place.

To be sure that the results of my analysis do not depend on the selection of 1948, I have replicated the process using 1946 and 1947 as base years, and I have also analyzed expanded and reduced sets of states as the stakeholders. The results are the same. The EUM predicts changes in policy positions—that is, support for the United States or the Soviet Union—in response to the pulls and tugs of competing coalitions of interest. In the simulations run for this study, the model was allowed to iterate over twenty-five periods (which we can think of as each being two years in duration, though the model is not instructive on calendar time), with the salience variable permitted to change randomly for each country during each round.[32]

The randomization of salience is intended to capture the range of possible fluctuations in the relative importance of security issues compared to other issues, including, for instance, domestic political concerns, economic policy, humanitarian concerns, and the like from period to period and from country to country. It allows the possibility to test the model while controlling, in a sense, for the potential impact of exogenous random shocks—domestic or foreign policy earthquakes—that alter the relative importance of security issues from state to state and from time to time.

The introduction of random salience is an innovation from earlier applications of this model. One problem in doing long-term analysis, whether it is post-diction or real-time prediction, is that the likelihood of an exogenous random shock to the initial data increases over time. A central problem in long-term assessments is anticipating the seemingly unpredictable. For instance, the assassination of President John Kennedy in 1963 could certainly not have been foreseen in 1948. Nor could anyone in 1948 readily foresee and so model the effects of the launch of Sputnik in 1957 or the sudden death of Prime Minister Lal Bahadur Shastri of India in 1965, or Watergate or the Profumo scandal in England and so forth. Each of these events could potentially influence the attentiveness of a government toward security or toward domestic affairs. Such shocks arise more or less randomly in time and space. By randomizing salience across stakeholders (space) and across iterations (time), the model allows us to estimate a wide array of such "unanticipated" events. By doing so, we can see whether there are strong pushes in the general configuration of the data that generally favored the continuation of the Cold War or an American or a Soviet victory. Indeed, this innovation appears to be an important step in devising long-term counterfactual scenarios as a means to test alternative states of history, both past and future.

The methodology applied here does not attempt to replicate the actual history of the past fifty years. That would be subject to ex post biases based on knowing how things turned out. Instead, the model simulates alternative histories to see to what extent the actual end of the Cold War was strictly path dependent and to what extent the peaceful collapse of the Soviet Union can be seen to have emerged from the starting conditions in 1948, given an array of alternative historical paths from 1948 forward. That is, the simulations indicate the degree of path interdependence over the half-century between 1948 and the end of the Cold War.

Each random distribution of salience scores represents a critical element in a different path that history could have taken. Indeed, we can see whether any of the 100 simulations I have run comes close to replicating the actual experience between 1948 and the present, and we can see whether the preponderance of paths led to an American victory, a Soviet victory, or the continuation of the Cold War. Note that the objective is not to predict the precise details of the actual path of circumstances and choices that led to the end of the Cold War, but to determine whether that precise path was part of a preponderant, interdependent set of paths favoring American victory. Specifically, through the randomization of salience we can see whether the American victory depended on a unique array of circumstances, a small bundle of possible circumstances, or a very broad range of feasible conditions. As the evidence makes clear, the end of the Cold War was one of a numerous and preponderant set of prospective paths that history could have traversed leading to American victory. The paths leading to other outcomes are far less numerous and, in that sense, less probable.

It is important to recognize that none of these simulations takes advantage of any information that could not, in principle, have been known in 1948. The data certainly were readily knowable. The model, of course, did not exist in 1948, but it makes no use of information about international politics after that year. The simulations do not update the national capabilities each year, for instance, because those changes are partially endogenous products of the Cold War, rather than its antecedents. The model predicts shifts in national positions on the pro-United States/pro-Soviet scale from iteration to iteration based only on its internal logic, the 1948 data, and random fluctuations in the values of the salience variable. The initial data assumptions are displayed in Table 4.1.

## Predicting the Cold War's End

Before turning to the analysis, let me say a word about how the results are to be interpreted. Each of the 100 simulations develops an alternative, plausible scenario or counterfactual history of the post–1948 years. The method I use does not provide an ex ante way to choose one scenario over another and say that the chosen scenario is the predicted path of the Cold War. We can, of course, find scenarios that look very much like actual history, and I will point to such scenarios (and others that do not look like actual history) as I go through the analysis. These are interesting cases that suggest a variety of alternative ways in which the Cold War could have ended or been prolonged. They are instructive about foreign policy making for the future, but they are not central to the predictions of interest.

The central predictions are about the likelihood that the Cold War would continue or would end with an American victory or a Soviet victory. Predictions about these likelihoods can be made with confidence by examining the relative probability of each of these three core possible outcomes. If the distribution of simulation outcomes that support, for instance, an American victory and a Soviet victory are about equal, then the model will have failed to predict the central feature of the end of the Cold War; that is, a peaceful victory by the United States. Such an approximately equal distribution would falsify my claim that this model could predict the end of the Cold War. So would a preponderance of predictions favoring a Soviet victory. If, however, the vast majority of simulations support the claim for a peaceful American victory in the Cold War, then the model will have succeeded in showing that the outcome of the Cold War was a predictable emergent property of the initial conditions reflected in the data in Table 4.1, with the actual path taken reflecting "noise" or a small perturbation around the preponderant central tendency of the predictions.

I begin the analysis with some summary statistics that speak to the model's predictions regarding the likely evolution of the Cold War. Then I

**Table 4.1**

Initial Data Conditions: 1948

| Country | Pro-American or Pro-Soviet Policy Preferences | | |
| --- | --- | --- | --- |
| | Resources | Position | Salience |
| Argentina | 0.972 | 9.6 | 100 |
| Australia | 0.889 | 1.3 | 100 |
| Belgium | 1.182 | 2.8 | 100 |
| Brazil | 0.993 | 89.6 | 100 |
| Bulgaria | 0.345 | −100.0 | 100 |
| Canada | 1.610 | 56.2 | 100 |
| China | 11.941 | 1.3 | 100 |
| Czechoslovakia | 1.401 | −91.0 | 100 |
| Denmark | 0.240 | 1.3 | 100 |
| Egypt | 0.408 | 3.2 | 100 |
| England | 7.863 | 3.6 | 100 |
| France | 3.597 | 2.8 | 100 |
| Greece | 0.418 | 1.3 | 100 |
| Hungary | 0.450 | −91.0 | 100 |
| India | 2.468 | 1.3 | 100 |
| Iran | 0.491 | 2.4 | 100 |
| Iraq | 0.157 | 3.7 | 100 |
| Israel | 0.125 | 1.3 | 100 |
| Italy | 2.426 | 1.3 | 100 |
| Mexico | 0.774 | 89.6 | 100 |
| Norway | 0.230 | 1.3 | 100 |
| Netherlands | 0.836 | 2.8 | 100 |
| Pakistan | 1.485 | 1.3 | 100 |
| Philippines | 0.408 | 1.3 | 100 |
| Poland | 3.273 | −91.0 | 100 |
| Rumania | 0.606 | −91.0 | 100 |
| USSR | 18.256 | −100.0 | 100 |
| South Africa | 0.680 | 1.3 | 100 |
| Saudi Arabia | 0.125 | 2.8 | 100 |
| Spain | 1.683 | 1.3 | 100 |
| Sweden | 0.648 | 1.3 | 100 |
| Syria | 0.104 | 2.8 | 100 |
| Thailand | 0.414 | 1.3 | 100 |
| Turkey | 1.347 | 2.4 | 100 |
| USA | 29.956 | 100.0 | 100 |
| Yugoslavia | 0.891 | −100.0 | 100 |

examine selected simulations to illustrate the characteristic paths the model suggests for the evolution of the Cold War. These suggest the main alternative histories that the model indicates were likely. The 100 simulations allow us to estimate the probability of alternative outcomes. The simulations also allow us to see the extent to which the end of the Cold War was attained optimally or might have been achieved earlier with the same or fewer costs.

They also allow us to speak of counterfactual strategies for ending the Cold War and compare them to the course actually followed.

The 1948 data reflect a system of nations highly centralized around neutrality, uncertain of whether to invest their futures with the Soviet Union or the United States. The initial locus of power was centered at 2.4 on the policy scale. The scale, you recall, varies between -100 and +100. The locus of 2.4 reflects the position of greatest national security in the sense that at position 2.4, power was evenly balanced between those more pro-American and those more pro-Soviet. From a structural realist perspective, this can be described as the policy that maximized security; it reflects a decision to balance one side against the other. From a spatial modeling perspective, 2.4 represents the location of the median power unit on the security issue dimension in 1948 and is analogous to Duncan Black's (1958) median voter. The 1948 structure reflects a seemingly stable system in which neither the United States nor the Soviet Union had enough support to defeat the neutral center so long as everyone remained focused exclusively on security. Thus, a neorealist view, in which security remains the focus, could not predict the end of the Cold War. Rather, such a view seems to favor stasis. The Cold War's end depended on at least some states being diverted from security concerns by other issues, whether domestic or foreign.

The randomization of the salience variable in the 100 simulations was utilized exactly to see what happens to the powerful neutral center as the security concerns of states waned and waxed in response to fluctuating hypothetical domestic or other pressures. By allowing salience to vary on the security dimension, my analysis departs from neorealist or structural realist precepts. In that view of the world, which is tested as a separate simulation (number 101), security is always the paramount concern of states, so that domestic, economic, humanitarian, or other concerns could never become more salient than security.

We can see how the waning and waxing of security concerns may have influenced the unfolding Cold War by looking at changes in the locus of the balance of power at different times across the simulations. By the end of the fifth iteration of the 100 random simulations of the model, for instance, the policy stance that represented the average point of maximal security against defeat by either extreme was 19.6. Remembering that positive values reflect a pro-American stance, this indicates a decidedly more pro-American world by about 1958 than was true on average in 1948. The average, however, can be misleading. The 100 simulations include examples at this stage for which the balance of power position is as pro-Soviet as -91 and as pro-American as 99.7. That is, a broad range of system evolutions away from neutrality were feasible in the early years of the Cold War, including quick American victory over the Soviet Union and quick Soviet victory over the United States.

By the fifteenth iteration of the model, roughly equivalent to the year 1978, the position that balanced power on average across all of the simulations was located at 12.5, still more pro-American than at the outset, but not quite so much so as in the simulated world of 1958. This fits nicely with the emergence in the 1970s of détente, including the recognition of the Soviet Union as a more or less equal super power. By the hypothetical average world of 1978, the variation in possible outcomes had decreased, both in the sense that the most pro-Soviet outcome is now -84.9 instead of -91 and the most pro-American outcome is 86.5 instead of 99.7, and in the sense that the standard deviation around the average policy outcome had dropped from 44 to 33 and continues to drop thereafter.

Table 4.2 summarizes the overall pattern of evolution of the emerging Cold War. The columns define four generic outcomes: a strongly pro-Soviet outcome, a weakly pro-Soviet outcome, a weakly pro-American victory, and a strongly pro-American victory. The weak outcomes are defined to reflect "balances of power" within ten points on the policy scale of the original situation (that is, a weakly pro-Soviet outcome ranges from -7.6 to 2.4, and a weakly pro-American outcome is greater than 2.4 up to 12.4), with strong outcomes being more than ten points above or below the initial condition.

Table 4.2 clarifies several important generalizations about the likelihood of American victory in the Cold War. It is evident that, though the system started out as neutral (100 percent of first-round "balance of power" positions are at 2.4 on the policy scale), it strongly tips in the pro-American position in the vast majority of cases. More than two-thirds of outcomes in the simulations are favorable to the United States compared to the initial condition. The Soviet Union was engaged in an uphill struggle from the outset. Furthermore, the simulations indicate that the United States had a very good prospect of emerging victorious fairly early on, much earlier than it ultimately did. This suggests that the policies the United States followed during the Cold War may have slowed its end, or the policies the Soviet Union followed may have prolonged the USSR's quest, while ultimately proving futile. Interestingly, John Gaddis has come to a similar conclusion (1997). He notes that the United States, by focusing on presumed (and knowingly exaggerated) Soviet military power over, for instance, economic might, may have unintentionally prolonged the Cold War. The long peace, then, may have been due to poor strategy rather than any stabilizing effects of bipolarity. In

**Table 4.2**
Distribution of Policy Outcomes: The Emergent End of the Cold War

| Round/"Year" | Pro-USSR | Weakly pro-USSR | Weakly pro-USA | Pro-USA |
|---|---|---|---|---|
| Round 5: "1958" | 14 | 15 | 29 | 42 |
| Round 15: "1978" | 24 | 5 | 20 | 51 |
| Round 25: "1998" | 23 | 9 | 18 | 50 |

this regard, it is interesting to note that already by the fifth iteration of the model, it was predicted that the United States would gain a strong victory over the Soviet Union in 42 percent of the cases and would gain victory in 71 of the 100 simulations. In contrast, the Soviets were expected to achieve a decisive victory in only 14 percent of the simulated states of the world. How more rapid American victories might have been achieved and how the Soviet Union might have won are topics discussed in the next section.

Table 4.2 depicts a coarse view of the distribution of likely outcomes of the Cold War as estimated through simulation. Now we may consider a somewhat more refined view, particularly with regard to defining what constitutes a U.S. victory. The model simulations lead to five generic sets of predictions: a slow American victory, a quick American victory, a continuation of the Cold War, a quick Soviet victory, and a slow Soviet victory. Victory is defined for these purposes as arising when the policy stance of the United States, the Soviet Union, and the majority of the remaining power in the world converge to either a pro-American or a pro-Soviet position. The Cold War is said to continue if such convergence does not take place, with the two superpowers remaining on opposite sides of the neutral position of zero on the security policy scale.

Another view of victory is that the preponderance of global power endorses the American or the Soviet perspective. Here the notion is that even if the Soviet Union and the United States failed to converge, if enough power favored one or the other viewpoint, then the remaining superpower could be viewed as marginalized and isolated. Figure 4.1 depicts such a perspective. It shows the cumulative probability distribution for the policy stance of the balance of power position in the global setting across the 100 simulations. Figure 4.1 displays the likelihood, if you like, of a pro-American or pro-Soviet world by the final iteration of each simulation.

Figure 4.1 shows quite dramatically that the cumulative probability of a pro-American world view or of American hegemony was extremely high. Only 22 percent of the simulations lead to predicted pro-Soviet Cold War resolutions by this definition. Seventy-eight percent yield a pro-American world outlook by the end of the simulations. This is a key view of the emergent property of American hegemony. It is ironic that the simulations capture this—which certainly has been echoed in the real world—while much of the academic community in the 1980s focused on the apparent decline of American hegemony (Gilpin 1981; Keohane 1984; Krasner 1981; but for a view consistent with the finding here, see Russett 1985; Kugler and Organski 1989).

We can attain another viewpoint by looking at examples of each of the five generic evolutions of the Cold War. In one such generic outcome—the dominant one—the policy stance of the United States, the Soviet Union, and the majority of the remaining powers in the world rapidly converge (say in fewer than ten model rounds, or about twenty years) to a pro-American outcome.

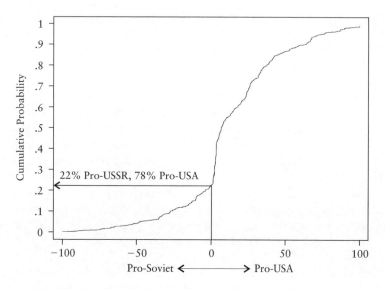

**Figure 4.1** The Evolution of the Balance of Power

Figure 4.2 illustrates an example of such a case, which I identify as Simulation 8. Figure 4.3 (Simulation 19) illustrates the second generic outcome, which most closely mirrors what actually happened. The United States and the Soviet Union remained far apart for a long time, ultimately converging, along with much of the rest of the world, to a decidedly pro-American posture after about twenty iterations or forty years. This is the next most common outcome in the simulations. It supports the notion that the Cold War would end around 1990. Chapter 5 shows that this timing is also overwhelmingly predicted to be the period when the Soviet Union would abandon its old-style autocratic structure. As we will see, that prediction is based on completely replicable data about the international system in 1980. So, this pattern, discerned repeatedly based on 1948 data, emerges even more strongly with information from 1990, reinforcing the idea that the end of the Cold War could have been predicted had the EUM been applied to known information in the years before the actual collapse of the Soviet political system.

Figures 4.4 and 4.5 reflect mirror image outcomes in which the United States relatively quickly (Simulation 3) or slowly (Simulation 5) adopts a pro-Soviet position along with the majority of the rest of the world. These each occur infrequently in the simulations.

Finally, Figure 4.6 (Simulation 96) shows a decidedly pro-American world in which the Soviet Union and many of its predicted allies (essentially the Warsaw Pact countries) nevertheless remain aloof from the pro-American system. Figure 4.6, then, illustrates an example in which the Cold War continues and reminds us that American victory was not at all inevitable (see

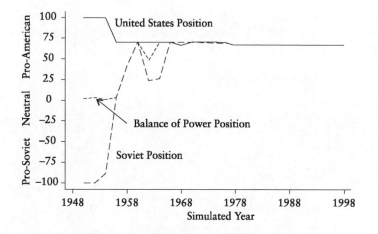

**Figure 4.2**   A Quick American Victory: Simulation 8

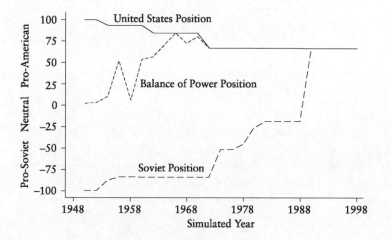

**Figure 4.3**   An American Victory: Simulation 19

also Greenstein 1996; Zelikow and Rice 1995). The predicted histories supporting each of these figures are explained in the next section.

These five generic cases remind us that the "balance of power" could shift to a pro-American or a pro-Soviet position without Soviet-American convergence. This is important because the simulations indicate that there were significant opportunities for the Soviet Union to hang on in not-so-splendid isolation even after the United States won the support of the vast majority of states and the vast majority of global power. The simulations include sixteen instances in which the Soviet position remains below -50 on

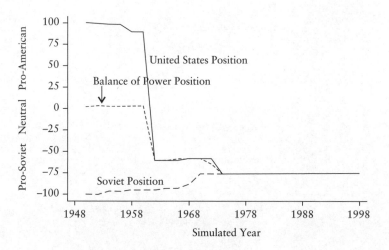

**Figure 4.4** A Quick Soviet Victory: Simulation 38

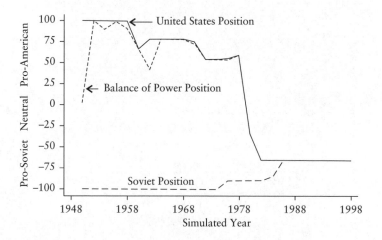

**Figure 4.5** A Soviet Victory: Simulation 58

the scale while the forecast is for a pro-American "balance of power." *There are no instances in the simulations in which the United States maintains a position above 50 and yet the predicted outcome is for a pro-Soviet "balance of power."* Apparently the Soviet Union was vastly more likely to hold out in ideological or political isolation against all odds than was the United States. Put differently, the United States manifests more policy flexibility than the Soviet Union or a greater preparedness to accept even an unfavorable resolution of the Cold War in those few instances in which the Soviet Union remains firm. The United States, however, more often remains firm than does

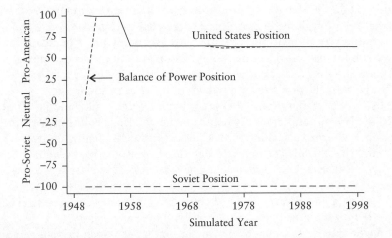

**Figure 4.6**   Cold War Continues: Simulation 96

the Soviet Union, so the number of instances when the United States might have faced the choice of giving in to Soviet preferences or remaining firm is only a small minority of cases. We must not lose sight of the fact that 68 percent of the simulations end with the Soviet Union accepting an American victory and 78 percent with the vast majority of the world's powers sharing in a pro-American victory whether the Soviet Union participated or not.

So far we have seen that the simulations show that the United States had a better than two-thirds chance of winning the Cold War. They also highlight the observation that the actual path to victory was not the only way there. Many policies could have helped foster the end of the Cold War and the establishment of a pro-American balance of power. I turn now to an examination of the five hypothetical worlds depicted in the figures above. In doing so, I provide additional details of the politics and policies that support the counterfactual histories represented by these EUM simulations. These are useful to compare to the actual history of events between 1948 and the fall of the Berlin Wall in 1989 or the collapse of the Soviet Union in 1991.

## Counterfactual Histories

I begin with the "history" that produces Figure 4.3, the circumstance most like the actual events of the Cold War. Then I turn to the "histories" associated with the other figures. A comparison between Figures 4.2 and 4.3 helps suggest alternative strategies for ending the Cold War.

As noted earlier, NATO was not yet in existence in 1948. In the sequence of events that makes up Figure 4.3 (Simulation 19), we can see that NATO begins to take clear shape by the third iteration (approximating 1954). During that iteration, Italy and France are predicted to shift positions from 3.6, or essentially from neutrality, to 90, or to a strongly pro-American stance. Great Britain also moves in this round from a relatively neutral position to 53, adopting a position clearly favoring the United States (currently at 94 on the scale) over the Soviet Union (which is at -84 at this juncture).

By the next iteration, NATO becomes quite solid, adding Turkey, Greece, Canada, and Spain. Israel, Iran, Egypt, Iraq, Pakistan, Argentina, Mexico, and Brazil also adopt pro-American policies. Meanwhile, the model estimates that the Soviet camp includes Hungary, Rumania, Poland, Czechoslovakia, Bulgaria, and Yugoslavia. The system is now clearly bipolar. The pro-U.S. nations control 56 percent of the power in the system, while the pro-Soviet forces are favored by 44 percent. Many states continue to remain neutral, with India being the most powerful in that category.

As the system continues to evolve, the bipolar character becomes emphasized further. By iteration 5 (roughly 1958), Greece moves away from its pro-American posture to a more neutral position, while Sweden, the Netherlands, Denmark, the Philippines, and Australia adopt an America viewpoint, further strengthening the American bloc. China, which had been pro-American—recall that the 1948 data precede the Communist Chinese victory over the Kuomindang—moves now to a decidedly more neutral stance. The Soviet bloc, looking much like the actual Warsaw Pact, continues to hold firmly at positions between -80 and -100.

During the next several iterations in the simulation, the system becomes increasingly polarized. The two main power blocs tighten while, in the neutral range, China becomes a major player. By the tenth iteration (roughly 1968), however, the neutral bloc begins to drift toward the American position. China moves in this period to position 35 on the scale. By round 12 (approximating 1972), the Soviet Union moves from -84 (they shifted early on to -84 from -100) to -51. They are still obviously strongly anti-American, but this movement indicates cracks in the solidarity of the Soviet bloc. This Soviet shift occurs at a time when American salience for security, randomly assigned in the simulation, is rather high (79), while the Soviet Union is more preoccupied with domestic problems (the USSR's salience for security = 24). The shift in the Soviet position takes place in an environment of remarkably low tension. The model estimates what percentage of dyadic relationships involve significant tension. While a value of about 30 percent is normal, at this point the model indicates only about 2 percent of relationships are sufficiently tense to impose real political costs. That is, the softening of the Soviet position (which is accompanied by a smaller softening in the American policy stance) is roughly equivalent to the policy of détente pursued during the 1970s.

After the Soviet Union adjusts its position to -51, the system stabilizes for the next eight rounds (or about 16 years). In the twentieth iteration, however, corresponding roughly to 1988, there is a sudden and dramatic turn of events. The United States and its NATO and other allies have occupied position 68 for eight or so rounds. The Soviet Union has hovered around -51 while its allies have remained even more staunchly anti-American, keeping themselves around -81. Now, however, the Soviet Union suddenly alters its posture, moving to +68. That is, it suddenly adopts a policy outlook in line with that of the United States.[33]

It is striking to note that this simulation produces an end to the Cold War, culminating in an American victory, in 1988. It was just then, of course, that Mikhail Gorbachev signaled his preparedness to allow the East European states to pursue their own destinies. As Margaret Thatcher observed in 1988, during her final official visit to Washington during the Reagan years, "We're not in a Cold War now" (Shultz 1993, 1131). As will be seen in chapter 5, the import of this simulation result is heightened by the fact that the exact timing for the end of the Cold War recurs in simulations derived from reproducible data known in 1980.

Just prior to Soviet acceptance of America's policy posture in the simulation, the entire world has subscribed to the American outlook, except for the Soviet Union and its East European allies. Shortly after the Soviet Union signals the end of the Brezhnev Doctrine, or, in the model's terms, shortly after the USSR moves to +68, the East European states abandon their stance and join in the new world order. The Cold War is over. The Soviet collapse does not occur because of a disparity in salience for security concerns. Both the United States and the Soviet Union have salience scores in the low 30s range at this point in the simulation. It seems that the preponderance of power on the American side ultimately makes the Soviet Union susceptible to accepting a deal at +68, rather than risk an outcome even more like the original American policy at 100. The Soviet leadership seems to have run out of the energy to resist the growing concentration of power in favor of the American perspective. In this instance, then, low salience for the security dimension (of about 33) supports the liberal hypothesis that internal problems (especially economic problems) broke the Soviet Union. The power concentration backing the United States supports the conservative claim that Ronald Reagan's military buildup and aggressive foreign policy posture made it clear to Mikhail Gorbachev that the Soviet Union could not compete successfully. Of course, still others contend that Reagan's "soft-line" policies in his later years, coupled with the Helsinki Accords, were the real key to the Soviet collapse (Deudney and Ikenberry 1991; Risse-Kappen 1991). The simulation reinforces both strands of argument for the end of the Cold War: The Soviet Union imploded because of internal failings and it collapsed because of external pressure.

The simulation may help to reframe what seems to be a fruitless debate between advocates of alternative points of view. Charles Kegley (1994), for instance, casts the debate in a seemingly either-or context, while favoring the liberal, internal implosion explanation. Yet, there is no compelling logical reason to view these as competing explanations. Quite the contrary, with the Soviet Union facing two sources of high costs for continuing the Cold War, the pressure to alter its behavior is greater than if it faced only one source. This is a point reinforced by analyses by others, including a prescient perspective expressed by Zbigniew Brzezinski as early as 1963 (Brzezinski 1963; George 1991; Greenstein 1996; Lepgold, Bueno de Mesquita, and Morrow 1996). Kiron Skinner and her collaborators provide deep evidence for the claim that Ronald Reagan actively sought to spend the Soviet Union into collapse, a claim reinforced, or should I say "replicated," in the simulation. Skinner et al. show that Reagan, as early as the 1960s, already was contemplating the possibility of achieving a peaceful American victory in the Cold War by spending the Soviet Union into a change in outlook (Skinner, Anderson, and Anderson 2001).

Simulation 19, of course, is not a replica of the actual events that ended the Cold War. Yet, in many details it provides a "history" rather close to actual events. NATO's formation is clearly evident early on, as is its growing strength as the system polarizes. The Warsaw Pact emerges as a resilient alliance, resistant to external pressure, but ultimately doomed by the superior capabilities of the United States to attract and hold allies and isolate the Soviet bloc and by the prospects of an internal crisis in the Soviet Union. The simulation produces a history in which Soviet-American relations are distant but stable for a long period, followed by a sudden and dramatic collapse of the Soviet bloc, much as actually occurred. In many other details, Simulation 19 reproduces important features of the Cold War, including the emergence of India as a leader of neutral states and the large swings in policy position of China. Again, remember the base year for the data, 1948, is before the communist victory over the nationalist forces in China so that the model was not informed of actual changes in China.

Figure 4.2 (Simulation 8) depicts a much faster transition from the Cold War to American success. In this simulation, the Soviet Union accepts the American approach to policy within three iterations or, roughly, by the end of 1954. The key to the rapid American success is that the Soviet Union early on is torn by domestic considerations that suggest internal instability. For instance, in round 2 of this simulation, even before a NATO-like alliance forms, Czechoslovakia, Rumania, and Hungary shift from their adamantly pro-Soviet position to neutrality (1.3 on the scale). This happens because the Soviet Union is not committed to holding its allies, being distracted by domestic politics or some other issue than security. The salience score for security in round 2 for the Soviet Union is only 13, leaving about 87 percent of its effort turned elsewhere, such as to domestic issues. This contrasts with America's 65 salience for security at this stage in the simulation.

Why might Soviet salience for foreign security have been so low in the early 1950s, as reflected by Simulation 8? Stalin's death could easily have precipitated an internal political crisis. Indeed, in important respects it did. Following his death, a power struggle ensued which took several years to resolve. During this period, the United States played a fairly quiescent role, not taking any bold steps to exacerbate the internal problems in the Soviet Union. Presumably, America's caution was out of fear of a war that might result or because the United States was preoccupied with its own problems in Korea.

Had the United States done more at that time to encourage internal turmoil in the Soviet Union and to support "separatist" movements, of which there were plenty in Warsaw Pact countries, then, at least in this simulation, war would not have resulted. Rather, the simulation suggests that the Soviet system, weakened internally and not yet recovered from World War II, would have collapsed and the Cold War would have been nipped in the bud. This is broadly consistent with views expressed by members of the Committee on the Present Danger in the early 1950s. Simulation 8 highlights the benefits that American firmness might have produced early on. It also reminds us that while NATO greatly facilitates the defeat of the Soviet Union by coordinating the capabilities of a large and powerful bloc, NATO was not essential in the early days. Certainly this does not remain true by the late 1950s. No simulation that ends in American success after ten rounds fails to produce a NATO-like European alliance. So, we can infer that NATO was critical to the Soviet defeat once the Cold War became well entrenched, but that its entrenchment might have been averted by a more aggressive American foreign policy in the early 1950s even without resort to NATO. The generalization that NATO was instrumental to bringing about a successful, pro-American end of the Cold War once it was well under way holds true in the simulations regardless of whether NATO just coordinated a powerful bloc, deterring the Soviet Union, or whether the leaders of the USSR never intended to attack the West (Vasquez 1991).

The important role that NATO played and the dangers that might have plagued the United States without NATO are evident from Figure 4.4 (Simulation 33). In this simulation, the European states fail to band together to form a NATO-like alliance. The United States seems to be pursuing an isolationist foreign policy.

By the sixth iteration of the model, roughly equivalent to 1960, the United States alone can no longer forestall a Soviet victory. Although American salience for security is high, so is that of the Soviet Union and its Warsaw Pact allies. What is more, the leaders of the Soviet Union perceive themselves in a highly conflict-prone, tense environment. Over 96 percent of their relationships are seen as conflict-prone by iteration 6. This suggests that a war was likely and that the war, without European assistance for the United States, would have ended in victory for the Soviet bloc. Failure to stop the Soviet Union early on and failure to form NATO by the mid-1950s apparently could have been a disastrous recipe for the United States or for those who advocate democratic government. The isolationist posture for which some argued after World War II seems to have promised to produce a Soviet-dominated world order, violently imposed.

Figure 4.5 (Simulation 58) tells a somewhat different story. NATO does form in this case by the end of iteration 3. In this instance, the NATO alliance, rather than tightening over time, unravels during round 6 (roughly equivalent to 1960) while the Warsaw Pact countries remain staunch in their support of the Soviet Union's foreign policy. Despite the unraveling of NATO, the United States holds steadily at 78 on the scale, indicating a strongly anti-Soviet viewpoint. The stress level is very high, with nearly 70 percent of American relationships being tense and strained while 100 percent of Soviet relationships have the same characteristic.

Despite the tension, no sudden shifts in policy occur. Rather, the system languishes in a heated-up state for another four rounds, equivalent to about eight years. At that point, a small crack occurs in the Warsaw Pact as Poland and Czechoslovakia distance themselves a bit from the Soviet Union, moving to -33 on the scale. With NATO having come apart and with tensions being very high, the United States seeks new partnerships. It links up with Czechoslovakia and Poland in an effort to redirect the system. However, American salience then drops markedly, suggesting an internal political crisis around 1972 (round 12). The internal distraction, combined with the loss of NATO, leads the United States down a gradual path of rapprochement with the Soviet Union on their terms. By round 17 (approximately 1982), the United States is in a new world order dominated by Soviet policy. The new balance of power is located at -66 on the scale. Of course, it is important to remember that the simulations indicate that such a scenario, though possible, was exceptionally unlikely to arise in reality. Recall that the vast majority of randomly selected scenarios yield a peaceful American—not Soviet—victory.

Figure 4.6 (Simulation 96) reinforces the view that the end of the Cold War was not inevitable. We can already see NATO emerging by round 2 in this simulation. By then, Canada, the Netherlands, France, Britain, Turkey, Norway, and others have shifted to a strongly pro-American position. The Warsaw Pact is also well formed. NATO continues to consolidate, adding Italy in the third iteration and Greece in the fourth. Most Asian and Middle Eastern states also shift to a pro-American posture, while the Soviet Union and its Warsaw Pact allies (and a few other states) remain anti-American and pro-Soviet. Although minor jockeying back and forth takes place after round 5, the system is essentially stabilized in a long-term, unchanging bipolar structure.

Interestingly, there is another scenario in which the Cold War, bipolar structure persists. If the salience variable is not permitted to change but is fixed across all iterations at 100, indicating that security remains the *paramount* concern, then the model emulates the structural, neorealist view of the world. Under those conditions, the Cold War persists in a highly stable environment. That is, the neorealist simulation fails to predict the end of the Cold War. It is consistent with Gaddis's claim that neorealism failed to anticipate this critical event. Indeed, neorealism's prediction of bipolar stability is borne out by the simulation while reality showed us quite a different outcome. Fluctuations in the relative importance of nonsecurity issues, such as domestic politics, economic or humanitarian concerns, as well as security issues, were an essential part of the actual end of the Cold War.

## Conclusions

The end of the Cold War did not depend on going down one unique path. Consequently, it is not important to establish that any one simulation was more likely to arise than any other. What is important is to see what the preponderance of possible paths lead to. Depending on how we define victory, between two-thirds and 78 percent of the simulated histories or paths from 1948 forward produced predictions that the Cold War would end on pro-American terms. The specific path may have been unique, but many paths or combinations of policies yield the same conclusion. This means that the end of the Cold War certainly was predictable as a function of path-interdependence. Predicting the particular details of the history that culminated in the American victory in the Cold War would, of course, require considerably more data, but then the model has also pointed out that ex ante there were "superior" histories to the one that actually played out. That is, there were alternative policies that could have led to a quicker, peaceful end to the Cold War on terms favorable to the United States. The few cases of Soviet victory, by contrast, were considerably more likely to arise through violence than through peaceful transition. The counterfactual histories simulated here give us insight into how we might plan the resolution of future policy disputes.

The end of World War II appears to have planted the seeds of a Cold War termination that took time to germinate. The ultimate end of the Cold War appears to have been an emergent property whose essential antecedents could already be detected in the world structure at least as of 1948. Finally, this retrospective analysis based on prospective data highlights the possibilities of using the EUM to evaluate long-term changes in foreign policy based on short-term perturbations in interests, much as the Concordat of Worms illustrated a short-term shift in policy with dramatic long-term consequences.

FIVE

# Global Democratization

LOOKING AT THE WORLD AT THE BEGINNING OF THE CURRENT MIL-lennium inevitably leads to a radically different perspective than one would have expected just two decades earlier. Then the Cold War was in full swing. Today it is just a fading memory. Then the vast majority of states in the world were hard-core autocracies. Today most of the states around the world are democratic. Then there was a raging struggle between socialist, planned economies and market forces. Today market forces dominate, with few socialist holdouts still in existence. Then everyone lived in the shadow of the threat of a nuclear holocaust. Today, while war is still far too commonplace, the threat of nuclear war seems remote. We live in a time of transition to a new world order, but what will be the outlines of that world order? I address this question now, in stages. In this chapter, I utilize the EUM and data from 1980 to project how *international* foreign policy pressures might have reshaped the world up to the present and beyond to approximately 2030. Later I use the EUM to investigate how domestic pressures might dampen or reinforce international conditions influencing the shape of future international politics. My focus here is on democratization.

Political leaders come and go, but the structure of a country's political system rarely undergoes drastic alteration. Dramatic changes in political institutions rarely occur incrementally and even less frequently arise without a major crisis. The sorts of situations that precipitate structural changes in regimes include financial crises that preclude incumbents from continuing to maintain the loyalty of cronies, as well as or accompanied by war, revolution, or coup d'état. The end of World War II, like the end of World War I, saw substantial global shifts in governance. As we saw in chapter 1, both of these world wars—won by democratic forces fighting autocratic rule—precipitated a sharp decline in the median country's level of democracy. How much of that decline was due to international pressure is difficult to say, though it would seem that domestic issues following on the war's end were more important. I say this for several reasons.

The victors in both World War I and World War II, on balance, favored greater democratization over less democracy, yet global developments run in the contrary direction. It is true that at the end of World War II the Soviets exerted substantial influence over the countries of Eastern and Central Europe, imposing and ensuring the maintenance of nondemocratic regimes. But it is equally true that the United States, Britain, and France exerted great influence over those West European countries they liberated from Nazi control just as they exerted political influence in Japan and other parts of Asia. Their influence might be thought to strongly favor democratization, though Bueno de Mesquita et al. (2003) offer an account of why democracies might favor promoting autocracy elsewhere. Certainly developments around the world favored autocracy and petty dictatorship.

Decolonization was one consequence of postwar allied emphasis on democracy and self-determination. The pressure for decolonization emerged in some places even before World War I, but was given strong impetus by Woodrow Wilson's fourteen points. Recall that the fourteen points emphasized the right of self-determination as a fundamental human right. Although often with substantial resistance and reluctance by democratic imperial powers, decolonization pushed forward after World War II. Virtually every state that gained its freedom did so under initially democratic institutional arrangements. However, the leaders in a vast majority of these newly liberated states, having attained office, then found ways to suspend competitive elections and resort to rigged systems which ensured that they would retain power. There are perfectly understandable incentives that make this regrettable development predictable. Leaders who rule over rigged electoral systems are better able to keep themselves in office than are their democratic counterparts. As long as an autocrat's economy produces sufficient wealth to bribe the few cronies or military officers whose support is needed to keep them in power, autocrats can survive fairly readily as political leaders even in the face of war, pestilence, famine, and misery (Bueno de Mesquita et al. 2003). The post–World War II changes in favor of autocratic institutions were the product of domestic choices—reinforced by democratic imperial incentives—based on altered circumstances unleashed in the aftermath of war.

The postwar choices over rules of governance are noteworthy particularly with regard to two points. First, leaders, if unconstrained, prefer rigged electoral systems over democracy. This was the choice made by postcolonial leaders who won straight-out victories over the imperial powers. Where coalitions were victorious, as in India, rigged electoral systems did not take hold. Second, democratic leaders are more likely to be turned out of office than are autocrats. The risk of being deposed is much higher for democrats than for autocrats either when their domestic policies fail or when their state is vanquished in war (Bueno de Mesquita and Siverson 1995; Bueno de Mesquita et al. 2003). This means that there are more opportunities for democratic institutions to mutate into autocratic systems than there are for autocracies to mutate into democracies simply because the turnover rate in leaders is much higher in democracy than in autocracy.

While domestic factors probably play a larger immediate role in producing new patterns of governance than do international pressures, these domestic considerations often depend on or are the consequence of international circumstances. The sharp move toward democratization in the late 1980s and early 1990s illustrates this point. I investigate international factors in this chapter and then focus on domestic considerations in the next chapter.

## Helsinki: The New International Environment

To see how international circumstances set the stage for domestic decisions to shift toward a more democratic order, I begin with a brief discussion of the Final Act of the Helsinki Conference, generally referred to as the Helsinki Accords, signed in 1975. Thirty-five nations attended the Helsinki Conference with an eye to establishing agreement on the definition, protection, and promotion of human rights. The attendees included representatives from all of the then existing sovereign states in Europe (except Albania), as well as the United States and Canada. All thirty-five participating states signed the final act.

The Helsinki Accords occurred against the backdrop of a willingness of the participants to recognize the separate sovereign status of the German Democratic Republic (East Germany) and the Federal Republic of Germany (West Germany). Thus, Helsinki provided the basis for officially ending World War II and codifying the partition of Germany. The permanent division of Germany had long been an issue of contention between the former allies of World War II: the United States, Britain, and France on one side, and the Soviet Union on the other. The Soviet Union was eager to gain recognition of the permanent division of Germany and the western powers were equally eager to promote a human rights agenda. Helsinki was convened to resolve these interests. Ironically, and as an unintended consequence of the final act, Helsinki set in motion changes that a mere fifteen years later resulted in the reunification of Germany and the dissolution of the Soviet "empire."

The Soviet Union agreed to the Helsinki Accords in order to ensure recognition of the independence of its dependent and allied state, the German Democratic Republic. In exchange for this recognition, the Soviets, probably unwittingly, set the stage for tremendous international pressure designed to foster democratization across Eastern and Central Europe. Much as the Concordat of Worms, 850 years earlier, precipitated significant unexpected changes in international affairs, so may have the Helsinki Accords. In the case of Worms, substantial changes in political institutions started right away, picked up momentum by 1139, and became truly dramatic by the mid-twelfth century. With that time line in mind, I examine likely developments between 1975 and 2030.

The thirty-five signatories to the final act reached seemingly innocuous agreements stipulating that:

> The participating States will respect human rights and fundamental freedoms, including the freedom of thought, conscience, religion or belief, for all without distinction as to race, sex, language, or religion.
>
> They will promote and encourage the effective exercise of civil, political, economic, social, cultural, and other rights and freedoms all of which derive from the inherent dignity of the human person and are essential for his free and full development. . . .
>
> The participating States recognize the universal significance of human rights and fundamental freedoms, respect for which is an essential factor for the peace, justice and well-being necessary to ensure the development of friendly relations and co-operation among themselves as among all States. (http://www.civnet.org/resources/historic/helsinki.htm)

Through these seemingly innocent terms, the Helsinki Accords permitted western states to assert something approximating a right to oversee and to influence domestic policies regarding human rights in any or all of the signatory states. Because the Soviet Union and its allies in the Warsaw Pact agreed to the final act, the other signatories had a legitimate basis to claim that they could question human rights policies in those states without being accused of infringing on the internal sovereign rights of the Soviets and their allies in Europe.

Human rights watchdog groups sprang up almost immediately within the Warsaw Pact countries and in the West. Both the former and the latter groups reported on human rights violations in the Soviet Union and especially in its allied states. They fomented government-to-government pressures to improve human rights conditions. Movements such as Solidarity in Poland and equivalent forces for free expression throughout Eastern Europe were bolstered by intense, legitimate scrutiny from the outside world, scrutiny fostered by the Final Act. Whereas the Soviets easily argued against foreign intervention during similar efforts to promote freedom in Hungary in 1956 or Czechoslovakia in 1968, their signature on the Helsinki Accords made such arguments hollow in the late 1970s and early 1980s. Thus, Helsinki established the foundation for international pressure to see democratic principles spread to the Soviet Union and Eastern Europe. Just how successful these pressures were can be gleaned by looking at how the world has changed since 1975.

In discussing global changes in systems of governance, I do not want to leave the impression that the Helsinki Accords stand alone as the cause of change. As at other times throughout history, an economic crisis accompanied many of the changes in political institutions. Helsinki did not precipitate or contribute to the economic pressures that the Soviet Union faced by the late 1980s. Those pressures are more likely the products of several circumstances, two of which stand out. One was the gross inefficiency of the Soviet, centrally planned economy (Gorbachev 1996). Soviet restrictions on market forces ensured that resources could not easily and flexibly flow within the economy in response to supply, demand, and comparative advantage. The inefficiency of the Soviet economy ensured a gradual descent into a financial crisis.

Second was Ronald Reagan's recognition that sooner or later Soviet military spending, if put under severe pressure by the United States, could not be maintained without resulting in economic collapse. As touched upon in chapter 4, by 1963 Reagan already contemplated that the Soviets could eventually be cajoled peacefully to change their system by American defense spending. His idea was that the United States could impose a choice on the Soviets between prohibitive defense spending and economic viability (Skinner, Anderson, and Anderson 2001). He recognized that America's huge economic advantage might permit the United States to win the Cold War by significantly increasing its military might. Reagan reasoned that the Soviet leadership would recognize that they could not keep up and might resign themselves to fundamental political changes. He had the good fortune to be president at a time when economic circumstances were right for this plan to work and when a new Soviet leader, Mikhail Gorbachev, rose to power and immediately set about the task of revising the Soviet economy (Gorbachev 1996) to ward off economic collapse. These and other factors, both domestic and international, contributed to the seemingly unforeseen changes that appear to have transformed the world.

## The Global Swing toward Democracy

The world has become vastly more democratic than it was at the time of the Helsinki Conference. Just how much more democratic can be gleaned by examining the median country's democracy rating according to the Polity IV data. Recall that I measure the degree of democracy as Polity's democracy indicator minus its autocracy indicator. The measure is normalized by adding 10 and dividing by 20. I multiply the result by 100 so that the index of democracy varies between 0 and 100 by intervals of 5 points. The result is a commonly used 21-point scale, with 100 being the score of the most democratic regimes and 0 the score for the most autocratic states.

The median country's score from 1975 through 1985 remained constant at a meager 15. By 1990 the median had risen to 60, and since 1992 the global median has maintained a score of 80. Figure 5.1 shows the distribution of scores across five-year snapshots up through 1999, the most recent year for which data are available. These snapshots show several points of interest.

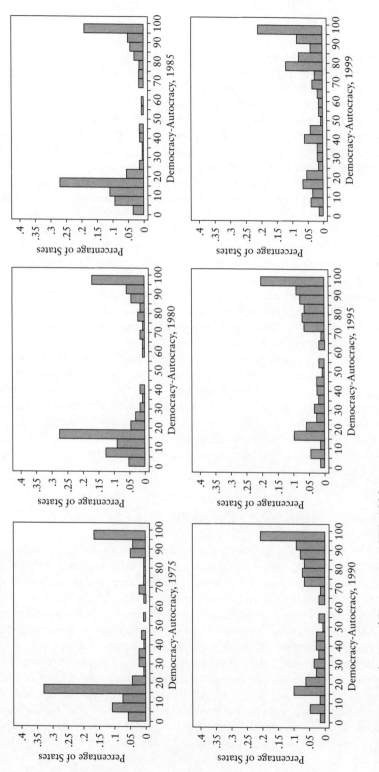

**Figure 5.1** Evolution of Democracy, 1975–1999

During the years 1975–1985, even as the median remained constant, regimes were shifting their structure of governance, albeit slowly. The world of this period was bipolar not only in terms of the rivalry between the United States and the Soviet Union, but also in terms of rivalry between autocracy and democracy. Societies with decidedly mixed systems were rare indeed. Of the thirteen nations for which Polity provides data in 1975, only four (Honduras, El Salvador, Guyana, and Singapore) had governance structures that fell within the range 40–60 on the democracy scale. Ten years later, six countries (Nicaragua, Senegal, Thailand, Zimbabwe, Nepal, and Singapore) fell in this range, with only one holdover from 1975 (Singapore). Of the three mixed regimes of 1975 that no longer were mixed in 1985, one (Guyana) slid toward greater autocracy, with a shift in score from 55 in 1975 to only 15 in 1985. Honduras and El Salvador, however, moved up from 45 to 75 and 80 respectively, supporting greater democratization. Perhaps even more telling of things to come, only Zimbabwe downgraded its democracy meaningfully over this ten-year period, shifting from a score of 70 in 1975 to a middling 55 in 1985. Thailand also backslid, but only by 5 points, to 60 from 65. By 1985, Senegal, Nepal, and Nicaragua all had scores between 40 and 45, up from scores between 5 and 20 in 1975.

The decades of the 1970s and the 1980s generally saw little large-scale change in governance. Though individual countries made sharp moves toward or away from democracy, the basic bipolar structure remained as a steady state. However, Figure 5.1 makes clear that the bipolar governance structure was severely eroded by 1990 and has remained eroded to the present. Was it possible to have predicted this dramatic shift while still correctly predicting the essentially steady state of the previous years? That is the question to which I now turn.

## EUM and Governance, 1980–2000

The Polity democracy-autocracy indicator can readily be used to infer the governance structure supported by each country, partially in response to domestic considerations and partially in response to international pressures. I select 1980 as a benchmark year and construct a data set appropriate for the EUM based on national positions on a scale reflecting preference for autocracy (0) or democracy (100). The Polity score is used as a replicable, objective indicator of stated national positions on preference for governance type as of 1980. I have selected the year 1980 for both substantive and practical reasons.

None of the spectacular changes that brought an end to the Cold War and fostered interest in the new world order was readily apparent in 1980. Ronald Reagan had not yet assumed the presidency of the United States. Leonid Brezhnev remained in control of the Soviet Union. America's attention was riveted on the just-ended Iran hostage crisis, while the Soviets were enmeshed in their Afghan war. A year earlier, that war brought efforts at détente between the United States and the Soviet Union to a crashing halt.

In Asia, the Asian miracle was only just underway. Deng Xiao Ping was beginning to stimulate economic growth in China, while holding firmly to autocratic rule. Taiwan and South Korea, key Asian "tigers," also remained firmly autocratic. Taiwan's democracy score, like China's, was 15 while South Korea earned a meager 10.

The few examples I have offered illustrate the difficulties 1980 presents as a baseline for predicting radical changes in governance around the world. That alone makes 1980 an attractive starting point. A practical consideration, however, adds to the attraction that 1980 holds. The data necessary to produce indicators of salience, power, and position are available for over 100 countries in 1980. This means that I can conduct a rather comprehensive simulation. Thus, 1980 is chosen as the benchmark.

I have already explained the source of data with which I measure stated policy positions. To evaluate relative national power, I take advantage of World Bank data for 1980. The indicator of national power is Gross Domestic Product, assessed as real per capita GDP multiplied by total population for each country. Salience, not surprisingly, is the most challenging variable to estimate.

I begin by assuming that national leaders seek to maximize their tenure in office. How long a leader lasts depends strongly on the institutional setting in which the incumbent governs. Incumbents in democracies have good reason to expect to be out of office much sooner than incumbents in autocracies. Indeed, the average autocrat (democracy-autocracy is less than or equal to 25) survives in office more than twice as long as the average democrat (score of 75 or higher). How focused a leader is on governance structure may well vary with how much longer the leader expects to remain in office. Regime change, when it happens at all, occurs relatively early in a leader's term in office. This suggests that salience for institutional arrangements is highest when a leader first comes to power so that the new incumbent anticipates a long remaining time in office and many opportunities to alter institutional arrangements. Salience, I assume, declines later as a leader has adjusted to existing arrangements or has utilized opportunities to restructure the system. With this in mind, I estimate longevity in office by regressing democracy-autocracy, tenure-to-date, current year, and per capita income on each leader's total tenure in office for the years 1950 through 1979. The length of the time period for the regression is determined in part by practical data considerations. I do not have per capita GDP data for years prior to 1950 and I wish to use each leader's information prior to 1980 to estimate his or her salience in 1980. The resulting regression analysis is summarized in Table 5.1.

The estimated values, which I call Longevity, serve as approximations of a leader's *expected* remaining time in office. I then use this information to

**Table 5.1**
Expected Tenure in Office

| Variable | Coefficient (Std. Error) | Probability |
|---|---|---|
| Democracy-Autocracy | −3.604 | 0.000 |
| | (0.341) | |
| Per Capita GDP | −0.0001 | 0.006 |
| | (0.00004) | |
| Time in Office to Date | 1.078 | 0.000 |
| | (0.015) | |
| Year | −0.296 | 0.023 |
| | (0.013) | |
| Constant | 65.347 | 0.011 |
| | (2.544) | |

N = 2990     F = 1635.88     $R^2 = 0.69$

approximate salience for the issue of governance by computing Salience = [(Longevity − Time in Office to Date)/Longevity] * 100. The estimated values for salience, along with the rest of the data used in the EUM simulation, can be found in the appendix. In essence, the indicator suggests that the longer a leader expects to remain in power, the higher the incumbent's salience for institutional arrangements. Salience, by this estimation method, averages 58.76, with a high of 100 and a low of 13.35.

Naturally, others may prefer to estimate salience using a different procedure or different underlying theory. One virtue of the EUM is that those who disagree with the assumptions behind my estimation of salience need not accept them. They can construct their own indicator and do their own simulation to see how alternative approaches to approximating salience influence the predicted unfolding of events. The particular method I have used is consistent with empirical findings regarding longevity in office and institutional change (Bueno de Mesquita et al. 2003) and is fully reproducible.

As in the simulation of the end of the Cold War in chapter 4, I treat each round of the EUM analysis of democratization as roughly equal to two years of actual time. This means that the simulation includes predicted values from 1982 through 2028 as well as real values for 1980. Since ex post, real estimates of democratization from 1980 to 1999 are readily available through Polity IV, we can compare simulated results to nearly twenty years of actual observations, as well as discussing predictions about an additional approximately thirty years of history yet to come.

The simulations are based on approximately 100 countries. The first question to ask is how well, on average, does the simulation do at capturing the dramatic changes in democratization around the world, with the world defined as the countries, listed in the appendix, for which I have sufficient data to undertake the simulation. To answer this question, I compare the global median according to the Polity estimate of democracy-autocracy to the median of the simulation in each time period. The result is displayed graphically in Figure 5.2.

Figure 5.2 highlights several important aspects of the EUM's first twenty years of simulated future based on 1980s data. The EUM simulation predicts that the Cold War would end around 1986 or 1987 when the median country reaches the relatively stable predicted level of post–Cold War democratization. In actuality, the Cold War did not end until slightly later, in 1988 or 1989. The ex ante level of democratization predicted by the EUM for 1988–1989 equals the ex post observed level of democratization recorded by Polity. The two lines—reality and simulation—intersect each other at the time the Cold War is generally said to have ended.

The EUM and reality parallel one another exceptionally well, albeit the EUM rises a little faster and levels off at a somewhat lower level. The actual correlation between the two series of median values is 0.90 (N=10). Although only ten time periods are tested here, still the correlation is high enough that it would occur by chance on only four out of ten thousand samples.

Reality as measured ex post by Polity IV shows a median degree of democratization equal to 90 from about 1992 onward. This is in comparison to a median score for this sample of countries of only 30 in 1980. The EUM predicts a median from 1990 forward of about 80. Anyone in 1980, using then current data and the EUM (its first incarnation was developed in 1979 and the first publication using it to make a real-time forecast was published in 1984), would have been dismissed as a hopeless optimist for

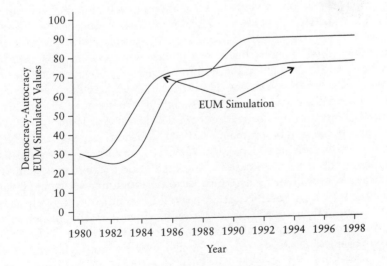

**Figure 5.2** Simulated and Actual Democratization

predicting that the median country around 1990 would have a democracy score of about 80. That the model actually *underestimates* the true democracy score by so little seems to indicate that the simulation provides a rather reliable picture of the world twenty years beyond the date of the initial known values. The model's dynamics that predict changes in positions seems to have captured the future accurately even though no information not known in 1980 was used.

The global median provides a powerful but limited perspective on change. To get a better picture of the reliability of the simulated results, I compare the true series to the predicted series of country scores across the time period and also year by year. In doing so, I use Spearman's rank order correlation rather than the product-moment correlation. The results are, of course, similar and all the product-moment correlations have a probability of being due to chance of 0.0000. This is also true for the Spearman correlations. I prefer the rank order statistic because the data are ordinal, not interval, and the relative degree of democracy, country by country, is of greater interest than the absolute and ultimately arbitrary score beyond ordering. When I say that the rank order is of greater interest, I mean this in a substantive and substantial sense. I will repeatedly return later to rank order information because national comparative advantages (or disadvantages) in securing investments, dispute resolution, and peace and prosperity will be shown to depend more on rank position than on absolute score in democratization. This observation has substantial implications with regard both to how we study the future and to how the future is likely to look.

Table 5.2 provides the Spearman rank order correlation statistics between simulated national positions on democratization and now known positions. These summary statistics measure how well the simulated ordering of states fits with reality on a year-by-year basis. Naturally the correlations decline as we move farther away from the starting point, but it is noteworthy how slowly they decline. The first correlation shows that over the initial two years of the simulation (that is, between the base data and the first iteration of the model) there was very little difference between actuality and prediction. Even a decade later the association remains very strong. From about 1990 onward, the correlation between the rank ordering of states in reality and in the simulation remains almost constant, and actually rises in the last year of available observed data (1998). The correlation across all of the time series is a very strong 0.77. The simulation reliably, though imperfectly, captures the evolving democratization of the countries in the sample.

Before looking at specific cases, we should examine one more especially tough test to evaluate the EUM's performance in anticipating democratization. I construct a variable called Δ Democracy and another called Δ EUM. The former measures the known change in democracy-autocracy score from 1980 to 1998 for each country. The latter does the same, but based on the simulated changes in position on the democratization scale. Remember that

**Table 5.2**
Year-by-Year Correlation: Simulated and Actual Democratization

| Year | Spearman Correlation | $N^a$ |
|------|---------------------|-----|
| 1982 | 0.92 | 97 |
| 1984 | 0.86 | 97 |
| 1986 | 0.79 | 95 |
| 1988 | 0.73 | 97 |
| 1990 | 0.69 | 94 |
| 1992 | 0.66 | 87 |
| 1994 | 0.61 | 88 |
| 1996 | 0.61 | 89 |
| 1998 | 0.66 | 86 |
| All Years | 0.77 | 830 |

[a] The number of countries varies from year to year because, while the set in the EUM is fixed, the set in the Polity data changes as a result of shifts in sovereignty. For instance, Polity notes the dissolution of Czechoslovakia into two states, while the EUM, based only on information known in 1980 and not having been used to model state emergence or dissolution, is unable to track the new countries that result from the dissolution.

the simulated changes are the product only of the initial data and the logic of the EUM. The results are not derived from some statistical procedure that continually takes into account the latest known information about any observation. No information goes into the simulation other than the initial data from 1980.

With this test we get a picture of how well the EUM does in shifting individual country scores correctly in the sense of reflecting the relative ordering of states in terms of their degree of democracy. To appreciate the difficulty of this test, consider the distribution of changes across the 84 countries in both the 1980 and 1998 samples. The average country's true democracy score increased 24.6 points, with a standard deviation of 32.3. The largest decline was 30 points and the largest increase was 85 points. The EUM predicts an average increase in democracy of 18.1 points, with a standard deviation of 33.6. It predicts the largest decline as 23 points and the largest increase as 67 points. Thus, both the EUM and reality show great variation in shifts. Yet the correlation between the true changes and the predicted changes is 0.73 (N=84). The Spearman rank order correlation for the change in scores indicates substantial success in predicting the correct change in the ordering of states.

## EUM and the Future of Democratization

The results reported thus far are intended to lend credibility to the forecasts made beyond the year 2000. Clearly, the detailed reliability of a long-range forecast must deteriorate the farther one looks into the future. Exogenous events outside the frame of reference of the issues examined can perturb the system in ways that deflect it from the otherwise anticipated course of events. For example, domestic affairs, which are partially evaluated in the next chapter, can significantly disrupt trends based solely on external, international influences. Later in this chapter I introduce random shocks in the form of randomized changes in salience scores to evaluate the robustness of the predictions. Before turning to these checks on robustness, however, some comment is in order on expected and observed patterns of democratization regarding specific countries.

The standard of what constitutes a fully democratic, mostly democratic, somewhat democratic, somewhat autocratic society changes over time. Polity, for instance, scores the United States as a perfect 100 on the democracy-autocracy index from 1871 onward, and also scores the United States as a 100 from 1845 to 1849. But a country today that follows governance practices equivalent to those followed by the United States in the late nineteenth or early twentieth century probably would not be considered fully democratic by current standards. After all, the United States imposed severe restrictions on voting rights. As a legal matter, women could not vote in national elections. As a practical matter, African Americans could not vote in much of the country. Likewise, we should be cautious in holding the belief that a country that scores 100 today will measure up to the highest standard in thirty years if it continues to follow current practices.

When I raise the issue of how a country will measure up in the future, I have several practical considerations in mind. The EUM predicts a fairly stable leveling off of global democratization over the next thirty years. That is, the impressive burst toward greater global democracy that arose in the late 1980s and early 1990s seems unlikely to be repeated again soon. Much as we saw earlier periods of flatness in movement toward democratization in the past (see Figure 1.1, especially the years between 1875 and 1900), the model anticipates such flatness in the next few decades. Within this global flatness, however, countries continue to shift up or down in their democratization. The most dramatic aspect of this change is in the compression of regime types. For instance, across all states, the average democracy score in 1980 was 40.78, with a standard deviation of 39.05. By 1998 the mean had risen to 63.76 while the standard deviation shrank to 34.29. The comparable values in 1998 for the EUM countries were 69.69 and 16.89. The EUM estimates that by 2020 the mean score will be 73.59 with a standard deviation of only 9.24. What does this mean? If the past is a guide, it means that what people come to expect of a government will change. The bar will be raised in terms of what constitutes democratic governance.

We can already see the standards or expectation being raised. Consider Russia in 2000 and in 1980. Clearly, Russia was vastly more democratic and freer in the year 2000 than was the Soviet Union in 1980. This fact is certainly reflected in Polity's ex post assessment and in the EUM's ex ante predictions. Russia's democracy-autocracy score rose between 1980 and 1998 from 15 to 70, while its EUM score rose from 15 to 77. Yet it was common in 2000 and it is common today to express concerns about the commitment Russian leaders have to democratic practices. One possible explanation for this continued concern is Russia's position in the global "pecking order." In 1980, many states had very autocratic governments; today only a few do. The result is that Russia's score in 1998 of 70 would have earned it a ranking of 54.5 out of 74 ranks (with many ties) in 1980. At the turn of the millennium that same democracy value earned only a ranking of 23.5 out of 84 (again with many ties). In 1980, Russia's actual score of 15 earned a ranking of 28.5, *a higher relative position than Russia achieved in 1998.* So the perceived improvement in absolute democracy is accompanied by a deterioration in freedom for Russia relative to global freedom. This difference is extremely important because how others react to a government is partially determined by its relative advantage.

Consider the decisions of prospective investors seeking places to build or support businesses. Institutional guarantees of property rights, civil liberties, rule of law, and so forth play an important part in influencing decisions about where foreigners invest. Investment and the economic benefits it can bring flows to places that offer comparative advantage in terms of larger expected marginal returns on funds placed at risk. More democratic governments generally offer more protection to investors by promoting rule of law, property rights, transparency and the like than do less democratic systems. Consider, for instance, the difference in the experiences of Russia and Hungary between 1980 and 1999.

Polity scored both Russia and Hungary as 15 on the democracy-autocracy scale in 1980, tied at 28.5 in ranking. By 1998, as we just saw, Russia's rank position dropped, while Hungary's rose to 74, the highest rank score achieved in 1998, based on 87 countries and many ties. Hungary has done exceptionally well at attracting investment and improving its economy; Russia has not. Chapter 7 demonstrates that this is no fluke. With this in mind, let me speculate about places that will become relatively much more or much less attractive between 1998 (the most current estimates for both the EUM and Polity series) and 2010.

Table 5.3 identifies the five best and five worst risks in terms of *improvement* or *deterioration* in their democracy ranking between 1998 and 2010. Let me be clear—these are not the most democratic or the least democratic countries. Europe, the United States, and so forth remain at the top of the democracy rankings, but then the marketplace already knows that they are good places to invest.[34] The question is who becomes much more attractive than they currently are and who becomes much less attractive.

Again let me emphasize that the "worst" countries in Table 5.3 are not necessarily becoming absolutely less democratic. Rather, much of the rest of

**Table 5.3**
The "Best" and the "Worst" Changes in Democraticness: 2010–1998

| Country | Best Change in Rank (EUM rank in 2010- Polity Rank in 1998) | Country | Worst Change in Rank |
|---------|------|---------|------|
| Malaysia | +54.5 | Uruguay | –47.5 |
| China | +45.0 | Bolivia | –46.0 |
| Venezuela | +43.5 | Philippines | –34.0 |
| Mauritania | +42.5 | Haiti | –31.0 |
| Cameroon | +40.5 | Rumania | –30.0 |

the world is becoming more democratic faster, placing these countries at a relative disadvantage, just as the "best" performers are gaining relative institutional advantage. Of course, many other considerations, such as the cost of the factors of production, proximity to markets, particular skills in the labor force, and so forth enter into investment decisions. Still, all else being equal, Table 5.3 points to those who are likely to see significant improvement (the "best") or significant deterioration (the "worst") in their economic performance. Some on the list, like Haiti, already are in terrible straits, so the failure to improve its institutions reinforces an already tragic set of conditions. The others among the worst performers are countries about which, for various reasons, many are more hopeful. If the predictions are correct, these countries will diminish further in their attractiveness to investors. Interestingly, some Latin American countries are expected to do exceptionally well (Venezuela and Colombia, ranked third and sixth respectively in improvement in democracy), while others are expected to do exceptionally poorly (Uruguay, Bolivia). Among these Latin American states, all had rather democratic political institutions as of 1998. The difference is that the poor performers are expected to stagnate or backslide while the good performers are expected to maintain or improve their position while others around them slip. The most exciting prospect, in terms of global freedom and global markets, accompanies the prediction that China's degree of democracy will improve dramatically both absolutely and relatively. If this proves correct—I examine domestic political pressures in China on this issue in the next chapter—then the portion of the world's population living in freedom will take a great leap forward by the end of the first decade of the current millennium. Alas, as we will see, any note of optimism must be sounded with great caution.

By 2028, further compression in the range of democracy scores takes place, raising expectations still more. By that time, Europe loses considerably in terms of its political comparative advantage, not because it abandons democracy, but because so much of the world catches up with it. Those playing catch-up and performing particularly well by about 2028, like Pakistan and Bangladesh, Zambia, Bolivia, Algeria, and even Haiti, are also places that investors have generally avoided. Though many of these countries fail to attain or even come close to European levels of democracy, their strides forward coupled with their relative underdevelopment economically should make them more attractive investment sites in the longer-term future than they were in 2001. If the EUM is right, I cannot be equally sanguine about Mozambique, Somalia, Togo, Sudan, Tanzania, Guyana, Rumania, Bulgaria, and others. Although they do not deteriorate a lot, they do deteriorate. Since they are generally starting at relatively modest levels of democracy and even more modest levels of investment, their long-term prospects look bleak.

## Random Shocks and Robustness

The predictions discussed thus far assume that salience remains fixed across the entire time period and all of the countries. This is, of course, unrealistic. To evaluate the robustness of the general tendencies found among the pre-dictions—as opposed to exact values—I allow any country's salience score to vary randomly each period, that is, each iteration in the model. Country salience values are chosen by chance each round, with each country having a 20 percent probability of being selected. If selected by the random draw, the salience score is allowed to move randomly up or down within the range of admissible values. Across many simulations, these random changes are a way of capturing the expected effects of currently unforeseen shocks such as major domestic events, major upturns or downturns in the global or local economy, and so forth. The point is that these are unforeseeable events and so the random shocks simulate unspecified social, political, or economic earthquakes that heighten or dampen attentiveness to the mode of gover-nance. The shock can raise one country's score while decreasing another's and while leaving about 80 percent of such scores unchanged from its value in the previous iteration in any given round.

Figure 5.3 displays the pattern of predicted democratization values for Russia and China only. They are not terribly unlike the rest of the sample in showing strong central tendencies toward the baseline case discussed thus far. What is more, these two countries are of great interest to foreign policy decision makers and they are the focus of simulations of domestic processes in the next chapter.

The dotted lines in Figure 5.3 reflect, from top to bottom, China's most democratic performance, simulation to simulation and round by round; China's median simulated score each round; and China's lowest democrati-zation score each round. The solid lines, in the same order, reflect the same information about Russia. Recall that this graph and all of the analysis in

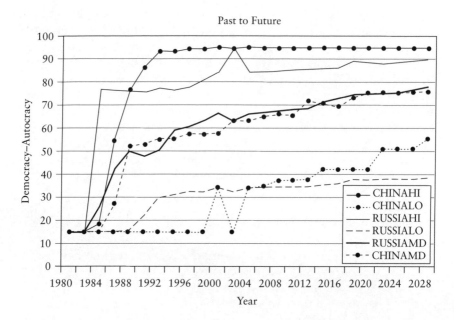

**Figure 5.3** Random Shocks to Democratization: Russia and China

this chapter is based *only* on external, international pressures for and against democratization.

There are important insights to extract from Figure 5.3. The simulations with random shocks almost always produce the patterns displayed here. Russia almost always democratizes sooner than China. Russia almost always democratizes less than China by the end of the simulated time period. Russia almost always follows a smoother path to a limited democracy, whereas China experiences more frequent fits and starts. When democratization is delayed, as in the two lowest curves, it is always delayed much longer for China than it is for Russia. This is especially important to keep in mind as we turn toward an investigation of domestic pressures.

The central tendency across all of the simulations is to indicate that the Cold War was unlikely to survive past about 1990. Whether examined from the perspective of the base case data or from the distribution of values across many simulations with random shocks, this is the fundamental insight of the simulations regarding the period up to the present. The simulations show a strong likelihood that democratization will improve very modestly on average over the next three decades. It is unlikely that we will see consequential global retrenchment, though individual countries ebb and flow in their commitment to democracy. The robustness of the predicted increase in democratization is reflected in Figure 5.4 where the median democratization values, round by round (or year by year) are plotted for a representative sample

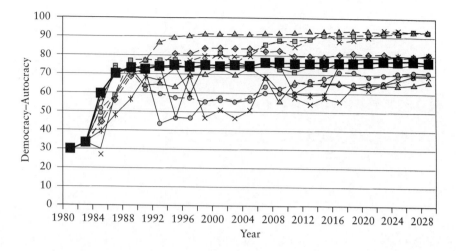

**Figure 5.4** Random Shocks and Democratization

of simulations. The darkest line is the median of all simulated median values for each round and so represents the average expectation across the simulations.

It is evident from Figure 5.4 that the simulations produce a consistent expectation that the world would democratize substantially starting around the late 1980s. Some simulations suggest smooth progress while others show fits and starts, but still, all seem to converge on a high degree of global democracy by the year 1990 or so. Even the worst case scenarios show marked improvement in democracy over the levels of the early 1980s.

It is evident from Figure 5.4 that social, political, and economic earthquakes are unlikely to undo the path toward further modest improvements in democratization. Even the worst case scenario in Figure 5.4 indicates a global median of nearly 70. While this is not as attractive as the world we currently live in, it is a great improvement over the last years of the Cold War. Anyone who wonders whether the end of the Cold War is just an inconsequential blip in history would do well to reflect that both reality to date and the future as predicted by the EUM indicate that we live in a new age, an age of democracy. How will this international trend toward democratization react to domestic pressures in key countries? That is the topic on which the next chapter focuses.

# SIX

# Democratization
# and Domestic Pressures

CHANGES IN GOVERNANCE POLICIES DEPEND TO A SUBSTANTIAL degree on what goes on inside individual states. Foreign pressure often sets the stage for institutional change, but domestic political calculations usually determine how external pressure translates into internal action. What is more, internal circumstances often prove sufficient to produce institutional changes in the absence of international pressure. International pressure alone is neither necessary nor sufficient to produce fundamental restructuring of political institutions. Domestic calculations of the costs and benefits associated with alternative political arrangements are sufficient, though they are not necessary for institutional change. They are not necessary because victors in war may externally impose such changes with or without the support of domestic interests in the vanquished state.

The two most influential autocracies of the post–World War II years were the Soviet Union and the People's Republic of China. Though often at odds with one another, these two states led the movement against competitive democracy, fostering revolution around the world and promoting autocratic rule wherever their allies succeeded in taking control of government. The primary successor to the Soviet Union, Russia, is no longer an autocracy. China remains firmly in the now greatly diminished camp of autocratic states. In this chapter I investigate domestic political pressures in each of these societies. The object is to see what the EUM suggests about the future of democracy in Russia and China.

## Simulating Russia's Future

The Cold War ended without a violent confrontation between its main protagonists, the United States and the Soviet Union. The leaders of the Soviet Union, faced with external pressure arising from the Helsinki Accord and international movements, and also faced with domestic pressure in the form of economic malaise and political unrest, made momentous decisions that resulted in a mostly peaceful collapse of the Soviet Union and its replacement by a host of independent states. Russia is the largest and perhaps strategically most important among the successor states of the old Soviet Union. This is not to underestimate the importance of the Ukraine or others; rather, it is simply recognition that Russia above all others is the successor to the Soviet Union.

We saw in the two previous chapters that the Soviet Union faced enormous difficulties in surviving as an autocracy. Simulations based on data from 1948 clearly showed that the Soviet Union had only a small chance of winning the Cold War. Recall that only 11 percent of the simulations ended in that eventuality. Simulations based on data from 1980 reinforce the view that the Soviet system of autocratic rule was endangered. It appears from the simulations almost inevitable that external forces would, by the late 1980s, shift the tectonic plates of the seemingly encrusted Soviet government. But what about domestic responses after the collapse of the USSR? In the wake of severe economic dislocations and political depression, is it likely that the Russian leadership will sustain a democratic government or is it more likely that Russia will slide toward a new form of autocracy?

As with the previous two chapters, I simulate the pattern of domestic political pressure within Russia based on data collected several years ago. In this instance, the data are from 1995. These data were gathered by Decision Insights, Incorporated, a New York–based consulting firm, for the purpose of analyzing likely developments in Russia following the 1996 presidential election. Decision Insights has generously permitted me to use their data.

The 1995 Russian domestic data are useful from several perspectives. We have the opportunity to see how events turned out for several years since the data were gathered. This allows for a check on the reliability of the simulations over a period of known outcomes, while still allowing for an assessment of future trends. Unlike the earlier simulations, however, these data are not extended out for fifty years. Rather, because the data were collected with the idea of making predictions one and one-half years in advance, I treat each round as equal to approximately six months, as most data sets resolve according to the model's time discount rule (see chapter 3) in about three rounds. The simulations apply, then, from 1995 through about 2008.

## Base Case Analysis

Naturally the domestic forces and sources of influence in Russia, or in any country, change from time to time. Boris Yeltsin, a stakeholder in the 1995 data, is no longer a significant political force in Russia. But the stakeholder identified in the data set as Yeltsin, displayed in Table 6.1, is not just Boris Yeltsin as an individual. The stakeholder represents Yeltsin and other influential players identified as part of his bloc. Thus, we can draw inferences about the rise and decline of blocs of influence through the simulations.

**Table 6.1**
Russian Data, 1995

| Stakeholder | Description of Stakeholder | Resources | Position | Salience |
|---|---|---|---|---|
| Army | Army | 70 | 35 | 85 |
| Bus&Banks | Big business and banks | 80 | 85 | 85 |
| CPZiuganov | Communist Party–Ziuganov | 85 | 55 | 90 |
| Chernomyrd | Chernomyrdin and Industrial Complex | 85 | 75 | 75 |
| EastEur | East Europe | 20 | 85 | 60 |
| Gaidar | Gaidar and Russia Choice Bloc | 60 | 100 | 85 |
| IndepReps | Independent Republics | 20 | 65 | 65 |
| Lapshin | Lapshin | 50 | 25 | 85 |
| MassMedia | Mass Media | 85 | 75 | 80 |
| MilDefCmpl | Military Defense Complex | 65 | 65 | 70 |
| ModDems | Gorbachev Moderate Democrats | 40 | 70 | 60 |
| NATO and USA | NATO and USA | 30 | 100 | 40 |
| ProRusRepb | Pro Russia Republics | 30 | 70 | 70 |
| RadComNat | Radical Communists and Nationalists | 25 | 0 | 100 |
| Regionals | Regional Authorities | 70 | 65 | 70 |
| RusMafia | Russian Mafia | 80 | 45 | 70 |
| Rybkin | Rybkin and Moderate leftists | 45 | 60 | 80 |
| SecForces | Security Forces | 60 | 35 | 70 |
| SkokovLebd | Skokov and Lebed | 75 | 65 | 65 |
| Unions | Independent Trade Unions | 65 | 35 | 80 |
| YabFedGrp | Yablinski and Federov group | 70 | 100 | 85 |
| YeltsinLoy | Yeltsin and Loyalists | 65 | 60 | 70 |
| Zhirnovsky | Zhirnovsky | 50 | 25 | 65 |

The first point of note in Table 6.1 is that even as late as 1995 there were Russian interests promoting the idea of a return to extreme authoritarianism. Included among these were the army, Lapshin, Zhirnovsky, the independent trade unions, security forces, and the radical communists and nationalists. Collectively, these antidemocratic interests represent nearly 25 percent of domestic Russian political influence or power. These pro-authoritarian interests cannot be taken lightly. The strongly pro-democracy interests—say, those whose position is at or above 85—are not as powerful. They represent less than 20 percent of political power in Russia, at least as of 1995.

Barring events sufficient to alter the landscape of salience for Russia's political institutions, the domestic picture is consistent with the international picture for Russia. By around 2000 the situation is expected to have pretty much stabilized. The stable equilibrium level of democracy rooted in the domestic base case analysis is almost identical to the level predicted as a function of international pressure: 75. This level is reached around 1999 or 2000.

Although, as we saw in the previous chapter, a score of 75 makes Russia only a middling democracy at the turn of the millennium, with the world marching toward greater democratic commitment faster than is Russia, 75 is still a far cry from the backsliding desired by leaders who represent about one-fourth of Russia's domestic political resource base. On an encouraging note, the most antidemocratic forces recognize, at least in the base case simulation (that is, without random shocks), that their political stance as of 1995 is a losing proposition. As long as circumstances do not alter the focus on political institutions, the antidemocratic hardliners are predicted to adjust their viewpoint. Most accept the idea of a middle-of-the-road position, not strongly autocratic and not strongly democratic, roughly equivalent to around 50–55 on the democracy scale. Put in perspective, this is the 1999 democracy score in the Polity IV data for Ethiopia, Liberia, and Zambia. These states certainly are far from paragons of democracy, but they are a substantial improvement in governance style over Belarus, China, Angola, Cameroon, or Saudi Arabia. These latter states have governments that meet the structurally autocratic goals of Russia's hardliners as of 1995. That is, they share a Polity rating roughly equivalent to the expressed preferences of Russia's hardliners reflected in Table 6.1.

### Random Shocks

The base case analysis is suggestive, but the likelihood that Russia will not experience political shocks is remote indeed. Therefore, the base case is a starting point, but hardly represents a firm foundation for predicting future political developments. To make such predictions, I return to the method used in chapters 4 and 5 by introducing random shocks into the data set. The shocks take the form of a 20 percent chance that any stakeholder in any round will experience a change in focus on political institutions. Salience can move up or down any amount within the admissible range of values, with the exact magnitude of movement for any stakeholder being determined by a random draw of values between 1 and 100. By allowing salience to shift, the model introduces random shocks to several of its elements. First, realized power, that is, actual influence, is reflected by the product of power and salience so that a shift in salience is tantamount to a change up or down in a player's actual influence. Second, salience reflects attentiveness to an issue. Players with lower salience are more susceptible to "making deals" or to stumbling into disputes and those with higher salience tend to behave as if they are more committed to their policy stance. Third, the estimated rates at which stakeholders trade off between policy satisfaction and personal political satisfaction vary as a function of salience. So, varying salience allows for a wide variety of nonlinear effects on round-to-round bargaining.

Most importantly for the purposes here, random shocks simulate the impact of unforeseen, unspecified exogenous changes in the Russian domestic political environment. Thus, this method provides a way to assess how vulnerable Russia is to substantial improvement or deterioration in its degree of democracy as a function of as-yet unknown changes to the political environment.

The first perspective I examine regarding the effects of random shocks is what these shocks suggest about the overall degree to which Russia is or will remain committed to a democratic path. The base case forecast started out at 65 on the democracy index, rose slowly to 72 and then, around 1997, dropped to 59, only to rise again, reaching the predicted steady-state equilibrium of 75 by century's end. Across fifty simulations with random shocks, the EUM leads to the conclusion that the base case assessment is overly optimistic. The median forecast with random shocks starts at 65 and does not rise above 68. Again to help with perspective, a score of 65 equals the actual Polity IV rating of Iran and Peru in 1999. If the EUM is right, Russia stands to lose about eight places in the ranking of states in terms of its degree of democracy. For a country already struggling to attract investment and to meet its people's needs, such slippage, if it proves correct, could be extremely costly.

There is another, perhaps more troubling way to think about Russia's prospects as predicted by the EUM with random shocks. Figure 6.1 displays a sampling of simulated Russian futures based on the domestic assessment. The dark solid line with circles punctuating it reflects the median predicted outcome across the sample of simulations with random shocks. The dark dashed line near the top of the figure shows the base case prediction round by round. The other lighter dotted lines depict the range of predicted outcomes, from most optimistic to most pessimistic, based on simulations with random shocks.

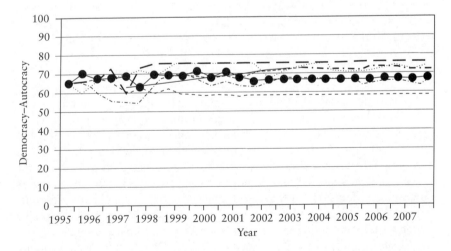

**Figure 6.1** Random Shocks and Russia's Domestic Views of Democratization

Two features of the figure are striking. First, the range of values predicted year by year and simulation to simulation is very narrow. That is, shocks to the Russian political system are unlikely to precipitate a great expansion or contraction of Russian democracy. Second, the base case appears to be a rosy, best case scenario. No simulation predicts Russia will be more democratic than the initial, "unshocked" data suggest, and most predict a less democratic Russia. This is evident from the fact that the median value round by round of the simulations is generally at a lower level of democratization than is the base case prediction.

The political faction identified in the data with Boris Yeltsin has been and remains the dominant political grouping in Russia. Though Yeltsin has personally passed from the political scene, his hand-picked successor, Vladimir Putin, replaced him as the Russian president. Putin, the former head of the KGB, is suspect among many western democrats who fear that he harbors antidemocratic ambitions. The fact that prominent individuals who oppose Putin politically have found themselves accused by the Putin government of corruption and other crimes lends some credence to western concerns. It is reasonable to inquire, then, about the prospects of a marked shift in orientation toward governance structure by the Yeltsin/Putin bloc, Putin's cooperation with the U.S. during its war against terrorism in Afghanistan notwithstanding.

This bloc's stance on democratization as of 1995 placed them at 60 on the scale, favoring less democracy than the Polity IV data set attributed to Russia as of that year. Polity gave Russia a rating of 70. The EUM domestic data predict an equilibrium level of democracy in 1995 equivalent to 65 on the Polity scale, while under international pressure the EUM predicts Russia's score in 1995 as 77. So, the predicted scores based on the EUM baseline data closely approximate reality in 1995. Both Polity and the EUM score overall are consistent with the idea that Yeltsin's bloc is less democratic than the norm for Russia.

By about 1997, that is, the fifth round in the model, the simulations of Russian domestic governance interests indicate that there was an 82 percent chance that the Yeltsin/Putin faction would backslide, generally to a score in the mid-50s. But, after that initial predicted retrogression, the EUM offers a modestly optimistic view for Russia's currently primary political faction. By the end of the century, the predicted likelihood that the Yeltsin/Putin faction would become less democratic than the initial score of 60 drops from 82 percent to 45 percent. By 2002, there appears to be a 71 percent chance that the faction will become modestly *more* democratic, falling approximately in line with the overall Russian democracy rating of 70. The odds that this faction will become more democratic continue to improve, reaching an 84 percent chance of supporting a level of democracy commensurate with a rating of 70 or so by 2008. By 2008, the chance of retrogression below the 1995 score of 60 for this group drops to only 16 percent. This encourages the belief that

Putin's support for the U.S. following the terrorist attacks of September 11, 2001, is the beginning of a moderately positive trend predicted by the EUM.

It is noteworthy that the Yeltsin/Putin faction has a good chance of continuing to dominate Russian presidential politics. The shift in their domestic stance on democracy places this faction very close to the median voter position in Russia from the year 2002 onward. Though still slightly below the median voter at this point, the faction greatly narrows the gap they established earlier. According to the simulation results, the Yeltsin/Putin faction was, on average, more than 10 points below the projected Russian median voter position in the period from 1997 to 2000, narrowing the gap to under 3 points by 2001 and continuing to narrow the gap through 2008. That the Yeltsin/Putin group could control the presidency while being so far below the national median is revelatory of how far Russia still has to go to be a full-fledged democracy.

That the governance structure overall was closer to the median voter viewpoint than to the Yeltsin/Putin faction's point of view is suggestive of how much real influence more democratically oriented groups exert. Finally, one reason the Yeltsin/Putin faction is narrowing the gap between their own point of view and that of the median voter is that the Yeltsin/Putin bloc is becoming more democratically disposed. However, another reason is that the Russian median voter's projected position, given random shocks, is becoming less and less democratic. So the gap narrows both because Yeltsin/Putin rise a little and because the median voter preference declines a little. This latter observation casts a gloomier shadow over the optimistic view that the dominant political group is improving in its attitude toward democracy.

Whether we examine Russia's prospects for democratization by focusing on its susceptibility to international pressure or on its domestic political circumstances, the conclusion is the same. Russia is unlikely to make substantial strides forward, at least over the next decade, in its commitment to democracy. Though Russian society today probably is freer than it has ever been in the past, the sad fact remains that Russia is farther behind the "average" country today in democratization than it was twenty years ago. Its fall in rank casts a giant shadow on its prospects for the future.

## Simulating China's Future

China's rapid economic expansion during the 1980s, and somewhat slower economic growth during the 1990s, encourages many observers to believe that political liberalization cannot be far behind. It certainly is true that wealthier states tend to be democratic and that democratic states tend to be wealthy. China, though having enjoyed rapid growth until recently, is still a poor country. While the trend in wealth is in the right direction, it is not clear whether we should expect the improving prosperity to create the foundations for political change any time soon. For one thing, there is little theoretical basis for thinking that wealth causes a shift to democracy. There is some theoretical and empirical basis for claiming that causality runs the other way; greater degrees of governmental inclusiveness promote growth (Bueno de Mesquita et al. 2003). In this section I address the expectations for democratization in China formed by the EUM simulations.

Table 6.2 displays the data used for the simulations of Chinese domestic political debate over institutional reform. These data were originally collected in 1991 for a talk I gave on the forecasting model at Florida State University. The results, however, have never before been published, nor did I undertake an analysis that included random shocks for my Florida State talk.

Professor Yi Feng provided the required expertise to assemble these data. I am extremely grateful to him for his assistance. Although Deng Xiao Ping was still alive when the data were collected, Yi Feng wisely built a data set under the assumption that Deng had passed from the scene. This made it possible to analyze likely developments regarding democratization in the post–Deng era. The scale fortunately matched the general parameters of the Polity scale and other data I have used throughout this volume oriented toward

**Table 6.2**
Chinese Data, 1991

| Stakeholder | Resources | Position | Salience |
|---|---|---|---|
| Baibing | 85 | 15 | 85 |
| Boyibo | 75 | 20 | 70 |
| China All Democracy Movement | 20 | 100 | 90 |
| Chenyun | 100 | 10 | 85 |
| China Spring | 20 | 100 | 90 |
| Europe | 55 | 90 | 30 |
| Guandung | 30 | 50 | 70 |
| Hong Kong | 25 | 100 | 85 |
| Japan | 50 | 60 | 50 |
| Li Peng | 90 | 15 | 80 |
| Peng Zhen | 90 | 15 | 80 |
| Qiao Shi | 85 | 15 | 80 |
| Ruihuan | 60 | 30 | 75 |
| Shanghai | 30 | 35 | 50 |
| Shangkun | 100 | 20 | 85 |
| Students/Intellectuals | 40 | 100 | 90 |
| Tian Jiyun | 50 | 20 | 40 |
| United States | 70 | 100 | 40 |
| Wang Zhen | 85 | 15 | 80 |
| Wan Li | 60 | 25 | 60 |
| Xiannian | 60 | 20 | 60 |
| Zeming | 80 | 25 | 50 |
| Zhu Rongji | 60 | 35 | 80 |
| Zou Jiahua | 80 | 15 | 75 |

assessing the preference of individual stakeholders regarding democratization. The data were explicitly designed to give a long-term view of developments. With that in mind, I treat each bargaining round as a bit longer than I did for the data on Russia. In that case, each round was interpreted as equal to about one-half year. I treat the China rounds as equivalent to approximately two-thirds of a year. This has the effect of making the forecast range from the years 1991 through 2008, so that the upper bound is the same as with the Russian data. I reinforce this view in the analysis of the impact of random shocks by increasing the probability of a shock for each stakeholder each round from 20 percent to 30 percent. This is equivalent to capturing more potential shocks in the twenty-five simulated rounds than would have been captured in the Russian data or the global data. By capturing more shocks in the same number of rounds I am, in essence, extending the length of time over which the simulations are likely to be valid, since more shocks surely take place over a longer time horizon than a shorter one.

## Base Case Analysis

The strongly pro-democracy forces (i.e., a score of 90 or greater on the stated preference scale) assumed to have leverage on China's domestic affairs include China's All-Democracy movement, a group referred to as China Spring, Chinese students and intellectuals, those representing the interests of Hong Kong, Europe, and the United States. Collectively, however, these pro-democracy interests represented only about 13 percent of the total power within the Chinese political context in 1991. What is more, as one would expect, the pro-democracy stakeholders external to China (i.e., the United States and Europe) have low salience and so exert much less influence than they could. Those occupying the democratic middle ground also are weak, suggesting little initial reason to be optimistic about China's institutional evolution given domestic political considerations. Indeed, the base case scenario leads to the expectation that China's institutional arrangements would reach a score of only 20 in 1991, suggesting a strongly autocratic government. Polity scored China as a 15 during that same period. The domestic estimate based on the EUM is very close to the Polity score. This is of great significance because it underscores an important difference between the Russian analysis and the Chinese analysis.

In the case of Russia, the EUM produced scores exceedingly close to the ex post Polity values regardless of whether the EUM assessment was based on domestic pressure or international pressure. This is not true for China. Recall that the international analysis for China showed that Chinese democratization would lag behind Russian democratization, but that it would occur by the very late 1980s. The EUM's estimate for China's democratization based only on international influence equals 77 on the democracy scale by 1991. The domestic prediction, as mentioned above, is only 20. Why such a large difference?

Recent developments help clarify an important subtlety captured by the EUM simulation. To appreciate the significance of the domestic assessment and its ability to capture what was going on between competing political factions inside China, I pause to provide a bit of information about some of the key Chinese political stakeholders in the years since 1989. This will provide the context for understanding the major differences between the domestic and international analysis.

According to the EUM, China's government would have succumbed to political liberalization in the late 1980s in response to international pressure, provided that the central leadership was in internal agreement. In the international assessment, China, like all countries, was treated as if the central leadership reflected a united point of view. Many in the West believed by 1989 that Deng Xiao Ping, extremely elderly and in failing health, had turned the reins of government over to Zhao Ziyang and that Zhao Ziyang was, therefore, the heir apparent in the Chinese government. Recent evidence strongly reinforces the claim that when, in June 1989, students called for political reform in China, Zhao Ziyang wanted to initiate significant moves toward democratization. He was, however, overruled in a bitter internal political battle. Zhao Ziyang was ousted from office and placed under house arrest. His defeat came at the hands of hardliners, removing him from the list of players in Chinese politics.

Jiang Zemin, previously a virtual unknown, at Deng Xiao Ping's insistence was brought to Beijing during the Tiananmen uprising and elevated to the position of General Secretary of the Communist Party. Widely believed to have no personal base of power, many observers expected Jiang Zemin to fade from the scene in the post–Deng era. However, he skillfully consolidated power to become the most influential figure in China. Jiang Zemin held the three most powerful offices in the country, an unprecedented consolidation of authority. He became president, general secretary of the party, and chair of the party's Central Military Commission.

Li Peng is generally regarded as the key henchman who presided over the violent suppression of the democracy movement centered in Tiananmen Square in 1989. He was elevated to the Politburo in 1985 and became prime minister in 1987 when Zhao Ziyang was made general secretary of the party, a post Zhao Ziyang lost to Jiang Zemin in 1989. Because of reforms pushed through by Jiang Zemin that created mandatory retirement, Li Peng was compelled to give up his official position in 1997, but still remained powerful. He was widely regarded as the second or third most influential figure in China as of early 2001.

Zhu Rongji, an economist by training, was mayor of Shanghai from 1987 to 1991 and a protégé of Jiang Zemin. After leaving Shanghai he became one of six vice prime ministers. When Li Peng retired, Zhu Rongji replaced him as prime minister. Considered a reformer, he was generally viewed as the third most powerful person in China by early 2001. It is noteworthy that he seems to be on his way up while Li Peng and his backers appear to have been diminished in authority.

Two other figures are worthy of brief discussion, though they no longer are prominent figures. Each was at one time a prospective central figure in China. Qiao Shi headed the National People's Congress (the NPC) until Jiang Zemin ousted him (with support from Li Peng) in 1997. Prior to his leadership of the NPC, that body was a rubber stamp that routinely accepted party directives. Under Qiao Shi's leadership, however, the NPC occasionally voiced opposition to such directives. Qiao Shi, a rival for authority to Jiang Zemin and Li Peng, was the third most powerful leader in China before his ouster. His defeat marked a major turning point in determining that Jiang Zemin would succeed in consolidating power in his own hands.

Yang Shangkun was president of China and had close ties to the military. Until the early 1990s, he was regarded as the number two power in China and the person most likely to be the power broker determining the post–Deng succession. In a major success for Jiang Zemin, Yang Shangkun was forced out of office in early 1994.

Apparently China in 1989 came close to the dramatic political reforms that the international version of the EUM forecast. Zhao Ziyang staked his political future on promoting such reforms. Unfortunately, because of internal dissent from hardliners including especially Deng, Li Peng, and others, the reformist faction was ousted from power and China stuck to its authoritarian form of government, as suggested by the domestic EUM analysis (Nathan 2000).[35] The domestic forces trumped the international pressure because the international actors with influence inside China did not attach sufficient salience—perhaps wisely at the time—to that country's democratization to interfere in its internal affairs. The international community briefly imposed economic sanctions in response to Tiananmen, but these were lifted in short order and with little consequence. There was nothing equivalent to the Helsinki Final Act to justify foreign political intervention oriented toward changing China's domestic course. Absent that intervention, reformers like Zhao Ziyang lacked the domestic support to carry the day. Reformers in reality and in the EUM simply were neither sufficiently influential nor sufficiently well positioned strategically to impose their reformist attitudes on China's government structure. This, of course, still leaves the question of what China's government is expected to be like in the future.

### The Base Case for Likely Chinese Governance

The base case simulation predicts that after sticking with extreme autocracy in 1991 (i.e., a score of 20 on the preference scale), internal pressures lead to modest liberalization in 1994 (53 on the scale), followed by steady and significant retrenchment. The EUM base case predicts a value of 41 in 1997, 32 in 2000, and 31 in 2004 and 2008.

To put the predicted absolute democracy scores for China in proper perspective, consider what these values indicate about China's ranking on democratization. In 1991, using the Polity data, China ranked between fifth and sixth lowest among the about ninety countries in the sample on the democracy-autocracy scale. The domestic prediction for China (20) would have yielded a ranking of between 3 and 4. China's actual ranking in 1994 based on the Polity data equals 14, whereas its seemingly more liberal government as predicted by the EUM (i.e., EUM prediction of 53) renders a ranking of only 20, putting the domestic predicted score at the same level as Mozambique in 1994. By 1997, China slips from a rank of fourteenth to between third and fourth least democratic based on the Polity data. The EUM also shows a substantial retrenchment in ranking, with the domestic score for China placing it between the eighth and ninth least democratic regime. The domestic EUM prediction is equivalent to the predicted value for Algeria based on the international data. By 2000, the observed ranking based on Polity and predicted by the EUM are identical. Although only 15 on the Polity scale and a seemingly more liberal 32 based on the EUM estimate, still within their respective rankings, each shows China again as between the third and fourth least democratic government with a ranking equal to that for Saudi Arabia. In 2004 and 2008, the EUM prediction retains China at the same rank position as in 2000, a dismal showing in terms of democratization. In fact, reality as estimated ex post by Polity and as estimated ex ante by the EUM match rather closely.

## Individual Political Winners and Losers

The base case can be investigated in greater detail to see how well it does at ferreting out important shifts in political power within China. The EUM calculates the nature of the relationship between every pair of stakeholders during each simulation round. Specifically, the EUM reports what are called "Verbal Summaries" that indicate which relations are expected to yield compromises, which interchanges lead to a conflict in which the stakeholder of interest is expected to win or to lose. The reports also indicate those relations in which the stakeholder of interest can compel the rival to accept the stakeholder's position or in which it may have to accept the rival's position. They point out those situations in which there is a stalemate between the stakeholders so that the status quo prevails or in which the players have no policy disagreement. These classifications can readily be divided into three categories of interest:

1. The proportion of situations in which if stakeholders challenge one another's policies then the stakeholder in question is expected to lose
2. The proportion of cases in which the player can find a credible compromise
3. The proportion of times the stakeholder in question is expected to obtain an outright win.[36]

If we sum the number of relationships a stakeholder has that lead to an outright win or to the opportunity to reach a compromise agreement with others, we can see the chances the player has to resolve political differences and gain increased political influence. Those who experience many out-and-out losses are unlikely to prevail politically. The wins and compromises are the opportunities to alter other people's policy positions. I call the sum of these two categories Advantage. Those who have the highest values on Advantage have the best opportunity to change the political landscape in ways that are favorable to them. Therefore, they are the expected political winners in the contest for political control over the form of governance.

I have already provided brief summaries of the political fortunes of Jiang Zemin, Zhu Rongji, Li Peng, Qiao Shi, and Yang Shangkun. All five of these leaders were in significant positions in 1991. By 1994, Yang Shangkun was ousted. By 1997, he was joined by Qiao Shi, and in 1997, though certainly not out of power, Li Peng's position was diminished because of his forced retirement. Over the same period, Jiang Zemin and Zhu Rongji clearly grew in stature and authority. Jiang Zemin, obscure until 1989, became the foremost power in China. Zhu Rongji, obscure until 1991, has risen steadily since and is, as of early 2001, at least the third (and maybe second) most powerful person in the country. Might the EUM have helped predict the emergence of Jiang Zemin and Zhu Rongji as the big political winners in China by 1997 and Qiao Shi, Yang Shangkun, and (though to a lesser extent) Li Peng as the losers?

To address winners and losers, I compare the scores on Advantage among these five stakeholders. With hindsight we know that the year of greatest interest is 1997. In 1997, Jiang Zemin and Zhu Rongji consolidated their control. It is in that year that Qiao Shi was forced out and that Li Peng, under a constitutional provision pushed through at Jiang Zemin's initiative, was compelled to retire. Yang Shangkun had been ousted three years earlier but, of course, his faction of supporters still existed. So, by the end of the 1997 Party Congress, Jiang Zemin and Zhu Rongji were the clear winners.

In 1997, an extraordinary 70 percent of Jiang Zemin's relationships were advantageous. Second highest on the variable Advantage for 1997 among these key figures was Zhu Rongji with 48 percent. Li Peng and Qiao Shi followed at 39 percent, and Yang Shangkun had a low Advantage score of only 26 percent. Note that while Yang Shangkun was out of power by 1997, the EUM data, collected in 1991 when he was still in a strong position, were not updated to include his ouster. The EUM correctly identified his weak position among key leaders.

It is evident that the EUM's assessment of political fortunes in 1997—based on 1991 data—sorts out the political winners and losers. Of course, the number of observations is small. Still, with five politicians of interest, there are 120 possible ways to rank them, of which only six would place

Jiang Zemin at the top and Zhu Rongji second in rank. Of these six, only two can also put Yang Shangkun at the bottom of the ranking. So, the probability that political advantage in 1997 was correctly assessed occurred by chance at worst with a 5 percent probability (6/120) and perhaps with as low as a less than 2 percent probability (2/120).

A similar story can be told for 1994. Zhu Rongji and Jiang Zemin again show the greatest political advantage (65 and 39 percent respectively). Bolstering the opposition by counting as an advantage those cases in which others agreed with the position of the politician in question, Li Peng and Qiao Shi's political advantage lies between 13 and 35 percent, behind the two clear subsequent winners. Yang Shangkun only scores 30 percent, again signaling his anticipated beleaguered position.

The political defeat of Yang Shangkun, Qiao Shi, and the diminution of Li Peng were neither inevitable nor obvious in 1991. Likewise, Jiang Zemin's success and that of Zhu Rongji were very much in doubt in 1991. Their policy stance on the issue of political reform alone is insufficient to guess who the winners and losers would be. After all, the data in Table 6.2 suggest that Yang Shangkun was something of a moderate among the top leaders. His stance on democratization in 1991 equals 20 on the scale, precisely the location of the 1991 median "voter." Zhu Rongji favored 35, Jiang Zemin 25, Li Peng and Qiao Shi each supported the autocratic status quo at 15. What is more, the 1991 assessment of the EUM gives second lowest political advantage to Jiang Zemin and least to Yang Shangkun. Thus, the initial data share the common view in 1991 that Jiang Zemin was a political lightweight unlikely to survive in the rough and tumble world of Chinese domestic politics. Yet, once the EUM's dynamics are considered, we see Jiang Zemin and Zhu Rongji consistently rise politically while the others fall by the wayside. With this in mind, we can consider what the EUM suggests for the future, say in 2008.

In looking through the EUM "crystal ball" to 2008, I note a difference in leadership style between Jiang Zemin and Zhu Rongji, the two leading contenders for supreme political domination. Jiang Zemin's political advantage, as reflected in the EUM simulation, stems from his remarkable willingness to compromise rather than impose his will on others. He is about four times more likely to look for a way to make a deal with opponents than he is to try to force them to accept his perspective. This is true in almost every round of simulated negotiations within China's power elite. Zhu Rongji appears more inclined to put views forward forcefully and win by convincing others to accept his viewpoint rather than by striking a deal. This difference in style persists through at least 2008, but with a twist. Jiang Zemin continues to be a consummate negotiator, finding his way through a maze of policy differences to ensure his political success. Zhu Rongji continues as an effective persuader for his point of view, but he also is likely to become more willing to accept compromises. If the EUM is correct, by 2008 Zhu Rongji is about as likely to prevail politically through persuasion as he is through compromising with his rivals. This suggests that he is likely to grow further in stature as he consolidates his position by forging coalitions through accommodation. Unfortunately, this seems to offers little hope for democratization in China. Zhu Rongji, often touted as a reformer, never takes a stance in the EUM simulation that is above 35 on the scale, nor does he ever dip below 30. He is, relative to China's status quo institutional arrangements, only a modest reformer. Jiang Zemin very much appears to follow Zhu Rongji's lead on views toward governance. Though he starts out as more conservative, he slowly rises throughout the simulations to a position close to that of Zhu Rongji.

## China's Governance and Random Shocks

China's politics, perhaps more so even than Russia's, is likely to experience random shocks. The leadership tends to be very elderly so that key figures can pass from the scene at any time. Rapid economic growth is helping to create rival interests emanating from the wealthy coastal provinces like Guandung and Hong Kong. As noted earlier, I have simulated shocks to the salience variable at a higher rate than was done for Russia or the international system. This does not markedly influence the results, though it does allow for more opportunities for change round by round. We saw that shocks did not materially alter expectations regarding Russia as they did do for the analysis in chapter 4 of the end of the Cold War. Now we can see how unanticipated shocks might influence the course of Chinese politics.

Figure 6.2 shows the course of six out of more than fifty simulated futures for China. The dark solid line punctuated by circles depicts the median democracy score for China for each round across all of the simulations. The dark dotted line accompanied by diamonds displays the base case scenario. The other, lighter lines show the most optimistic and most pessimistic simulation results. The actual simulations are well dispersed across the observed range. The range falls between the high twenties and the low fifties. By round 5, equivalent approximately to 1994, about one-fourth of the simulations fall below 40 on the scale, one-third between 40 and 50, and about 45 percent fall above 50 on the scale. Five rounds later, approximating 1997, less than one-third fall between 40 and 50, with the remainder equally divided between scores below 40 and scores above 50. The modest bimodal distribution of round 10 is strengthened by approximately the year 2000. At that point (round 15) less than one-fourth of predicted results fall between 40 and below 50, with more that 40 percent being in the 30s or 20s and 36 percent being above 50. In round 20 (equivalent to the year 2004) the low end still is most prevalent at nearly 40 percent. The middle and high categories (40–49 on the scale and 50 or above, respectively) each reflect about one-third of the simulations. Finally, the odds of liberalization by 2008

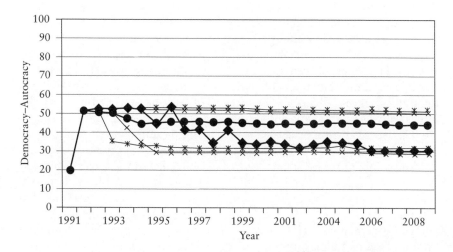

**Figure 6.2**   China's Domestic View of Democratization, with Random Shocks

are poor, with 40 percent of the simulations below 40 and about 30 percent in each of the two more democratic categories.

Figure 6.2 tells a story dramatically different from the comparable figure for Russia (Figure 6.1). The Russian figure reflected a very narrow range of likely outcomes in which the base case was the most optimistic. China's prospects for democratization are not nearly as good as Russia's. The scores even from the most optimistic Chinese simulations tend to be lower than the Russian values for the most pessimistic Russian simulations. What is more, the base case for China undergoes a discouraging transition over time. In the early years of the simulation, the base case forecast is among the most optimistic views for the future. That is, very few of the simulations with random shocks lead to the expectation of more democracy for China than is reflected in the early years in the base case. But then the base case prediction steadily deteriorates, equaling the most pessimistic simulation from about 2005 through 2008, the last year simulated. This provides a reason for some optimism about the years to come.

Random shocks that deflect China from the base case course are virtually inevitable over such a long time period. The vast majority of simulations with random shocks lead to a more democratic China than is expected from the base case. To be sure, it is not a particularly democratic China, but the odds of progress at least look excellent.

If China experiences the sorts of shocks simulated here, how much more democratic might it be? To address this question, I look at the predicted rank for China in 2008 based on the base case and compare it to the rankings China might achieve according to the simulations with random shocks.

Recall that the base case democracy score of 31 for China ranks it third or fourth worst in the simulated world of 2008. If it reaches a score of 50 to 55, a range achieved in about 30 percent of the simulations for 2008, then China's ranking would be about tenth or eleventh. This is equivalent to the predicted positions of such countries as Guyana, Lesotho, Togo, and Tanzania. This is about the same rank as Togo earned in 1998 based on the Polity data and is about twenty ranks lower than Guyana achieved in 1998. So, even the optimistic view is not at all rosy.

China's attraction as a place to invest may not improve, all else being equal, as the rest of the world becomes democratic, with transparent rule of law and secure property rights, faster than China. Perhaps such a decline may trigger the random shocks that help propel China at least to the upper bound of the simulations. For now, I can only predict slow, limited progress toward a gradual weakening of the autocratic reigns of power in China. This loosening of control may itself be stymied by the prospects that China's abysmal democracy ranking may, in the future, also reduce its prospects for continued economic growth.

SEVEN

# War in the Future

THE ANALYSIS HAS HELPED ILLUMINATE PROSPECTIVE CHANGES IN
global democratization and has illustrated the EUM's potential to make
detailed predictions about the internal workings of specific governments.
Using the simulations as the basis for more extensive analyses of prospective foreign policy futures, I now turn to an investigation of how some
major social forces in the world are influenced by the projected changes
in democratization. Specifically, the first chapter examined historical patterns in democratization, the spread of prosperity, and population movements through immigration. Now I ask two sets of questions: (1) How, if
at all, are prosperity and immigration influenced by changing patterns in
global democratization? and (2) How do changes in democratization, prosperity, and immigration influence the prospects of international conflict,
including war?

## Relationships among Social Forces: Democracy and Income

I begin with a statistical investigation of the relationships among the three
social forces emphasized in the first chapter. My initial focus is on explaining national and global shifts in prosperity.

One sensible indicator of a population's prosperity is its real per capita
income, the very factor examined in chapter 1. The Penn World Tables provide such data for most countries in the world every year from 1950 through
1992 (http://datacentre.chass.utoronto.ca:5680/pwt/docs/subjects.html). I
convert these values to their logarithm. This change recognizes that the
marginal increase in welfare from a dollar of added income is greatest
for those with the lowest incomes and smallest for those with the highest
incomes. That is, I assume decreasing marginal utility for money as people
become more prosperous. The logarithm focuses attention on relative
magnitudes of income. Although I do not report them here, the statistical
results are comparable if I use the actual real per capita income rather than
its logarithm.

To evaluate how, if at all, the degree of democracy influences subsequent income levels, I construct several different tests. The democracy-autocracy scores derived from the Polity data are used for the statistical analysis. Because I am interested in how democracy influences income, I lag the democracy variable. Three different lag periods are used: one year, three years, and five years. As they generally produce the same results, I focus on the one-year lag to preserve observations. The tests are conducted in three different setups. First I examine the bivariate relationship between democracy and per capita income. Then I add control variables. Both in the bivariate case and in the tests with control variables, I run the analysis with no fixed effects, with fixed effects for geographic region and year, and with country-specific fixed effects. The two sets of tests with fixed effects add substantial constraints and represent extremely demanding assessments. The region-year fixed effects controls for general changes over time within geographic divisions of the globe. These tests, then, are tough evaluations of the cross-sectional impact of variation in democracy on prosperity. The country-specific fixed effects are even more demanding, perhaps too demanding. These tests look within each country to see whether changes in the degree of democracy correlate with subsequent income levels, thereby looking at temporal but not cross-sectional effects. The reason these tests are especially demanding is that many countries have little or no variation in their institutional arrangements over the years 1950–1992. The impact of the United States, Canada, and Western Europe, for instance, is virtually eliminated by the country-specific fixed effects models because these countries did not experience changes in their Polity democracy-autocracy score over the years investigated. Thus, this test treats the degree of democracy as equivalent to simply naming the country, and attributes the variance in per capita income to characteristics of the country rather than to democracy.

Prosperity surely does not depend only on political institutions. Economic productivity as well as receptivity to trade are two useful indicators of national economic policies that should be expected to foster greater per capita income. Fischer (1993) provides cross-sectional time series estimates for national economic productivity based on Solow's research (Fischer's variable esolow), and on openness to trade (Fischer's variable open). Some types of economic activity, of course, can also dampen per capita income. Black market exchange rate premiums over official exchange rates (Fischer's variable exchprem) are a useful indicator of restrictions in the national marketplace that create off-the-books business transactions and opportunities for corruption (Fischer 1993). These may well be an economic drag. Although productivity, openness to trade, and black market exchange rates may themselves be partially shaped by the political environment, my interest here is in these factors as controls to see whether even in the face of their impact on prosperity, democraticness continues to exert a separate, significant effect. If democracy proves beneficial (or detrimental) to per capita income, then we can infer something about future prospects for prosperity.

Tables 7.1a–c shows the cross-sectional time series results, including the effects just of democracy lagged by one year, as well as results with control variables. Table 7.1a shows the association without fixed effects. Table 7.1b shows how democracy influences per capita income with fixed effects controlling for geographic region and year. Finally, Table 7.1c replicates these estimates, but controlling instead for each country so that cross-sectional effects are removed, leaving within-country temporal effects only with a slow-moving explanatory variable (democracy) that is, itself, a significant feature of the variance captured by each country's fixed effect.

The two tests in Table 7.1a strongly support the expectation that democracy promotes prosperity. Though not shown in the table, similar findings arise when democracy-autocracy is lagged by three or five years. In each of those cases, the democracy coefficient remains about the same and the significance level is the same. The surprise in Table 7.1a is that the independent impact of productivity is not significant. This, however, is not the concern here.

Table 7.1b offers a more demanding test than Table 7.1a. The results reinforce the conclusion from 7.1a that the degree of democracy greatly influences the magnitude of per capita income. The tests in this table make clear that, looking across countries, political institutional arrangements directly help shape prosperity even after removing important economic inducements or drags on the economy. Both this and the previous table suggest that a substantial portion of the variation in per capita income is dependent on politics.

Results like those in Tables 7.1a and 7.1b help explain how it is possible that places with the same natural resources and even the same culture can so often show such different patterns of economic performance. Consider the dramatic differences in per capita income, for example, in China, pre–1997 Hong Kong, and Taiwan. All share a common culture, while the latter two are disadvantaged in terms of natural resources and were, at one time, also equal to mainland China in their level of educational attainment, level of skill in the work force, and so forth. The three, however, differed markedly in political system in the past. China has never known democracy. Taiwan has shed its past autocratic structure and become a full-fledged democracy. Hong Kong, as a British Crown Colony, did not enjoy free elections and other aspects of democracy, but it did enjoy a scrupulous regime committed to rule of law and protection of property rights and individual freedom. Taiwan and Hong Kong, of course, have among the world's highest per capita incomes, while China languished far behind.

Perhaps an even more dramatic example can be found in comparing the Democratic People's Republic of Korea and the Republic of Korea, or the German Democratic Republic and the Federal Republic of Germany. In both of these comparisons, the two countries were devastated by war. Immediate postwar per capita incomes were not terribly different. Yet, in a relatively

**Table 7.1a**
Democracy and Prosperity[a]

| Variable | No Fixed Effects Coefficient (Standard Error) | No Fixed Effects Coefficient (Standard Error) |
|---|---|---|
| Democracy: | | |
| One-Year Lag | 1.42 (0.036) p=.000 | 0.71 (0.057) p=.000 |
| Free Trade | | 0.004 (0.0005) p=.000 |
| Productivity | | 0.23 (0.363) p=.527 |
| Black Market | | −0.41 (0.044) p=.000 |
| Constant | 7.04 (0.024) p=.000 | 7.27 (0.045) p=.000 |
| | Adj. R²=0.31, F=1586.81, N=3486 | Adj. R²=0.24, F=91.41, N=1152 |

[a] All coefficients are calculated with democracy-autocracy varying between 0 and 1.00 rather 0-100 to make it easier to see the coefficients.


**Table 7.1b**
Democracy and Prosperity: A Cross-Sectional Assessment

| Variable | 257 Region-Year Fixed Effects Coefficient (Standard Error) | 168 Region-Year Fixed Effects Coefficient (Standard Error) |
|---|---|---|
| Democracy: | | |
| One-Year Lag | 1.00 (0.031) p=.000 | 0.71 (0.057) p=.000 |
| Free Trade | | 0.004 (0.0005) p=.000 |
| Productivity | | −0.05 (0.322) p=.3 |
| Black Market | | −0.29 (0.044) p=.000 |
| Constant | 7.26 (0.019) p=.000 | −0.29 (0.039) p=.000 |
| | Adj. R²=0.31, F=1050.96, N=3486 | Adj. R²=0.24, F=104.08, N=1152 |


**Table 7.1c**
Democracy, Prosperity, and Country-Specific Fixed Effects

| Variable | 123 Country Fixed Effects Coefficient (Standard Error) | 52 Country Fixed Effects Coefficient (Standard Error) |
|---|---|---|
| Democracy: | | |
| One-Year Lag | 0.06 (0.031) p=.059 | 0.08 (0.057) p=.005 |
| Free Trade | | 0.010 (0.0005) p=.000 |
| Productivity | | 0.02 (0.109) p=.880 |
| Black Market | | 0.04 (0.017) p=.034 |
| Constant | 7.77 (0.017) p=.000 | 7.15 (0.03) p=.000 |
| | Adj. R²=0.31, F=3.56, N=3486 | Adj. R²=0.07, F=86.68, N=1152 |

short time in each case the more democratic polity's per capita income dramatically outstripped the more autocratic regime's per capita income.

Table 7.1c continues to support the fundamental account found in Tables 7.1a and 7.1b, though the support is weaker. The coefficient in 7.1c associated with democracy is smaller and the standard error is larger than in 7.1a or 7.1b, both suggesting a somewhat less reliable—though still statistically and substantively significant—impact of democracy on per capita income. Recall, however, that this test controls for each country so that the cross-sectional differences in regimes variable is removed from the regression analysis. Thus, the results in Table 7.1c tell us that temporal changes in governance within countries also contribute significantly to improved per capita income. As many of the other features that characterize a country—and are removed by the country fixed effects—also depend on democracy, Table 7.1c is perhaps the most remarkable result. The country fixed-effect model removes most of the variance of interest and yet democracy continues to produce a statistically significant impact even when I also control for key economic factors. This tells us that changes in governance that promote greater democracy also promote improvements in per capita income.

The results from the regression analyses suggest that the world of the future will continue to become more prosperous. More democratic regimes are also polities with higher per capita income. The statistical findings thus far, when coupled with the EUM predictions, encourage confidence in the diminution in poverty in the future. Those countries expected to make a large move away from autocracy and toward democracy are especially likely to enjoy significant improvement in their prosperity. Before discussing who these states might be, let us continue the statistical exploration to approximate the way in which national and global income can be expected to improve if the statistical patterns in Tables 7.1a–c persist over time and across countries.

To evaluate the impact that expanding democracy is likely to have on the world, I take the result in the second column of Table 7.1b and extrapolate its implications over various time periods. The result is the lagged effect of democracy on per capita income, controlling for region, year, openness to trade, labor productivity, and the vibrancy of the black market. This result suggests that democracy adds 0.71 orders of magnitude to per capita income. Now consider what this means about the difference in income for a country whose democracy score is 15 as typified the world in 1980, and a country whose score is 80 as typifies the world projected by the EUM into the future. To begin with, citizens in a country with a score of only 15 on democracy, ignoring all other factors, have an expected per capita income of about $1,500. All else being equal, if the country's democracy score were 80, per capita income would be $2,380. This is a rather dramatic difference, but it only tells part of the story. What is more, it understates the difference since the magnitude of the control variables can also be shown to depend in part on the degree of democracy, a factor not considered here.

Growth in per capita income, as implied above, depends on change in institutions. Thus far, however, I have only considered the absolute level of such income. Table 7.2 examines the annual percentage change in per capita income as a function of change in a polity's democracy score over a three-year period ending in the year growth is observed. That is, growth is measured as (real per capita income in year t minus real per capita income in year t-1)/(real per capita income in year t-1), and change in democracy is measured as (democracy-autocracy in year t) minus (democracy-autocracy in year t-3). The table controls for openness to trade, labor productivity, and the black market as well, respectively, as fixed effects for region-year and country by country. Now, looking at temporal change, the extremely demanding country-by-country fixed effects model and the region-year fixed effects model produce similar results, both in terms of significance and variance explained. As before, I focus on the region-year, cross-sectional fixed effects results.

The results on income taken from Table 7.1b showed a substantial difference in "base case" per capita income, depending on whether a country's democracy score typified that of the world before the Cold War ended or that of the world projected for the coming decades by the EUM. Taking these two base incomes as the starting point, we can now use the results in Table 7.2 to evaluate how differences in growth rates associated with institutional arrangements influence changes in per capita income in years to come.

At the outset, a country with a democracy score of 15 has a per capita income about $900 lower than a country with a score of 80 on democracy. After a decade of growth, having sustained a democracy-autocracy value of only 15, the country's per capita income would have grown from about $1,500 to about $1,880, roughly a 25 percent improvement. Moving up to a democracy score of 80, however, suggests a per capita income of about $2,100, or 40 percent growth over the initial income of $1,500. After

**Table 7.2**
Change in Democracy and Growth

| Variable | 165 Region-Year Fixed Effects Coefficient (Standard Error) | 52 Country Fixed Effects Coefficient (Standard Error) |
|---|---|---|
| Change in Democracy | 0.0178 (0.008) p = .021 | 0.0143 (0.007) p=.056 |
| Free Trade | 0.00008 (0.00004) p=.025 | −0.0001 (0.00005) p=.000 |
| Productivity | 0.69 (0.030) p=.000 | −0.05 (0.0001) p=.396 |
| Black Market | −0.006 (0.003) p=.076 | 0.73 (0.028) p=.000 |
| Constant | 0.02 (0.003) p=.000 | 0.03 (0.007) p=.000 |
| | Adj. $R^2$=0.42 F=144.79, N=1105 | Adj. $R^2$=0.40, F=182.48, N=1105 |

twenty-five years, the difference in real per capita income is even more striking. The citizens of an autocracy that stays an autocracy can expect incomes of about $2,635, or a 75 percent improvement over their incomes a quarter of a century earlier. Those citizens living in a state that switched from autocracy to democracy could anticipate incomes of about $3,490, having started with the same $1,500 income. This is an improvement of more than 130 percent. Of course, if the polity became even more democratic, the differential would grow larger. Autocracy appears to be an important contributor to low growth and to poverty.

If the EUM simulations prove accurate and if the association between democracy and per capita income persists into the future, then we may be living in the century in which poverty is largely eradicated from the earth. This is an exciting prospect for the future of humankind.

## Relationship among Social Forces: Democracy and Immigration

Population movement, though relatively erratic, has been increasing with the passing years. On a global scale, immigration appears to occur in waves. The first quarter of the twentieth century and the third quarter saw especially large population migrations. Certainly some factors that contributed to the waves of immigration were the improving technology for moving people and the reduced costs of air and sea travel.[37] One question, then, that is associated with the growth in immigration over time is the extent to which it might be explained by changes in democratization and in personal income. In chapter 1 we saw that both democracy and prosperity contribute significantly to immigration. Now I look at these questions more closely and more carefully.

Democratization and real per capita income both have been rising over time. What is the relationship between these two factors and immigration as a proportion of population when controlling for the passage of time? In fact, lagged democracy scores and lagged per capita income are both strongly and positively associated with immigration even when controlling for the passage of years. More interestingly, the association between democracy and immigration as a percentage of population is so strong that it has only a five in one thousand probability of having arisen by chance. The association between per capita income and the same dependent variable is even stronger, while the effect of the passage of the years washes out (p=.513, N=652). So, democratization and high per capita incomes in the recipient country directly encourage immigration.

Not too surprisingly, international conflict involvement, and especially war involvement, dampen immigration. Democracies are attractive destinations for prospective immigrants during times of peace or in the aftermath of war. Interestingly, during wartime nondemocracies are neither especially attractive nor unattractive destinations for immigrants, but *during* wartime, democracies become less attractive. One possible reason for this is that democracies pour more resources into their effort to win wars and so have less left over with which to assist newly arriving immigrants in times of war (Bueno de Mesquita et al. 2003). Autocracies do not make this extra effort to win during war, so they are not less attractive in wartime than they are in peacetime for immigrants. Immigrants simply never find autocracies especially attractive places to go.

If the EUM simulations are reliable, then the future is likely to witness more population migration than has the past. The increase in immigration that is likely to occur as more societies become attractive destinations for immigrants also, however, contains the seeds of diminished future migration. There is a statistically and substantively strong association not only between immigration and democracy, but also between net migration and regime type. That is, if we consider immigration minus emigration, the flow of people strongly favors movement to democracies, especially populous and wealthy democracies. But as democracy spreads around the world and helps foster increased prosperity, the incentive people have to shift from their homeland to a new country will diminish. Thus, the initial spread of democracy should expand population migration, but as democracy takes a firm hold across more of the world, migration should gradually diminish. The comparative advantage for immigrants offered by democracies clearly is greater in a world in which democracy is scarce than it is in a world in which democracy predominates as the form of government.

## Democracy, War, and the Future

Over the past few decades, studies of war have identified strong empirical patterns and theoretical bases for interpreting those empirical results. The theoretical foundations provide justifications for projecting certain correlates of war into the future, based on expected values on key variables. That is, we can use the empirical knowledge acquired about war and the predicted values on democratization set out in chapters 4–6 to generate comparative static predictions about the prospects of peace or war. These prospects can be projected globally, regionally, for specific pairs of states, or even for individual countries. In performing this task, I take advantage of the links between the social forces investigated in chapter 1 and the prospects of war or peace.

The evidence suggests that the world's governments are continuing to become more democratic. Although the statistical evidence amassed thus far in the literature on regime types and war is insufficient to say with confidence that democratic states are less war-prone than autocratic states (Maoz and

Abdolali 1989), the evidence overwhelmingly supports the proposition that democracies almost never fight wars with other democracies. Indeed, so strong is the evidence in favor of the claim that democracies do not fight one another (Maoz and Abdolali 1989; Bremer 1992; Oneal and Russett 1997; Ray 1995; Gartzke 2001) that Jack Levy has described this regularity as a law of politics (Levy 1988). Despite numerous challenges to the "democratic peace" generalization (Layne 1994; Spiro 1994; Farber and Gowa 1995; Schwartz and Skinner 1999), numerous rigorous statistical tests all show a significant propensity for democracies to have been virtually immune from wars with one another (Russett 1993).

Another body of evidence examines the motives behind war. It is clear throughout history that wars have commonly depended on the quest for expanded territory. Indeed, there is a remarkably strong and robust finding that territorial disputes are the most common motivation behind war (Vasquez 1993, 1995; Huth 1996; Senese 1995, 1997; Hensel 1996). But this result is contingent. Bueno de Mesquita et al. (2003) offer a theory and show evidence that the motivation behind war depends on the regime types involved. Autocracies are disproportionately more likely to fight for territorial gain, but democratic regimes are more likely to fight for the opportunity to alter the rival's regime and impose new policies on it. Naturally, as the number of democracies increases in the world, the implications of these results suggest many important changes in the frequency and purpose of war.

The Polity data indicate that the median government in 1980 was an autocracy with a score of only 15. Twenty years later the median government was a democracy with a score of 80. If the democratic peace hypothesis is in fact a law of politics, then the opportunities for war are diminishing.

To see how much more pacific the future might be than the past, let us consider all countries with a Polity/EUM score of 75 or more as democratic. About 40 percent of the world's countries met this criterion in 1980. By 1990, nearly 60 percent of the countries satisfied this threshold. In 2000, the percentage rose to encompass two-thirds of the world. If the EUM is correct, the percentage will continue to increase, reaching three-fourths of all countries by 2028. Whereas once the world's democracies were mostly limited to Western Europe, North America, India, Israel, Australia, and New Zealand, by 2028 this form of governance will prevail almost everywhere. This means that few states will not border on democracies. As shared, disputed borders are a common cause of war, especially between autocracies or autocracies and democracies, the proliferation of democracies will largely eliminate this source of war. Democracies with shared borders are more likely to negotiate their way through differences or for one to bully the other into submission without a war than they are to fight with one another.

Still, certain parts of the world are likely to remain as significant pockets of international conflict and even war. Using the EUM's assessment of international pressure to foster democracy, Table 7.3 shows the twenty countries

**Table 7.3**
Most Autocratic States: High Risks for War in the Future[a]

| 2010 | 2020 | 2028 |
| --- | --- | --- |
| Swaziland | Swaziland | Swaziland |
| Saudi Arabia | Philippines | Philippines |
| Philippines | Tunisia | Saudi Arabia |
| Tunisia | Saudi Arabia | Tunisia |
| Congo | Zambia | Lesotho |
| Bolivia | Congo | Algeria |
| Zambia | Tanzania | Bolivia |
| Algeria | Mali | Haiti |
| Haiti | Lesotho | Bulgaria |
| Togo | Togo | Togo |
| Somalia | Central African Republic | Mali |
| Sudan | Guyana | Somalia |
| Tanzania | Mozambique | Central African Republic |
| Guyana | Rumania | Rumania |
| Rumania | Haiti | Guyana |
| Lesotho | Bolivia | Zambia |
| Mali | Bulgaria | Mozambique |
| Central African Republic | Somalia | Sudan |
| Bulgaria | Algeria | Argentina |
| Mozambique | Sudan | Congo |

[a] Some countries were not considered because of missing data, including such otherwise probably good candidates for war as Iraq and Syria. Listed from most undemocratic to less autocratic.

each decade predicted to be most autocratic. These states are expected to be at especially high risk of war with their neighbors in the future. They also constitute the states most likely to slip in relative per capita income.

The countries in Table 7.3 are heavily concentrated in a few geographic areas. North Africa and the Middle East are particularly prominent in their regrettable representation. As the world becomes more democratic, these parts of the world appear to lag far behind. This suggests that the prospects of a peaceful Middle East are dim, at least as viewed from an international perspective. In the absence of internal pressure for political reform, such societies as Sudan, Somalia, Tunisia, Algeria, and Saudi Arabia show little prospect of being pacified through democratization. On a more hopeful note, the EUM does suggest that Egypt and Iran will move up somewhat, reaching the middle ranks of quasi-democratic states over the next few decades. Neither becomes a full-fledged democracy, so even if their neighbors do, as seems unlikely, they will not be strong pacifying elements, but perhaps they are heading in that direction.

Just how dramatic the changed prospects for war or peace are can be gleaned from an investigation of the statistical relationship between democracy, per capita income, and war or other forms of militarized international disputes.[38] These show an informative pattern of links between democracy, prosperity, and international conflict.

To evaluate the interdependence between democracy and prosperity, I construct a binary variable, bi-democracy, that equals 1.0 if the democracy-autocracy score is equal to 75 or more. Otherwise, the variable is coded as 0. I then multiply this variable by the logarithm of per capita income and examine a logistic regression in which the dependent variable, War, is evaluated against the effects of democracy-autocracy, bi-democracy, the logarithm of real per capita income, and the interaction of the two (which I call Democracy*Income). Table 7.4 shows the results, with odds ratios rather than coefficients reported for ease of interpretation.

Table 7.4 tells an important and complex story about the prospective future. The odds ratios reported in the table tell us the effect that the variable in question has on increasing (odds-ratio > 1) or decreasing (odds-ratio < 1) the probability of war. On average, we see that a doubling of per capita income cuts the risk of war nearly in half. This bodes well for the future as per capita incomes seem to be on the rise. However, this beneficial effect does *not* carry over to the most democratic societies. For those whose democracy score is above 75, increased wealth, at the margin, significantly increases the risk of war. The net impact of the two income factors together (i.e., Log [Per Capita Income] and Democracy*Income) is essentially to indicate no change or a small increase in the risk of war.

The direct impact of democracy on the danger of war is more encouraging for the future. Moving up the democracy ladder seems at first blush to increase substantially the risk of war. The odds ratio associated with democracy-autocracy is 4.51, presaging a near quadrupling in the risk of war. However, this effect is not only muted, it is reversed at the highest reaches of democracy. Thus, the odds ratio associated with bi-democracy is .001. This tells us that those countries with government structures that equal or surpass 75 on the democracy scale have a reduction in the likelihood of war to one-thousandth of what that risk is on average. The net impact of increasing democracy is that there are several order of magnitude *reductions* in the risk of war once nations reach at least 75 on the democracy scale. The beneficial

**Table 7.4**
Democracy, Prosperity, and War

| Variable | Odds-Ratio (Standard Error) |
|---|---|
| Democracy-Autocracy | 4.51 (3.53) p=.054 |
| Bi-Democracy | 0.001 (0.003) p=.010 |
| Log(Per Capita Income) | 0.56 (0.13) p=.014 |
| Democracy*Income | 2.18 (0.71) p=.016 |
|  | $\chi^2$ =10.29 p=.036 N = 711 |

effects of democratization are progressively weakened as we step down the democracy ladder, redefining bi-democracy to have a lower and lower cut point. So, those closest to pure democracy as indexed by the Polity scale or the EUM are least likely to be embroiled in war. As much of the world is expected to meet these conditions in the next few decades, there is great hope that, in John Mueller's terms (Mueller 1989), war is becoming obsolete.

The prospective obsolescence of war can be seen in further detail by evaluating the risk of such conflicts from a somewhat different perspective. As the world becomes more democratic, one issue is how likely disputes are to escalate to the level of warfare as a function of the characteristics of the participants in the dispute. I address this issue by evaluating the risk that war arises if a democracy initiates a dispute or if initiation falls to a nondemocratic state, again taking into account also prosperity and absolute degree of democracy. Initiation is a binary variable called Initiate, and coded 1 if the state in question is the initiator of a militarized dispute, and coded as 0 otherwise. This variable is also interacted with the democracy-autocracy score (called Initiate*Democracy), the income score (Initiate*Income), and jointly with income and democracy (Initiate*Democracy*Income). Table 7.5 summarizes the logistic regression, again reporting odds ratios rather than standard coefficients for ease of interpretation.

Most disputes do not become wars. Therefore, the variable Initiate by itself should not be expected to influence whether a dispute escalates to war or not and it does not, as can be seen from the inconsequential significance level. The variable is included as a benchmark against which to compare the likelihood of escalation when the initiator happens to be democratic. Disputes involving democracies are highly likely to become wars (p=.004), but they are wars of self-defense. When we consider the odds of a war given that a democracy initiates the dispute, the probability of escalation to war is vanishingly small, on the order of $10^{-13}$ (p=.001). Even taking into account the substantial preparedness of democracies to engage in self-defense, the net effect of democracy on the risk of war, given that the democracy initiates the

**Table 7.5**
War, Democracy, Prosperity, and Dispute Initiation

| Variable | Odds-Ratio (Standard Error) |
| --- | --- |
| Initiate | 86.64 (378.62) p=.307 |
| Democracy-Autocracy | $8.32*10^7$ $(5.22*10^8)$ p=.004 |
| Log (Per Capita Income) | 0.95 (0.44) p=.907 |
| Initiate*Democracy | $2.50*10^{13}$ $(2.10*10^{12})$ p=.001 |
| Initiate*Income | 0.43 (0.27) p=.179 |
| Democracy*Income | 0.15 (0.11) p=.011 |
| Initiate*Democracy*Income | 24.76 (25.33) p=.002 |
| | $\chi^2$ =141.24 p=.000 N = 711 |

dispute, is still vanishingly small, on the order of $10^{-6}$. So, in a world with mostly democracies, there is little room for escalation to war unless a hapless surviving autocrat initiates a dispute against a democrat. Income effects barely influence this decidedly pacifying aspect of democracy. Whether rich or poor, the key to escalation seems to be a world with few democracies and that does not appear to be the state of the future world.

One final piece of analysis will help in projecting the future state of the world, especially with regard to specific pairs of countries or flash points. Earlier I noted that the rise in democracy scores around the world could be somewhat misleading. Russia, for instance, has risen markedly in its degree of democracy over the past two decades, but the rest of the world has risen farther. Thus, Russia's ranking on the democracy-autocracy index has actually fallen. In projecting the prospects for peace or war in the future, we should also investigate the role played by rank position in degree of democracy. Such a test recognizes that in some important ways democracy is not an absolute condition; it is relative.

In terms of projected behavior, a score of 75 today may not be the same as such a score twenty, ten, or even one year ago. To assess this possibility, I construct a variable that is a country's percentage ranking (that is, its rank divided by the maximum rank for the year to correct for changes in the number of countries) on democracy. This variable is called %Rank. I also interact this term with the log of real per capita income to see what effect, if any, high or low ranking in rich or poor states implies about the risk of war involvement. I do so while also controlling for the actual democracy score and the actual log of per capita income. Table 7.6 contains the findings.

Being democratic, per se, has a weak positive effect on the likelihood of a country becoming embroiled in war. However, that risk is mitigated if its absolute score places the country high on the democracy ranking. Those with lower rankings, like China or Russia, are more likely to become involved in war. Rich countries are also less likely to engage in war than are poor countries, although this is not true of highly ranked democracies. Those with high rankings exacerbate the danger of war, albeit not nearly so strongly as to offset the generally beneficial effects of high ranking and high per capita income.

**Table 7.6**
Democracy Ranking, Prosperity, and the Risk of War

| Variable | Odds-Ratio (Standard Error) |
|---|---|
| %Rank | $7.24*10^{12}$ $(1.01*10^{10})$ p=.066 |
| Democracy-Autocracy | $1.90*10^{7}$ $(2.07*10^{8})$ p=.123 |
| Log (Per Capita Income) | 0.21 (0.12) p=.006 |
| %Rank*Income | 79.91 (153.47) p=.023 |
| Democracy*Income | 0.06 (0.08) p=.053 |
| | $\chi^2$ =23.33 p=.0003 N = 711 |

The one effect that significantly increases the danger of war pales when compared to the odds of war given a high democracy ranking. When the ranking is high, the probability of war is nearly zero.

## Flash Points and the Future

The world will probably become wealthier and generally more pacific as it democratizes. The twenty-first century might well mark the end of broad-based poverty, though pockets of poor governance may help ensure the continuation of poverty in some parts of the world. After all, over 40 percent of the variance in investments made in different polities are explained just by %Rank and the logarithm of per capita income. The actual democracy score contributes much less to investment than does the ranking, a value that reflects comparative institutional advantage.

Poor governance may also help promote pockets of international conflict outside of what Singer and Wildavsky (1996) call the zone of peace. We already know that countries with low democracy rankings are especially prone to find themselves engaged in warfare. So are poor countries. Since a low ranking—that is, relatively poor governance—contributes to low incomes for the citizenry, low rankings serve up a double effect: they directly and indirectly increase the danger of war.

Not all countries are expected to become democratic or wealthy. Those that fail to do so are especially at risk for international conflict. With that in mind, I close by surveying prospective hot spots around the world to see if the EUM forecasts give hope for bringing these disputes to a peaceful resolution.

The contemporary world offers up no shortage of flash points with the prospect of escalating to warfare. Taiwan and the South China Sea, especially including territorial claims over the Spratly Islands, provide two locales in which there is a real danger of violent conflict involving China. The Sino-Russian border remains another locale to look at. The relations between North and South Korea likewise are current points of concern with a long history of hostility. The same might be said for China and Vietnam. What does the EUM suggest about changes in risks in these parts of Asia?

China's position in the global pecking order of democracy may well be dropping rather than increasing. Domestic pressures have kept China from making institutional changes that could improve its absolute or relative position in terms of democracy. On the positive side, China's economy has been growing at a strong rate for two decades, though it appears now to be slowing down. Though growth has been strong, China remains a poor country with a per capita income approximately one-tenth that of the United States. China also has a recent history of militarized disputes with many of its neighbors. Unless China succumbs to international pressures to democratize or unless growth in income pacifies China, those flash points that involve this country remain relatively high risks for war.

Statistical evidence shows that if China's per capita income increases, say, 25 percent over a three-year period—an optimistic but not implausible amount given economic performance in China over the past two decades— then we can expect a subsequent three-year improvement in governance such that the country's ranking would move up fewer than two ranks. For every doubling of per capita income we can look forward to a seven rank improvement in subsequent degree of democracy. At 25 percent growth in three years, China's growth by itself cannot be expected to push it toward real democracy for many, many, many decades to come.

China remains a danger for war. This danger is particularly high if it initiates a challenge against Taiwan (or perhaps Thailand). As we saw earlier, democratic societies are very unlikely to initiate war, but they are not reluctant to escalate disputes to war if they find themselves challenged militarily. Taiwan has risen in its ranking on democracy. It is, however, a country with a high per capita income. As we saw in Table 7.5, the latter factor when coupled with democracy diminishes the risk of escalation, but not enough to offset the strong preparedness of democracies to defend themselves if challenged militarily. So, if China provokes Taiwan in a serious way, as it frequently threatens to do, then there is an especially grave danger of war.

Conversely, if China provokes Vietnam, that country's low democracy ranking makes it war prone, while its poverty also renders it a high risk for war. The combination of low ranking and low per capita income makes predicting who the initiator of a dispute might be exceedingly difficult, but it makes it relatively easy to say, if there is a military dispute, it has a higher than normal risk of becoming a war.

Thailand and Vietnam fit very much the picture of China and Taiwan. Thailand is rising in the democratic ranks and in per capita income. Vietnam may have begun meaningful economic growth, but it remains extremely poor and extremely undemocratic. These two countries must be particularly careful around each other. Thailand is unlikely to be provocative, given its rise in democracy ranking and in income, but it would not be overly reluctant to escalate a dispute to meet the threshold of war if it were challenged militarily by Vietnam.

The Russo-Chinese border is a continuing flash point of great danger. Though Russia is more democratic than it was decades ago, its ranking has fallen. China's was and is expected to continue to be low. This is a dangerous combination, especially when we consider that both countries are well armed, have expanding military establishments, and both have nuclear weapons. Many who subscribe to the idea of "the democratic peace" may be lulled into some sense of security regarding Russia in the future. They focus on its demonstrable improvement toward democratization since the end of the Cold War. They do not, however, attend to its relative decline in democracy as compared to the rest of the world. Yet, Table 7.6 urges upon us caution and attentiveness: Declining rank position makes war more likely even though a government has the general trappings of democracy.

Latin America paints a more upbeat picture. During the past few decades, Central and South America have been the locale of numerous militarized conflicts and war. With a few small exceptions, rankings on the EUM for predicted democracy improve for the Latin American countries over the next three decades. Guatemala, Chile, and Uruguay are especially notable for significant predicted shifts upward in their democracy ranking. Argentina and the Dominican Republic show a noticeable decline in their ranking, partially because of crowding near the top and partially—especially in Argentina's case—because of a failure to democratize very much. On balance, Latin America and North America enjoy unusually high average rankings, good economic growth prospects, and improved or steady rankings on democracy. All of this bodes well for a rather pacific, high investment region over the coming decades.

The Middle East picture is simply gloomy. If the EUM proves accurate based purely on international pressures, little change in political arrangements can be expected in the Middle East. Israel improves modestly on the EUM-based democracy ranking, while Saudi Arabia bounces around in a very narrow range. Algeria shows some consequential improvement, but from a very low base that still leaves it as a high risk for war or military disputes. Barring dramatic domestic changes in approaches to governance— changes that could be modeled with the EUM but have not been thus far— the Middle East remains a prospective source of conflict for the coming decades. Peace, alas, does not appear to be at hand as a consequence of prolonged and hearty international efforts.

Africa provides an interesting picture for the future. In terms of average democracy ranking, Africa is predicted to remain among the least democratic parts of the world. In terms of improvement, however, Africa does exceptionally well. Starting from a low base, much of Africa is expected to improve its institutional arrangements and become more democratic (and possibly more pacific) over the next few decades. Most notable for the expectation of becoming significantly more democratic are especially Benin, Burundi, the Comoros, Central African Republic, Mozambique, and Zambia. Mauritania, Ghana, and the Cameroons also show real promise of improved democratization, though often from a very low baseline.

A difficulty in the African context is that some of the countries that show the greatest promise for improvement also show the greatest prospect for decline, including particularly Ghana, the Central African Republic, Zambia, and Mozambique. If the EUM is correct, this suggests that these countries are likely to experience significant swings in governance, swings of the sort that often follow war or coups d'état. Thus, Africa displays a mixed picture with some reasons for optimism and, especially in the period from about 2020 on, some reasons for concern that there will be retreats from democratization and a resurgence in conflict and political instability.

Europe is the most democratic part of the world as measured by the average government's score. Yet it has become the seat of considerable international conflict in recent years, especially as states make the transition from former Soviet-dominated autocracies to nascent democracies. Ireland, among West European societies, appears to be the country at greatest risk of a meaningful decline in its degree of democracy. This may portend problems between Ireland and Northern Ireland as the latter progresses toward emergence as a fully sovereign state. In Eastern and Central Europe, there is not much reason to become optimistic. Although countries appear to be stabilizing in their governance, Rumania and Bulgaria especially continue to maintain poorly ranked, relatively undemocratic regimes. These two countries also have modest per capita incomes, particularly by European standards, and so stand out as significant threats to the prospects of peace in Europe.

One of Europe's historically hottest rivalries is between Greece and Turkey. They have a long and sad history that includes fairly frequent military engagements. The EUM provides an optimistic picture for Greece, a country expected to remain firmly and squarely near the top of the democratic ranks. Turkey, however, stagnates in the upper reaches of the middle ranks, neither autocratic nor firmly democratic. Turkey appears to be headed for a political system that falls between the somewhat more democratic forms expected in Poland over the next few decades and the less democratic, though improving, forms of governance projected in Egypt for the period around 2010. The threat of conflict between Greece and Turkey remains, though the EUM leads to the conclusion that it will be considerably muted. That is, rising incomes and improved degrees of democracy both help to make this long-standing rivalry less war prone in the future than it was in the past. The expected decline in the threat of war between these NATO allies is further improved by the prediction that Cyprus, too, is a fully committed, stable democratic polity.

## Conclusions

Several important lessons can be gleaned from the predictions of the EUM and the statistical assessment of the association between war and various indicators of democracy and individual prosperity. We have seen that the EUM simulations successfully foresaw the end of the Cold War and the global rise of democracy in the last decade of the twentieth century. In the extremely important case of Russia we learned important lessons. Russia's transition to a more democratic form of governance was predicted accurately both by the international and the domestic variant of the EUM simulations. At the same time we learned a harsh and discouraging lesson about Russia. Since the end of the Cold War, the rest of the world has democratized more than has Russia. One consequence of this fact is that Russia's relative position has fallen in the global democratic hierarchy. As we adjust our expectations about governance, Russia is likely to disappoint, looking less and less democratic.

Economic investments are much more strongly associated with rank position on democracy than they are with a country's Polity (or EUM) score. For Russia this means that economic malaise is likely to continue unless sharp changes in its internal politics lead to much more democratization. What is more, the risk of war is closely tied not just to the absolute level of autocracy or democracy, but especially to the rank position in the global pecking order. Russia's decline makes it a more likely threat to peace in the future than it has been over the post–World War II decades. This frightening realization is cause not only for concern, but also for a carefully focused foreign policy in the United States and elsewhere. American and West European policy toward Russia over the next two decades or so should be designed to encourage improved conditions of governance in that country, coupled with the military preparedness to deter the risks of expansionist designs into other parts of Europe or possibly Asia. The coming years do not appear to be a time when the United States should disengage from European security concerns.

We learned that, unlike the Russian case, the Chinese case shows a sharp difference between its domestic political attitudes toward democratization and its prospective vulnerability to international pressure for change. The simulations of China's responsiveness to international pressure hold out real hope for democratization in the future. But, the simulations of domestic political pressures and interests contradict such optimism. If the EUM is accurate in the future—and we saw that it was highly accurate in predicting now known events—then internal Chinese politics will produce only very modest improvements in democratic governance. China, with an extremely poor ranking on democracy and growing economic wherewithal, is a growing threat to peace in Asia. It has the characteristics that were shown to be statistically closely associated with a rising risk of war.

What can the international community do to heighten China's willingness to adjust politically to fall more in line with international expectations for democratization? We can anticipate that investment in China will trail off as other parts of the world, particularly Latin America and Africa, become more attractive to Asian, European, and American investors. If that happens, the pressure of declining investment tied directly to poor norms of governance may help foster changed internal attitudes toward political liberalization in China. Likewise, clearer preparedness to assist Asian democracies in defending themselves against Chinese military expansion into the South China Sea, the sea lanes between China and Taiwan and so forth, without being overly provocative may help promote more reformist attitudes within China.

The EUM correctly anticipated the rise and fall of political factions within China. It is not difficult to imagine that one could use a tool like the EUM to design precise and specific policy reforms to help promote future shifts in political factions within China. Such shifts might improve that country's standing in the global democracy ordering and diminish its potential to upset prospects for future peace and prosperity. China can sustain the advantages offered by its huge potential market. To do so, it must sustain the confidence of investors. That can most readily be achieved by political reform aimed at making China a more competitive, democratic society. Ultimately, prosperity and governance are intertwined; without good governance it is unlikely that China will achieve continued growth in prosperity.

The future of foreign policy can be enhanced by diminishing the current emphasis on reactive, stimulus-response fire fighting. Such enhancement in future policy requires a strong commitment to pro-active policy formation. An activist foreign policy requires a vision of the future, the tools to assess how best to promote that vision, and the will to implement the best strategies. The EUM cannot provide the vision, but it can increase the odds that a vision, once articulated, can be realized. By predicting with reasonable reliability, the EUM offers a way for policy makers to simulate the consequences of alternative tactics and strategies, finding the best approaches to help realize the desired foreign policy future. If tools like the EUM are used as a routine part of foreign policy formation to help promote peace and prosperity around the world, then the policy future will be brighter, indeed.

# APPENDIX

Chapter 5 EUM Simulation Data from 1980:
Predicting the Future to 2028

| Stakeholder | Resources | Position | Salience |
|---|---|---|---|
| Algeria | 3.16 | 5 | 86.20 |
| Argentina | 11.27 | 5 | 60.22 |
| Australia | 11.28 | 100 | 28.85 |
| Austria | 4.87 | 100 | 20.92 |
| Belgium | 6.71 | 100 | 65.22 |
| Benin | 0.24 | 15 | 45.27 |
| Bengladesh | 5.77 | 30 | 65.48 |
| Bolivia | 0.68 | 15 | 100.00 |
| Botswana | 0.11 | 100 | 21.91 |
| Brazil | 32.00 | 30 | 83.79 |
| Burundi | 0.12 | 15 | 61.45 |
| Bulgaria | 2.13 | 15 | 28.23 |
| Burma | 1.04 | 10 | 29.81 |
| Canada | 20.84 | 100 | 100.00 |
| Cameroon | 0.64 | 10 | 27.86 |
| Central African Republic | 0.10 | 15 | 85.95 |
| Chile | 2.66 | 15 | 47.07 |
| China | 58.49 | 15 | 61.24 |
| Colombia | 4.79 | 90 | 31.66 |
| Comoros | 0.01 | 25 | 74.50 |
| Congo | 0.19 | 10 | 96.03 |
| Costa Rica | 0.52 | 100 | 58.26 |
| Cyprus | 0.20 | 100 | 47.28 |
| Czechoslovakia | 3.49 | 15 | 54.90 |
| Denmark | 3.56 | 100 | 30.18 |
| Dominican Republic | 0.82 | 0 | 64.71 |
| Ecuador | 1.61 | 95 | 74.67 |
| Egypt | 4.12 | 25 | 38.85 |
| Ethiopia | 0.74 | 15 | 67.80 |
| Fiji | 0.14 | 95 | 26.51 |
| Finland | 3.18 | 100 | 13.35 |
| France | 38.84 | 90 | 29.85 |
| German Democratic Republic | 7.84 | 5 | 41.24 |
| Federal Republic of Germany | 45.00 | 100 | 26.59 |
| Ghana | 0.64 | 80 | 78.92 |
| Guinea-Bissau | 0.02 | 15 | 48.57 |
| Greece | 3.49 | 90 | 34.90 |
| Guatemala | 1.09 | 25 | 73.76 |
| Guyana | 0.09 | 15 | 33.31 |

(*continued*)

| Stakeholder | Resources | Position | Salience |
|---|---|---|---|
| Haiti | 0.34 | 5 | 43.98 |
| Honduras | 0.34 | 45 | 71.52 |
| Hungary | 3.28 | 15 | 23.63 |
| Iceland | 0.16 | 100 | 64.59 |
| India | 37.18 | 90 | 100.00 |
| Ireland | 1.42 | 100 | 70.25 |
| Iran | 8.24 | 20 | 84.91 |
| Israel | 1.88 | 95 | 46.20 |
| Italy | 35.73 | 100 | 100.00 |
| Jamaica | 0.31 | 100 | 100.00 |
| Japan | 72.13 | 100 | 100.00 |
| Liberia | 0.11 | 15 | 100.00 |
| Lesotho | 0.08 | 15 | 32.36 |
| Luxembourg | 0.27 | 100 | 64.11 |
| Mauritania | 0.08 | 15 | 100.00 |
| Malaysia | 3.21 | 90 | 45.19 |
| Mauritius | 0.24 | 95 | 20.13 |
| Mexico | 24.89 | 35 | 55.68 |
| Mali | 0.21 | 15 | 36.83 |
| Mozambique | 0.69 | 10 | 56.84 |
| New Zealand | 1.98 | 100 | 31.24 |
| Nigeria | 6.27 | 5 | 77.84 |
| Niger | 0.24 | 15 | 52.02 |
| Norway | 3.05 | 100 | 33.25 |
| Netherlands | 9.79 | 100 | 40.14 |
| Pakistan | 5.62 | 15 | 67.49 |
| Paraguay | 0.49 | 10 | 23.62 |
| Peru | 3.05 | 5 | 100.00 |
| Philippines | 5.57 | 5 | 33.15 |
| Papua New Guinea | 0.33 | 100 | 39.35 |
| Poland | 9.64 | 20 | 38.34 |
| Portugal | 2.98 | 95 | 42.73 |
| Rhodesia | 0.52 | 75 | 100.00 |
| Republic of Korea | 7.23 | 10 | 5.77 |
| Rumania | 1.94 | 10 | 32.76 |
| South Africa | 6.33 | 70 | 66.09 |
| Saudi Arabia | 7.90 | 0 | 52.34 |
| Senegal | 0.39 | 40 | 24.95 |
| Sierra Leone | 0.23 | 15 | 42.65 |
| Singapore | 0.99 | 40 | 22.39 |
| Somalia | 0.26 | 15 | 38.52 |
| Spain | 16.94 | 90 | 41.96 |
| Sri Lanka | 1.48 | 75 | 57.18 |
| Sudan | 1.02 | 15 | 38.48 |
| Swaziland | 0.11 | 0 | 34.60 |
| Sweden | 6.35 | 100 | 63.27 |
| Switzerland | 5.54 | 100 | 100.00 |
| Taiwan | 4.87 | 15 | 74.26 |
| Tanzania | 0.53 | 15 | 29.33 |
| Thailand | 6.24 | 60 | 100.00 |

(continued)

| Stakeholder | Resources | Position | Salience |
|---|---|---|---|
| Togo | 0.12 | 15 | 35.16 |
| Trinidad | 0.75 | 90 | 14.32 |
| Tunisia | 0.99 | 5 | 25.78 |
| Turkey | 7.83 | 25 | 84.64 |
| United Kingdom | 35.12 | 100 | 66.47 |
| Upper Volta | 0.20 | 15 | 33.84 |
| Uruguay | 0.91 | 15 | 59.41 |
| USA | 213.63 | 100 | 34.17 |
| Soviet Union/Russia | 99.64 | 15 | 29.43 |
| Venezuela | 6.75 | 95 | 32.32 |
| Yugoslavia | 7.61 | 25 | 18.34 |
| Zambia | 0.34 | 5 | 32.25 |

# ENDNOTES

1. A far from exhaustive or even representative sample of game theoretic approaches to international relations includes Brams and Kilgour (1988); Bueno de Mesquita and Lalman (1992); Fearon (1994), Kim and Morrow (1992); Kugler and Zagare (1990); Morrow (1994); Nicholson (1989); Niou, Ordeshook, and Rose (1989); Powell (2000); and Wagner (1983).

2. I personally, however, am not convinced of that point of view. See Bueno de Mesquita (2000a).

3. Path dependence is certainly evident, for instance, in the arguments of Gilchrist (1969), de Santillana (1955), or McNeill (1982), to name but a very few examples.

4. Much of the context in terms of changes in political institutions, shifts in prosperity, and movement of populations is, however, explained in Bueno de Mesquita, Smith, Siverson, and Morrow (2002).

5. Polity IV data are used to measure democracy against autocracy. The Polity autocracy scale is subtracted from the democracy scale, 10 points are added, and the result is divided by 20 to yield a score normalized between 1.0 and 0.0. Lower scores reflect greater degrees of autocracy; higher scores, more democracy.

6. Of course global population refers only to the set of countries included in the data set each year and not the true global population of the world. The world's true population and excluded regimes (colonies are not counted nor are many non-European states before 1920) probably, if included, would paint a still more autocratic, less democratic picture.

7. The trend lines are derived by regressing the median government's score and the median person's governmental experience against the year, its square and its cube (cube only for the population-based test). Higher order exponents do not add to the fit of the trend lines. The by-country regression yields the following results:

Median Country Democracy Score $= -116.855$ (std. error $= 8.633$) $+ 0.120$ Year (std. error $= .009$) $- .00003$ Year$^2$ (std. error $= 2.39e{-}06$); N $= 370$, F $= 267.71$, $R^2 = .59$.

The by-population regression yields:

Median Population Democracy Score $= -1698.421$ (std. error $= 69.229$) $+ 2.710$ Year (std. error $= 1.07$) $- .001$ Year$^2$ (std. error $= .0006$) $+ 2.56e{-}07$ Year$^3$ (std. error $= 1.00e{-}07$); N $= 348$, F $= 69.13$, $R^2 = .38$.

8. See the epistle *Unam Sanctam* (http://www.shrine.com/unam.htm) issued by Boniface VII and the commentary by John of Paris (1971).

9. The regalia, consisting of the ring and staff, were the symbols of the bishop's office and authority. In exchange for the return of these regalia to the bishop, that is, the return of authority over the bishopric to the church, the bishop promised to defend the king. As the Concordat stipulates, "The one elected, moreover, without any exaction may receive the regalia from thee [the Holy Roman Emperor] through the lance, and shall do unto thee for these what he rightfully should." The emperor's promise at Worms includes the critical passage, "I . . . do remit to God, and to the holy apostles of God, Peter and Paul, and to the holy catholic church, all investiture through ring and staff [that is, the regalia], and do grant that in all the churches that are in my kingdom or empire there may be canonical election and free consecration. All the possessions and regalia of St. Peter . . . which I hold: I restore to the same holy Roman church." The full text of the Concordat of Worms can be found in the Medieval Sourcebook at http://www.fordham.edu/halsall/source/worms.html.

10. That policy was influenced by the loyalties of bishops is evident from Philip Augustus's experience. Pope Innocent III interdicted Philip, depriving the king's subjects of access to the sacraments. The interdiction was faithfully observed by virtually every bishop whose background indicated close personal ties to the pope. Almost every bishop who was a blood relative of the king, in contrast, ignored the interdiction and continued to provide the king's subjects in their domain with the sacraments (Baldwin 1986, Appendix).

11. The church pointed to the account of Jesus throwing money lenders out of the Temple as evidence against usury, but others were quick to note that Jesus did not condemn money lending or money lenders, but rather objected to the pursuit of such money-making ways *in the Temple*.

12. Trial by ordeal was the process by which innocence or guilt was determined through the presumed intervention of God. Two common ordeals, both supervised by the church, involved submersion of the accused in deep water and forcing the accused to hold a red-hot piece of iron. Failure to stay submerged for a prescribed period of time was taken as proof of guilt, as was the inability to hold a red-hot iron for a specified period.

13. Judgments about expectations of loyalty are from the appendix of regalian Sees in Baldwin (1986). Newly appointed bishops are identified as blood relatives of Philip or known at the time to be under his influence or as relatives of the pope or within his circle. The judgments are all Baldwin's who, you recall, contends that Philip learned contrition toward the pope.

14. Practical models also exist to address logrolling or issue linkage. Win sets and the exchange model developed by Frans Stokman and his colleagues are but two examples (Bueno de Mesquita and Stokman 1994).

15. A veto player is any player whose agreement is required in order for a policy position to be enforced as the issue outcome. Veto players cannot necessarily impose their desired outcome on others, but they can prevent some other outcome from being chosen. Thus, either every veto player accepts the same proposed outcome or the issue remains unresolved.

16. Let $N = 1, 2, 3, \ldots, n$ be the set of actors or stakeholders trying to influence a multilateral decision. An actor might be a government representative, an official from a faction within a political party, or a bureaucracy, a leader of some interest group, an influential private citizen, and so forth. Let $M = \{a, b, c, \ldots, m\}$ be the set of issues in a multilateral negotiation and let $R_a$ be the line segment that describes the

unidimensional policy continuum for any individual issue *a* selected from among the larger set of issues M.

Let each actor i, i∈N (i.e., *i* is a member of the set of actors trying to influence the decision), have its own *preferred* resolution of issue a, with that preferred resolution denoted as $x^{\bullet}_{ia}$. $x^{\bullet}_{ia}$ is the outcome actor *i* has revealed to be preferred on issue a. It may or may not be *i's policy* ideal point. We generally do not know for sure what another actor's true ideal point is as there are strategic incentives for an actor to misrepresent his or her ideal point. Because the model as applied here assesses policy decisions on one issue at a time, I drop the issue-denoting subscript (a, or b, etc.) from the notation so that henceforth $x^{*}_{i}$ is the preferred position of actor i on the issue being evaluated at the moment.

For any feasible proposed outcome on issue a, say k's proposal, $x_k$, i's utility for $x_k$, $u^i x_k$, is a decreasing function of the distance between the proposal and i's preferred resolution, so that $u^i x_k = f(-|x_k - x^{*}_{i}|)$. This means that proposals farther away from actor i's preferred outcome are of less value to *i* than are proposals closer to i's preferred outcome.

17. Again I will drop the a subscript from the notation throughout, but the reader is alerted to the fact that the model does not assume that an actor's capabilities or potential power need be the same on all issues.

18. Denote the salience of issue a for actor i as $s_{ia}$, with $0 < s_{ia} < 1$. Each actor is described by the values of $u^i x_k$ for all i, k∈N, $c_i$, and $s_i$ on each issue. $S_i$ is assumed to be greater than zero because if it were equal to zero for more than one stakeholder then it is possible for division by zero to arise in the computation of the model. Strictly speaking, then, the model can tolerate one actor with a salience of zero. Still, this is an odd concept in that it implies that there is a stakeholder who does not care at all about the issue in question. In that case, the actor in question really does not have a stake in the decision. Each actor is described by the values of $u^i x_k$ for all i, k∈N, $c_i$, and $s_i$ on each issue.

19. Say j's proposal ($u^i x_j$), to another proposal, say k's ($u^i x_k$).

20. That is, selecting $x_i$ such that $u^i x_i - u^i x_j$.

21. That is, to alter $x_k$ so that $u^k x^{*} k = u^k x_k$.

22. To do so requires a focus on the three characteristics: $u^i x_j$ for all i, j∈N, $s_j$, and $c_j$.

23. I am grateful to Frans Stokman for bringing this similarity between the EUM and prospect theory to my attention.

24. A somewhat simplified version of the software is freely available for academic research and instructional use only at http://bdm.cqpress.com. That software can be used with user-created data sets. Replication of the results here is possible with that software, but will prove cumbersome and extremely time consuming. The software is not set up to provide some of the capabilities I use, though they can readily be introduced manually by the analyst. The data used in chapter 6 involve more than 100 stakeholders and will take several hours to solve. The amount of time required increases geometrically with the number of stakeholders and rounds. The model calculates approximately 3*N! interactions per round where N is the number of stakeholders.

25. I am grateful to Professor Yi Feng, now at the Claremont Graduate School, who prepared these data for me. I presented results from these data during a talk on "The Prospects of Reform in China" at Florida State University on October 31, 1991.

26. In a perhaps greater signal about the reliability of this model, Dr. Feder left

the government in 1998 and, using the original 1984 static version of the model, set up a business called Policy Futures that assists its clients in anticipating important policy choices. Two other companies make use of the more advanced dynamic model described here. These are Decision Insights, Inc. (DII, see diiusa.com), a New York-based consultancy that has been in business since 1981, and a Dutch firm, Decide bv, which uses the dynamic model under license from DII.

27. Within the commercial setting, the expected utility model is sometimes called Policon and sometimes called Factions.

28. By path dependence I mean here the extent to which a particular outcome could only have arisen through one unique combination of historical circumstances.

29. In Chapter 5 I simulate democratization based on more than 100 nations. Because such simulations take three to seven hours for each one, I have restricted the set here to a smaller number of key states, trading off the greater precision that comes with more stakeholders for speed to allow a larger number of simulation runs.

30. Others may wish to reconstruct the scale using Curt Signorino's and Jeffrey Ritter's S indicator (1999). There is little reason to anticipate much difference as their indicator and the tau b indicator are very highly correlated.

31. They actually sum to 99.692 because of rounding error.

32. As the model does not attach calendar time to its rounds or iterations, this is one place where we can say that hindsight was used. It is convenient to speak of each round as if it were of two years' duration, but the model is not informative on this. Given the nature of the data, we can be confident that a round reflects no less than a year, but might reflect two or more years.

33. I again remind the reader that the two-year interval associated with each round is ex post; the model does not specify how long a round lasts in calendar time. The use of two years is a convenience that corresponds remarkably well with actual events. Two years seems reasonable substantively as well in the sense that such major policy stances as are investigated here are unlikely to change over a more rapid time scale.

34. Significant parts of Europe, however, become relatively less attractive targets of investment as their ranking slips because of pressure from countries beneath them in democracy score who are becoming as democratic as Europe.

35. For what it is worth, I mention that I gave a talk on the EUM and China at Gettysburg College in February 1989. Based on the EUM analysis, the focus of my talk was the prediction that there would be a pro-democracy student uprising in China sometime within six months of the talk, that is by August 1989. At the time the prediction was received with great skepticism. Its basis was a domestic analysis of China at that time.

36. Those seeking to replicate the results using the Web-based software at http://bdm.cqpress.com can do so by checking the verbal summary tables. The category defined as lose includes –Give In, –Conflict and any Stalemate. Compromise includes both –Compromise and +Compromise from the verbal summary. Win includes +Compel and +Conflict.

37. The correlation between the passage of time and immigration as a proportion of population, assessed across 1829 nation-years, is 0.07, which is significant at p=.005.

38. I ignore migration in this analysis as the evidence suggests that migratory patterns are partially responsive to war, and to changes in democraticness and prosperity, but the likelihood of war is not significantly influenced by population migration.

# REFERENCES

Altfeld, Michael F., and B. Bueno de Mesquita. 1979. "Choosing Sides in Wars." *International Studies Quarterly* (March):87–112.

Angell, N. 1910. *The Great Illusion*. New York: G. P. Putnam's Sons.

Baldwin, J. W. 1986. *The Government of Philip Augustus*. Berkeley: University of California Press.

Banks, J. S. 1990. "Equilibrium Behavior in Crisis Bargaining Games." *American Journal of Political Science* 34:599–614.

Barzel, Y. 1989. *The Economic Analysis of Property Rights*. New York: Cambridge University Press.

Bates, R., A. Greif, M. Levi, J. L. Rosenthal, and B. Weingast. 1998. *Analytic Narratives*. Princeton, N.J.: Princeton University Press.

Black, D. 1958. *The Theory of Committees and Elections*. Cambridge: Cambridge University Press.

Bloch, I. S. 1991. *Is War Now Impossible?* Brookfield, Vt.: Ashgate.

Brams, S. J., and D. M. Kilgour. 1988. *Game Theory and National Security*. New York: Basil Blackwell.

Bremer, Stuart. 1992. "Dangerous Dyads: Conditions Affecting the Likelihood of Interstate War, 1816–1965." *Journal of Conflict Resolution* 26:309–41.

Brzezinski, Z. 1963. "After the Test Ban: the US must Take the Initiative in Europe." *The New Republic*, August 31, pp. 1–21.

Bueno de Mesquita, B. 1981. *The War Trap*. New Haven, Conn.: Yale University Press.

———. 1984. "Forecasting Policy Decisions: An Expected Utility Approach to Post–Khomeini Iran." *PS*, pp. 226–36.

———. 1985. "The War Trap Revisited." *American Political Science Review* (March 1985): 157–76.

———. 1990. "Multilateral Negotiations: A Spatial Analysis of the Arab-Israeli Dispute." *International Organization* 44:317–40.

———. 1996. "Counterfactuals and International Affairs: Some Insights from Game Theory," in P. Tetlock and A. Belin, eds. *Counterfactual Thought: Experiments in World Politics*. Princeton, N.J.: Princeton University Press, 211–29.

———. 1998. "The End of the Cold War: Predicting an Emergent Property." *Journal of Conflict Resolution* 42,2 (April):131–55.

———. 2000a. "Popes, Kings, and Endogenous Institutions: The Concordat of Worms and the Origins of Sovereignty." *International Studies Review* (Fall): 93–118.

———. 2000b. *Principles of International Politics*. Washington, D.C.: CQ Press.

161

Bueno de Mesquita, B., and D. Beck. 1985. "Forecasting Policy Decisions: An Expected Utility Approach." In S. Andriole, ed., *Corporate Crisis Management.* Princeton, N.J.: Petrocelli Books, pp. 103–22.

Bueno de Mesquita, B., and B. Berkowitz. 1979. "How to Make a Lasting Peace in the Middle East." *Rochester Review,* pp. 12–18.

Bueno de Mesquita, B., and D. Lalman. 1986. "Reason and War." *American Political Science Review* (December):1113–31.

———. 1992. *War and Reason.* New Haven, Conn.: Yale University Press.

Bueno de Mesquita, B., R. McDermott, and E. Cope. 2001. "The Expected Prospects for Peace in Northern Ireland." *International Interactions,* 27, 2: 129–67.

Bueno de Mesquita, B., J. D. Morrow, R. M. Siverson, and A. Smith. 1999. "Policy Failure and Political Survival: the Contribution of Political Institutions." *Journal of Conflict Resolution* 43, 2 (April):147–61.

———. 2000. "Political Institutions, Political Survival, and Policy Success." In B. Bueno de Mesquita and H. L. Root, eds., *Governing for Prosperity.* New Haven, Conn.: Yale University Press, pp. 59–84.

———. Bueno de Mesquita, A. Smith, R. M. Siverson, and J. D. Morrow. 2003. *The Logic of Political Survival.* Cambridge, Mass.: MIT Press.

Bueno de Mesquita, B., D. Newman, and A. Rabushka. 1985. *Forecasting Political Events: The Future of Hong Kong.* New Haven, Conn.: Yale University Press.

———. 1996. *Red Flag over Hong Kong.* Chatham, N.J.: Chatham House.

Bueno de Mesquita, B., and R. M. Siverson. 1995. "War and the Survival of Political Leaders: A Comparative Study of Regime Types and Political Accountability." *American Political Science Review* 9 (December):841–55.

Bueno de Mesquita B., and F. Stokman, eds. 1994. *European Community Decision Making: Models, Applications and Comparisons.* New Haven, Conn.: Yale University Press.

Cohn, J. 1999. "When Did Political Science Forget about Politics? Irrational Exuberance." *The New Republic,* October 25, pp. 26–31.

De Roover, R. A. 1948. *Money, Banking and Credit in Mediaeval Bruges.* Cambridge, Mass.: Mediaeval Academy of America.

———. 1974. *Business, Banking, and Economic Thought in Late Medieval and Early Modern Europe.* J. Kirshner, ed. Chicago: University of Chicago Press.

de Santillana, G. 1955. *The Crime of Galileo.* Chicago: University of Chicago Press.

Deudney, D., and J. Ikenberry. 1991. "The International Sources of Soviet Change." *International Security* 16:74–118.

Duby, G. 1991. *France in the Middle Ages: 987–1460,* Juliet Vale, trans. Oxford: Blackwell.

Eggertsson, T. 1990. *Economic Behavior and Institutions.* New York: Cambridge University Press.

Farber, H. S., and J. Gowa. 1995. "Polities and Peace." *International Security* 20:123–46.

Fearon, J. 1994. "Domestic Political Audiences and the Escalation of International Disputes." *American Political Science Review* 88:577–92.

Feder, S. 1995. "Factions and Policon: New Ways to Analyze Politics." In H. Bradford Westerfield, ed., *Inside CIA's Private World: Declassified Articles from the Agency's Internal Journal, 1955–1992.* New Haven, Conn.: Yale University Press, pp. 274–92.

Fischer, Stanley. 1993. "The Role of Macroeconomic Factors in Growth." *Journal of Monetary Economics* 32, 3: 485–512.

Gaddis, J. L. 1992. "International Relations Theory and the End of the Cold War." *International Security* 17:5–58.

———. 1997. *We Know Now: Rethinking Cold War History.* Oxford: Clarendon Press, pp. 291–92.

Gartzke, E. 2001. "Liberalism, Information and Peace: A Two-Level Game." Paper presented at the Annual Meeting of the International Studies Association. Chicago, February 20–24, 2001.

George, A. L. 1991. "The Transition in U.S.-Soviet Relations, 1985–1990: an Interpretation from the Perspective of International Relations Theory and Political Psychology." *Political Psychology* 12:469–87.

Gies, F., and J. Gies. 1994. *Cathedral, Forge, and Waterwheel: Technology and Invention in the Middle Ages.* New York: Harper Collins.

Gilchrist, J. 1969. *The Church and Economic Activity in the Middle Ages.* New York: Macmillan.

Gilpin, R. 1981. *War and Change in World Politics.* New York: Cambridge University Press.

Gorbachev, M. 1996. *Memoirs.* New York: Bantam Books.

Greenstein, F. I. 1996. "Ronald Reagan, Mikhail Gorbachev, and the End of the Cold War: What Difference Did They Make." In W. C. Wohlforth, ed., *Witnesses to the End of the Cold War.* Baltimore, Md.: Johns Hopkins University Press.

Greif, A. 1998. "Cultural Beliefs and the Organization of Society." In Mary C. Brinton and Victor Nee, eds., *The New Institutionalism in Sociology.* New York: Russell Sage Foundation.

Gurr, T. R. 1970. *Why Men Rebel.* Princeton, N.J.: Princeton University Press.

Henderson, E. F. 1910. *Select Historical Documents of the Middle Ages.* London: George Bell and Sons, pp. 408–9.

Hensel, Paul. 1996. "Charting a Course to Conflict: Territorial Issues and Militarized Interstate Disputes, 1816–1992." *Conflict Management and Peace Science* 15:43–73.

Huth, P. K. 1996. *Standing Your Ground: Territorial Disputes and International Conflict.* Ann Arbor: University of Michigan Press.

Interview. "A Conversation with Bruce Bueno de Mesquita: Where War is Likely in the Next Year or Two." *U.S. News and World Report,* May 3, 1982, p. 30.

*Izvestia.* April 3, 1995. "Russia is doomed to stability consider American experts." Translated by Foreign Broadcast Information Service. pp. 1–4.

John of Paris (1302) 1971. *De Potestate Regia et Papali,* translated by J. A. Watt as *On Royal and Papal Power.* Toronto: The Pontifical Institute of Mediaeval Studies.

Kahneman, D., and A. Tversky. 1984. "Choices, Values and Frames." *American Psychologist* 39: 341–50.

Kantorowicz, E. 1957. *The King's Two Bodies.* Princeton, N.J.: Princeton University Press.

Kaplan, M. 1957. *System and Process in International Politics.*

Kegley, C. 1994. "How Did the Cold War Die?: Principles for an Autopsy." *Mershon International Studies Review* 3:11–41.

Keohane, R. 1984. *After Hegemony: Cooperation and Discord in the World Political Economy.* Princeton, N.J.: Princeton University Press.

Kim, W., and J. D. Morrow. 1992. "When Do Power Shifts Lead to War?" *American Journal of Political Science* 36:896–922.

Krasner, S. 1981. "Transforming International Regimes: What the Third World Wants and Why." *International Studies Quarterly* 25:119–48.

Kugler, J., and A. F. K. Organski. 1989. "The End of Hegemony?" *International Interactions* 15:113–28.

Kugler, J., and Y. Feng, eds. 1997. *Special Issue, International Interactions* 23, 3–4: 233.

Kugler, J., and F. Zagare. 1990. "The Long-Term Stability of Deterrence." *International Interactions* 15:255–78.

Ladurie, E. L. R. 1971. *Times of Feast, Times of Famine.* Barbara Bray, trans. New York: Farrar, Straus and Giroux.

Lake, David. 1992. "Powerful Pacifists: Democratic States and War." *American Political Science Review* 86:24–37.

Lamborn, A. 1991. *The Price of Power.* Boston: Unwin Hyman.

Layne, C. 1994. "Kant or Cant: The Myth of the Democratic Peace." *International Security* 19 (Fall):5–49.

Le Goff, J. 1980. *Time, Work, and Culture in the Middle Ages.* Arthur Goldhammer, trans. Chicago: University of Chicago Press.

Lepgold, J., B. Bueno de Mesquita, and J. D. Morrow. 1996. "The Struggle for Mastery in Europe, 1985–1993." *International Interactions* 22:41–66.

Levy, J. 1988. "Domestic Politics and War." *Journal of Interdisciplinary History* 1 (Spring):653–73.

Lopez, R. S. 1966. *The Birth of Europe.* New York: M. Evans & Co.

———. 1976. *The Commercial Revolution of the Middle Ages, 950–1350.* Cambridge: Cambridge University Press.

Maoz, Z., and N. Abdolali. 1989. "Regime Type and International Conflict, 116–1976." *Journal of Conflict Resolution* 33:3–36.

McDermott, Rose. 1998. *Risk-Taking in International Politics.* Ann Arbor: University of Michigan Press.

McGurn, W. 1996. "We Warned You." *Far Eastern Economic Review,* June 13, p. 68.

McNeill, W. H. 1982. *The Pursuit of Power.* Chicago: University of Chicago Press.

Miller, E., and J. Hatcher. 1995. *Medieval England: Towns, Commerce and Crafts, 1086–1348.* London: Longman.

Morgenthau, Hans J. 1978. *Politics among Nations,* 5th ed. revised. New York: Alfred A. Knopf.

Morrow, J. D. 1994. "Modeling the Forms of International Cooperation." *International Organization* 48:387–423.

Morrow, J. D., B. Bueno de Mesquita, and S. Wu. 1993. "Forecasting the Risks of Nuclear Proliferation: Taiwan as an Illustration of the Method." *Security Studies* 2: 311–31.

Mueller, J. E. 1989. *Retreat from Doomsday: The Obsolescence of Major War.* New York: Basic Books.

Nash, J. F. 1950. "The Bargaining Problem." *Econometrica* 18:155–62.

Nathan, A. 2000. *The Tiananmen Papers.* New York: Harper Collins.

Nicholson, M. 1989. *Formal Theories in International Relations.* Cambridge: Cambridge University Press.

Niou, E., P. Ordeshook, and G. Rose. 1989. *The Balance of Power.* Cambridge: Cambridge University Press.

North, D. C., and B. R. Weingast. 1989. "Constitutions and Commitment: the Institutions Governing Public Choice in Seventeenth-Century England." *Journal of Economic History* 44 (December): 803–32.

Oneal, John R., and Bruce M. Russett. 1997. "The Classical Liberals Were Right: Democracy, Interdependence, and Conflict, 1950–1985." *International Studies Quarterly* 41 (June):267–93.

Organski, A. F. K. 1958. *World Politics.* New York: Alfred A. Knopf.

Organski, A. F. K., and B. Bueno de Mesquita. 1993. "Forecasting the 1992 French Referendum." In R. Morgan, J. Lorentzen, and A. Leander, eds., *New Diplomacy in the Post–Cold War World.* New York: St. Martin's Press., pp. 67–75.

Organski, A. F. K., J. Kugler, T. Johnson, and Y. Cohen. 1984. *Birth, Death and Taxes: Political and Demographic Transition.* Chicago: University of Chicago Press.

Persson, T., and G. Tabellini. 2000. *Political Economics: Explaining Economic Policy.* Cambridge, Mass.: MIT Press.

Powell, R. 2000. *In the Shadow of Power.* Princeton, N.J.: Princeton University Press.

Przeworski, A. 1991. *Democracy and the Market.* New York: Cambridge University Press.

Rabushka, A., and K. Shepsle. 1972. *Politics in Plural Societies: A Theory of Democratic Instability.* Columbus, Ohio: Merrill.

Ray, J. L. 1995. *Democracy and International Conflict.* Columbia: University of South Carolina Press.

Ray, J. L., and B. M. Russett. 1996. "The Future as Arbiter of Theoretical Controversies: Predictions, Explanations and the End of the Cold War." *British Journal of Political Science* 25:441–70.

Reiter, Dani, and Allan Stam. 1996. "Democracy, War Initiation and Victory." *American Political Science Review* 92: 377–89.

Risse-Kappen, T. 1991. "Did 'Peace Through Strength' End the Cold War?" *International Security* 16:162–88.

Robinson, I. S. 1990. *The Papacy 1073–1198: Continuity and Innovation.* Cambridge: Cambridge University Press.

Rosenberg, N., and L. E. Birdzell Jr. 1986. *How the West Grew Rich: the Economic Transformation of the Industrial World.* New York: Basic Books.

Rubenstein, A. 1982. "Perfect Equilibrium in a Bargaining Model." *Econometrica* 50:97–109.

Russett, B. 1985. "The Mysterious Case of Vanishing Hegemony; or Is Mark Twain Really Dead?" *International Organization* 39:207–31.

———. 1993. *Grasping the Democratic Peace.* Princeton, N.J.: Princeton University Press.

Schimmelpfennig, B. 1992. *The Papacy.* New York: Columbia University Press.

Schwartz, T., and K. Skinner. 1999. "The Myth of Democratic Pacifism." *Wall Street Journal,* January 7.

Senese, P. D. 1995. "Militarized Interstate Dispute Escalation: The Effects of Geographical Proximity and Issue Salience." Paper presented at the meetings of the Peace Science Society, October 13–15, 1995, Ohio State University, Columbus.

Senese, P. D. 1997. "Contiguity, Territory, and their Interaction." Presented at the Annual Meeting of the International Studies Association, Toronto, March 18–22.

Shultz, G. P. 1993. *Turmoil and Triumph: My Years as Secretary of State*. New York: Charles Scribner's Sons.

Signorino, C., and J. Ritter. 1999. "Tau B or Not Tau B." *International Studies Quarterly* 43:115–44.

Singer, M., and A. Wildavsky. 1996. *The Real World Order*. Chatham, N.J.: Seven Bridges Press.

Skinner, K., M. Anderson, and A. Anderson. 2001. *Reagan in His Own Hand*. New York: Free Press.

Spiro, D. 1994. "The Insignificance of the Liberal Peace." *International Security* 19 (Fall):50–86.

Tuchman, B. 1984. *The March of Folly*. New York: Alfred A. Knopf.

Van Caenegem, R. C. 1988. *The Birth of the English Common Law*, 2d ed. Cambridge: Cambridge University Press.

Vasquez, J. 1991. "The Deterrence Myth: Nuclear Weapons and the Prevention of Nuclear War." In C. Kegley, ed., *The Long Postwar Peace*. New York: Longman.

———. 1993. *The War Puzzle*. New York: Cambridge University Press.

———. 1995. "Why Do Neighbors Fight ?—Territoriality, Proximity, or Interactions." *Journal of Peace Research* 32:277–93.

Volgy, T. J., and L. E. Imwalle. 2000. "Two Faces of Hegemonic Strength: Structural versus Relational Capabilities." *International Interactions* 263: 229–52.

Wagner, R. H. 1983. "The Theory of Games and the Problem of International Cooperation." *American Political Science Review* 77:330–46.

Walt, S. 1999. "Rigor or Rigor Mortis." *International Security* 24 (Fall):5–48.

Waltz, K. 1959. *Man, the State, and War*. New York: Columbia University Press.

———. 1979. *Theory of International Politics*. Reading, Mass.: Addison-Wesley.

Weber, M. 1958. *The Protestant Ethic and the Spirit of Capitalism*. Talcott Parsons, trans. New York: Scribner.

———. 1968. *Economy and Society*, eds. Guenther Roth and Claus Wittich. Ephraim Fischoff, trans. New York: Bedminster Press.

Wesson, R. 1978. *State Systems*. New York: Simon and Schuster.

Wu, S., and B. Bueno de Mesquita. 1994. "Assessing the Dispute in the South China Sea: A Model of China's Security Decision Making." *International Studies Quarterly* 38:379–403.

Zelikow, P., and C. Rice. 1995. *Germany Unified and Europe Transformed*. Cambridge, Mass.: Harvard University Press, pp. 4–37.

# INDEX